DILEMMA AND DESTINY

The Democratic Party in America

Ralph M. Goldman

Copyright © 1986 by
Ralph Goldman

Madison Books

4720 Boston Way
Lanham, MD 20706

3 Henrietta Street
London WC2E 8LU England

Printed in the United States of America

Library of Congress Cataloging in Publication Data

Goldman, Ralph Morris, 1920-
Dilemma and destiny.

1. Democratic Party (U.S.)—History.   I. Title.
JK2316.G613   1986   324.2736   85-23191
ISBN 0-8191-4384-7 (pbk. : alk. paper)

All Madison Books are produced on acid-free
paper which exceeds the minimum standards set by the National
Historical Publications and Records Commission.

Madison
★ BOOKS ★

To
Adlai E. Stevenson
Hubert H. Humphrey
Walter F. Mondale

Distinguished Public Servants
Dedicated Party Leaders
Noble Runners-Up

In gratitude and frustration

Acknowledgments

James E. Lyons, vice president and managing editor of the University Press of America, thought that a discussion of the future of the Democratic party would render a substantial public service. I early suspected that he really believed any book about the party's future would consist mainly of blank pages. In any case, he has been magnificently cooperative in the advancement of this enterprise. Standing behind Jed Lyons and prodding him at strategic moments has been Elizabeth Carnes, editor of Madison Books. To both of them and their colleagues at UPA, particularly editor Patricia Buckley Bozell, I am most grateful.

My appreciation to David M. Bartlett, director of Temple University Press, for authorizing a republication of my *Search for Consensus: The Story of the Democratic Party*, originally published by that press in 1979. Instead of republication, the work has been extensively revised and, in effect, a new book written.

I beg the forgiveness of all the uncited sources and thank them for their contribution to my insights and arguments, for which only I bear responsibility.

Contents

*Twenty pages of illustrations
will be found following page 158.*

Preface

All through Presidential Year 1984 I noticed that everyone was talking about The Future. Gary Hart said that the time was now for a new leadership for the future. Walter Mondale picked up the theme to promise more taxes and other realistic approaches to a better future for America. Jesse Jackson proclaimed that "our time has come," meaning that ethnic justice must be implemented in the near future. Even Ronald Reagan, presumed spokesman for The Past, insisted that the future was here right now; enjoy it.

After the election, President Reagan, referring again to the future, said: "You ain't seen nothing yet!" Democrats simply declared that the party's future had to be different, and, once again, they started to work themselves over.

Were all these fellows avoiding discussion of 1984 because this was George Orwell's Year of the Future? Were The Past and The Present so dreadful that, with typical American optimism, only The Future seemed cheerful? After pondering the matter for some time, it hit me. If there is no future, what with the 50,000 nuclear bombs all over the place, who could be blamed for being all wrong about The Future? Besides, with the emergence of a whole new breed of experts called Futurists, there also has developed a new form of science fiction, that is, the extrapolations and guesses of these Futurists. It now seemed to me that the distinguished political leaders, when talking about The Future, were practicing a new campaign art form: science fiction.

I became intrigued, having myself tried to be something of a futurist. I recalled how at an early age I tried to plan my future so that I could wrap up several life projects by the time I reached sixty. I never anticipated so many interruptions and so much slippage. Then, too, for years I have been forecasting the emergence of a world party system that eventually would become the institutional alternative to warfare. The trends seem to be bearing this out, as many world leaders would agree. As a parties-and-elections specialist I have been making relatively informal election analyses and forecasts for at least two decades. My friends and colleagues insist that I have never been right, not even when I show them press reports of my correct forecasts.

My experience with futurizing has nonetheless been stimulating and instructive. When done seriously, forecasting the future requires special kinds of intellectual discipline. The futurist must separate out, carefully and explicitly, what he or she would *prefer* to have happen in the future from what is *likely* to happen. Hard-to-discern trends must be extrapolated over different time periods into the future; the farther into the future, the greater the fictional art form. These are only a few of the more demanding requirements. On balance, however, it is also likely that the futurist will be gone from the scene forever when his forecasted future comes to pass. If still alive, the futurist may, of course, blame Unpredictable Developments.

I have written two histories and two encyclopedia articles about the history of the Democratic party. I am deeply concerned about the party and its future. My bias is in the direction of liberalism and the primacy of the individual, both concerns reflecting the historic commitments of the Democratic party. My hope is to contribute to the party's deliberations about its future. This book, then, is how I think things will be for the party as it approaches the Year 2032, the year of its bicentennial.

However, the future is meaningless without history and optimism, both in short supply in much of contemporary political planning. In his book on *The Future as History*, Robert L. Heilbroner says it best:

> At bottom our troubled state of mind reflects an inability to see the future as an *historic* context. If current events strike us as all surprise and shock it is because we cannot see these events in a meaningful framework. If the future seems to us a kind of limbo, a repository of endless surprises, it is because we no longer see it as the expected culmination of the past, as the growing edge of the present. More than anything else, our disorientation before the future reveals a loss of our historic identity, an incapacity to grasp our historic situation.

Moving on to the matter of optimism, Heilbroner adds:

> [A]n attitude of optimism, for all its emphasis on personal striving and accomplishment, does not ultimately rest on a judgment about our private capabilities. It rests on a judgment about our historic capacities. At bottom, *a philosophy of optimism is an historic attitude toward the future*—an attitude based on the tacit premise that the future will accommodate the striving which we bring to it. Optimism is grounded in the faith that the historic environment, as it comes into being, will prove to be benign and congenial—or at least neutral to our private efforts.

Despite some of this book's bad news about the future that faces the Democratic party, it ain't necessarily so. My own optimism is derived from a faith in informed human choice within the context and momentum of observed historical tendencies. Tendencies can be modified by human choice. Democrats, be informed and choose. WARNING! DISCLAIMER! To demonstrate that I write this book with humility and a cloudy crystal ball, I refer the reader to Christopher Cerf and Victor Navasky's *The Experts Speak* (Pantheon, 1984). After all, Lord Kelvin *did* predict that x-ray would be proven a hoax, Herbert Hoover *did* say that prosperity was around the corner, and I *did* predict that a Republican would be elected president in 1960 (and, but for Mayor Richard Daley of Chicago, I think one was).

Ralph M. Goldman

Washington, D.C.

FOREWORD

The Lost Tribe Of Democrats

It was in the reign of Grand Old President XIV that the distinguished anthropologist Dr. Homer T. Pettibone, H.S.G., D.V.M., made a discovery that startled the nation: an enclave of elderly men and women practicing an ancient rite known as "a wine-and-cheese fund-raiser."

After several months of research, Dr. Pettibone tentatively concluded that these people were the remnant of a once-powerful pre-Reaganite tribal group known as "Democrats."

While occasional sightings of Democrats had been reported in the popular press down through the years, no concrete evidence of their existence had been brought forward. Scientists classified them with Bigfoot and the yeti. The supposed sightings, they said, were made by superstitious peasants who were probably frightened by one of those rare indigent Republicans or perhaps a wild goat.

Thus Dr. Pettibone's announcement electrified the country. ("Cult of the Living Dead!" was the headline in the National Enquirer.) He said he had found the group—18 males and 11 females—in an abandoned loft in Greenwich Village.

He said his curiosity was first piqued when they offered him square chunks of hard white cheese on toothpicks and sips of warm white wine from a plastic cup. It was then, he said, that he noted nine of those present were black, eight were Jewish and five were wearing white sheets with cut-out eyeholes.

"This is precisely the composition of the Democrats as it has come down to us in yellowed documents," said Dr. Pettibone elatedly. "And when I attempted to question them about their purposes, they replied in an indecipherable tongue from which I was able to pick out certain ancient Democratic buzz words like 'affirmative action,' 'separate but equal,' and 'CETA'—whatever a CETA might be."

Dr. Pettibone displayed a treasured artifact he had persuaded the Democrats to trade him for a handful of glass beads. It was a round button bearing the words "We Shall Overcome." Dr. Pettibone said one of the men had been wearing it on the breast of his white sheet. As far as the anthropologist could make out it referred to overcoming something called "racial hiring quotas," but of this he couldn't be positive.

Fortunately, Dr. Pettibone's field of study has been the ancient Democrats, who were thought to have been wiped out by radical changes in the political climate in the 1980s.

"While it is difficult to believe today," he said, "the Democrats were once the dominant species on the American political scene. They could be found in every town and hamlet, spreading government wherever they went. Back at the dawn of the present Eternal Republican Era, they did their utmost to adapt to the new conditions. They all went about crying, 'We suddenly realized we're for cutting government to the bone, too—but not quite as much to the bone as the Republicans.'

"Needless to say, such a weak survival mechanism was doomed to failure. What was believed to have been the last Democrat leaped from the Brooklyn Bridge in 1997 shouting, 'How could they do away with the Senior Citizens Bowling League Allocations Agency?'"

As a result, Dr. Pettibone said, few living Americans have ever seen a Democrat. He therefore expressed hopes that the little band from Greenwich Village could be put on display "in a tasteful manner" for the education of the public. "Let us look upon them," he said, "as political coelacanths."

Asked if he wasn't surprised that Democrats still existed, Dr. Pettibone shook his head. "No," he said, "I'm surprised they ever existed at all."

—Arthur Hoppe

ONE

The World and the United States in 2032

On May 21, 1832, Jacksonians came together from twenty-three of the twenty-four states of the Union to participate in their first national nominating convention (only Missouri refused to send a delegation). They referred to themselves as the Democratic-Republican party. They met in Baltimore, Maryland. And their absent leader, whom they were about to nominate for a second term of the presidency, was Andrew Jackson.

The formal birth of the Democratic party of the United States lasted three days. Delivery of the infant began on the last day under the sign of Taurus the Bull and concluded during the first days of Gemini the Twins. Thus, the party was born to stubbornness and divisiveness. That is how it was in 1832 and how it will probably be at its bicentennial in 2032.

The story of the Democratic party revolves around its leaders' efforts to join a large number of widely divergent constituencies into a winning electoral and governing coalition. Often these efforts have involved locating, mobilizing, and getting to the polls groups of citizens who are recently enfranchised or newly participating: immigrants, organized labor, blacks, women, Hispanics, youth, and so on. The party's search for coalition and consensus has stirred continual self-examination and self-reform.

One objective of these reforms has been to perfect the Democratic party as an institution of representation. A second objective has been to become well-enough organized to get its sometimes reluctant, other times forgetful, constituents to the ballot box. This includes those many occasions when the party has electorally activated particular groups. On other occasions the organizing impulse has gone the other way: particular groups have reorganized and revitalized the party.

The constituency-party interaction has been reciprocal, changes in one affecting the other. There have been times when each—party or constituency group—has had to wait for the other to pull itself together. Only then could the Democratic coalition become a winning one. This circle of relationships will continue.

To forecast whether the Democrats will be around for their bicentennial in 2032—they will—and under what conditions requires a long look at the party's history as well as guesses about the state of the world and the United States in the opening decades of the twenty-first century.

THE WORLD IN 2032

The world is the context for the politics of the United States. The United States is the context for the Democratic party. The obvious connection is simply that the Democratic party will be influenced by what is going on in the nation and in the world in 2032, probably more so than is the case today. The world in 2032 will be more crowded, more interdependent, and politically more integrated and dynamic than now. Today's demographic, communication, economic, scientific, technological, strategic, and political trends, even when loosely extrapolated into 2032, leave little doubt where the world is headed and what its problems are likely to be half a century from now.

Demographics

Politics is largely people management. Politicians have to know where people are, how many are there, what kinds of people are politically involved, what values and attitudes they have, and what types of messages and organizations will move them to political action. In office, politicians must be amateur demographers if they are to govern effectively. The Constitution of the United States recognizes this and calls for a census every ten years.

During the century from 1932 to 2032 the world's population will have quintupled, from 2 billion to 10 billion, assuming the present conservative growth rate of 1.7 percent per year. The rate for each continent differs, differences that are likely to continue over the next two or three generations. Africa increases annually at the rate of 2.9 percent, with Kenya and Algeria the highest in that continent; Latin America, at 2.4 percent, with Mexico and Peru highest; Asia, at 1.8 percent, with Iran and Bangladesh highest; North America, at 0.7 percent; Europe, at 0.6 percent. Demographers expect the world's population to level off at about 11 billion some time during the middle of the twenty-first century. By 2032 about 89 percent of the world's population will be living in less-developed countries (LDCs), 11 percent in the so-called First and Second Worlds.

A mere glance at these projections raises staggering

questions about feeding, housing, educating, providing medical care, and employing the work force from among 10 billion people. More immediately, however, is the question where these people will be. Most, as the projections above show, will be in Africa, Latin America, and Asia.

Population growth tends to lead to massive migrations from rural areas to cities and from poorer to wealthier countries. There will be cities of 30 million or more in 2032; Mexico City, San Paulo, Tokyo, and Shanghai, for example, are well on their way toward that figure. The mega-cities are bound to experience more congestion, crime, and violence. As for immigration, the United States alone is already admitting about 560,000 aliens legally a year, and another conservatively estimated half million are entering the country illegally. Migrant workers by the hundreds of thousands are moving from rural regions to wealthier urban centers throughout Europe. Immigration produces employment problems and social service burdens for the wealthier nations.

The problems arising from the quantity of people will be magnified by the greater longevity of many of them, particularly in the more-developed nations. Between 1975 and 1983, average life-span worldwide rose from 55 to 61 years. In the latter year, highest life expectancy—74 to 77 years—occurred in such developed nations as the United States, Israel, France, Denmark, Cuba, Canada, Switzerland, Australia, Sweden, Norway, the Netherlands, Japan, and Iceland, in ascending order. In contrast, longevity is and will continue to be lowest—40 to 50 years—in Ethiopia, Chad, Afghanistan, Mali, Congo, Cameroon, Bangladesh, Indonesia, and India. By 2032 the worldwide average may exceed 85 years for men and over 90 for women, with growing numbers of individuals living to 110. In the developed nations particularly, longer and healthier lives will bring new demands for health facilities, education, and work, not to mention new conceptions of retirement.

While decades of family planning and birth-control instruction will have slowed the rate of population growth in most countries, there will be important exceptions. Moslem societies, with ample space and severe labor shortages, will have grown in population at a 3 to 4 percent annual rate compared to zero growth in the United States and most of Europe. African nations, taken together, will be a close second in high birth rate, and the leader in mortality rate. Many Latin American countries, despite a weakening of the Catholic church's influence over family planning, will continue to be high among the population producers. Ironically, political and religious leaders tend to *promote* population growth, even though the solution to over population must eventually be found by them.

Economy and Technology

Feeding so many mouths is a recurrent crisis in many less-developed countries (LDCs). By 2032, hunger and starvation are likely to be common and continuing features of life in the LDCs. The hunger problem will be organizational and political rather than technical or economic. Despite the fact that much of the world's arable land is losing its topsoil through erosion at an alarming rate, at least half of the world's arable land is not yet used for agricultural purposes. Erosion control and space agriculture are feasible technologies and are likely to be major industries by 2032. "Farming" the oceans for microalgae and other food sources has hardly begun but is clearly on the agricultural horizon. What will continue to be lacking are political determination and the capacity to train and organize the necessary farmers and farm workers for the scale of food production needed.

Closely related to food supply is the supply of energy. A more positive note may be sounded here. Depletion of the world's oil reserves will continue, but at a pace slowed by conservation measures and alternative sources of energy. By

2032 renewable energy sources will have increased to more than 75 percent of the world's supply. Solar, wind, water currents, recycled garbage, grain alcohol, and nuclear fusion will be sources in wide use, particularly in the LDCs. Per capita usage will also spread around the world as LDCs achieve greater agricultural, industrial, informational, and consumer sophistication. Demand in the developed countries will increase exponentially as robots, computers, new forms of transport, expanding communication networks, and other new technologies line up for their share of the energy supply.

Problems of the environment and the depletion of natural resources will give rise to entire new industries, speeded by the realization that community housekeeping functions, such as refuse management and street-cleaning that once were local responsibilities, have now become continental and global in scope. Environmental problems, such as air and water pollution, will be dealt with not only by constraints upon polluters but also by the creation of new purification industries. The depletion of such natural resources as minerals, trees, and topsoil will be slowed by conservation, recycling, and replacement industries. Replacement industries will be those that produce alternatives such as synthetics and other man-made substitutes for natural materials. By 2032, the issue of mining the moon will undoubtedly have become as controversial as mining the ocean floor is today.

Science and technology will continue to inundate the world with new knowledge, new products, and new debates about the distribution of the wealth they produce. Futurists have their happiest hours extrapolating today's scientific and technological breakthroughs into the near future of the twenty-first century. A brief sampling suffices to give some hint of the political implications:

— Genetic engineering of dramatic new pharmaceuticals, "designed" (size, taste, shape, etc.) fruits, vegetables, animals, and fish

— Biochips, that is, semiconductors made of living cells rather than silicon

— Space manufacturing of pharmaceuticals, crystals, ball bearings, and countless other products best produced in gravity-free environments

— Two-way television permitting viewer participation in entertainment, educational, and political programs; and "talking" computers that will revolutionize language instruction, literacy education, home and office management

— Robots capable of performing almost every type of tedious, repetitive work in factory, farm, and home.

The list can go on. Many items are already at hand, in the design stage, or simply waiting to become an industry. While most consumption-oriented discoveries, technologies, and products will be found in the developed nations, development-oriented technologies such as agricultural genetic engineering, televised mass education, renewable energy systems, and the like will be welcomed in those LDCs where enterprising leaders are devoted to liberating their people from the shackles of illiteracy and poverty.

The International Labor Office has estimated that the world will need at least 1 billion new jobs by the year 2000— 100 million in the developed nations and 900 million in the LDCs. A rough extrapolation to 2032 forecasts a need for 2 billion jobs for the expected population of 10 billion. These figures do not reflect such factors as military employment, underemployment, useful employment for the elderly, unpaid employment, and other forms of work. Nor are these projections derived from solid statistics; current employment data for LDCs are not really reliable.

An optimist will see no employment problem; there is plenty of work to do in this world and never enough people to do it. A pessimist will focus on such matters as the failure of all economies thus far to provide full employment and fair income without underemployment or enforced employment. Nor have most societies been able to train people to their maximum capacities nor to meet the psychological as well as material needs of people in their role as workers. The issue of global unemployment will undoubtedly be high on the public agendas by 2032. It already is. Official data report 30 million unemployed in the industrialized nations in the mid-1980s, nearly 9 percent of the labor force. By adding those who no longer are seeking jobs, the total reaches closer to 50 million, or more than 12 percent . . . and going up. Unemployment concepts adopted by industrialized nations are not at all applicable in the LDCs, where, for example, it is common to employ children between the ages of nine and fifteen.

This pessimistic forecast about global unemployment is supported by other trends. Many economists who believe in boom-bust business cyle theories note that the cycle of boom-recession-depression-recovery in market economies usually takes fifty years. Their prediction is that a global boom will begin in the 1990s, reach its zenith around 2000, and be followed by recession and depression in the next two or three decades. The anticipated boom will begin in the United States with its many job-creating innovations, spread to Japan and Southeast Asia, but leave Europe lagging behind. The economies of the LDCs will not be sufficiently mature to experience the usual boom-bust cycle but are nevertheless bound to go through wrenching adjustments in their economic structures as they struggle to catch up.

Thus, during the decade of the 2020s, the world will probably endure a large-scale economic depression, in no small measure brought on by global unemployment and structural incompatabilities between developed economies and LDCs. World institutions capable of responding to such an economic crisis will still be lacking or merely emergent, and the crisis may drag even the most-developed and protected nations down. While it would be easy to make comparisons to the Great Depression of the early 1930s, world political institutions are not likely to be amenable to a global New Deal, let alone a global Franklin D. Roosevelt. (Who would close the banks temporarily, and how? How could a world social security and unemployment insurance program be established? And so forth.)

Two other trends further substantiate a pessimistic global economic picture for 2032: the debts of the LDCs and the arms race.

Much about the new requirements of international banking will undoubtedly be learned during the LDC debt crises of the 1980s and 1990s. In the mid-1980s about ninety LDCs are carrying a total outstanding indebtedness of about $700 billion, of which a third is owed by governments and two-thirds by private enterprises and projects. These debts add up to more than a fourth of the gross national products of these LDCs taken collectively. The interest service on the debts, as a portion of gross national product, has trebled in a single decade. Several nations with rapidly expanding economies—for example, Brazil and Mexico—are hard put to make loan payments without drying up their cash needs for domestic development. Other less-responsible or less-efficient LDCs and their business enterprises are failing to make loan payments.

The problems of international debt, capital investment, and cash flow that are becoming critical in the 1980s are probably a mere foretaste of the problems that will arise in the decades ahead as growing numbers of LDCs seek funds for domestic development and as international trade increases in volume and complexity. Without domestic economic and social development in each LDC, it is certain that their respective contributions to world trade and prosperity cannot be positive.

Multinational banks seeking quick interest earnings through loans to governments and business in LDCs will become more selective about the qualifications of and securities offered by borrowers. Supranational (e.g., the World Bank) and multinational lenders and underwriters of loans will charge different interest rates for different types of loans. Elements of a Global Marshall Plan, currently in the form of an International Development Association, are emerging to provide special low-interest or interest-free loans to selected

9

LDC governmental or business enterprises. "Needy" countries will continue to receive direct assistance from supranational agencies but less so directly from the more affluent developed nations such as the United States. By 2032, because of the developed nations' own domestic economic distress, popular support for direct foreign aid programs will have all but disappeared.

By 2032 the rapid growth in world productivity and international trade needs will have led to numerous international economic innovations. The requirements of cash flow, currency exchange, balance of trade, capital investment, profitability, and competition are likely to compel currency simplification and new balance-of-payment practices designed to make it easier for business to operate internationally and for governments to cooperate financially.

Multinational corporations—industrial, agricultural, financial, and informational—will abound, better protected from risks of nationalization, plant and natural disasters, and controversial cross-cultural ethical standards of business. Transnational unions will begin to design effective responses to their new roles in the world's labor market. As predicted by many economists, centralized and socialized economies will have adopted free-market principles in many fields of production and service and free-market economies will have explicitly and conditionally accepted monopoly enterprises in fields where the public interest is clear. The mixed economy will be the prototype, and theorists will be working on principles for rationalizing their operation. It is questionable, however, that these economic institutional advances, without concomitant political changes, will be enough to help combat global recessions and depressions.

The second trend that makes for pessimistic expectations about the global economy in 2032 pertains to the arms race. The continued militarization of the world will entail an economic burden that in 2032 will be even more onerous than it is today, particularly for the less-developed countries.

Strategic

The nations of the world are currently expending between $600-700 billion annually on their military security. The two largest spenders—almost at a par with each other—are the North Atlantic Treaty Organization and the Warsaw Treaty Organization; together, they expend up to two-thirds of the world's military outlays. The other third, and growing, is made up of expenditures by LDCs, primarily for conventional weaponry and at great cost to domestic economic and social development.

In economic terms, the United States defense budget has become increasingly controversial on grounds of its large part in the federal deficit and its questionable purchasing procedures. The annual defense budget of the Soviet Union—which has been officially reported at practically the same number of rubles for over a decade—has also become excessively burdensome to that nation's economy, as evidenced by its archaic industrial plants, its underemployed labor force, and the slow development of its consumer sector. For the two superpowers, economic considerations are likely to be the principal motivation for reaching arms-limitation agreements that will slow the race to a walk.

Other considerations, however, will limit this strong economic motivation for limiting arms expenditures. The desire to maintain their primacy within their respective alliance systems and their military duopoly throughout the world is likely to lead to new forms of military cooperation, which translates into joint spending by the two superpowers—for example, collaborative research on space and defensive weapons, greater direct involvement in United Nations peace-keeping missions, closer consultation on antiterrorist measures (the Kremlin will have been a target for bombings long before 2032), and joint monitoring of a comprehensive nuclear test ban. The inescapable pressures for researching new breakthroughs in military technology, particularly high-tech defensive systems, can lead the superpowers in no other direction than augmented research budgets; the United States alone spends over \$32 billion a year on defense research. Another source of pressure will continue to be the politics of their respective military-industrial complexes, involving domestic political coalitions that threaten to circumvent, if not overcome, each nation's constitutional policy-making apparatus.

Among the LDCs, the arms race is likely to accelerate and its costs reflect a greater proportion of the world's military expenditures. As part of the process of national integration, LDCs will continue to pursue religious, ideological, and nationalistic "crusades" against their neighbors or within their regions. For ruling oligarchies, displays of military strength will continue to be essential for imposing domestic order as well as for influencing external relationships. Domestic political and economic development in many LDCs will be increasingly tumultuous as superpowers learn to keep "hands off" or to exercise influence through surrogates. While democratic institutions will undoubtedly gain ground in many LDCs, authoritarian regimes in most will become more defensive, militarized, and enduring.

As a consequence of these developments, the world will acquire a two-tiered set of military institutions. The upper tier will consist of the military balance among the nuclear powers. At present, these are the two superpowers whose military capacities for mutual destruction provide the current deterrent balance that maintains the peace at this tier. By 2032 the bipolar balance will undoubtedly be destabilized by the increased nuclear capability of Mainland China and of new arrivals (Pakistan, Brazil, South Africa, etc.) to the nuclear club. The pressures for designing arrangements and institutions to control nuclear proliferation will have become irrepressible by this time. What nuclear ascendancy the superpowers may maintain will probably derive from their possession of high-cost defense systems resulting from advances in laser, satellite, and computer technology.

The second tier will include non-nuclear powers building and trading in what are now called conventional weapons. But the conventional weaponry of 2032 would be considered unconventional even today: "smarter" bombs and missiles, with precise target-finding capability; tactical field weaponry with nuclear components, as in the case of neutron bombs; laser-accurate defensive weapons; highly mobile infantry using individualized flying machines; nonlethal chemical and other weapons, such as psychochemicals, designed to immobilize rather than kill; space, ocean, and earth monitoring and intelligence systems that will put Mata Haris permanently out of business, and so on.

Regimes buying these and more old-fashioned conventional weapons will be doing so, first, because their neighbors are doing so and, secondly, in order to maintain themselves against domestic disorders. The limited national resources of LDCs will thus be funneled off into heavy military expenditures except in those few cases where small and friendly neighboring countries form alliances of mutual defense and internal police cooperation. In the more authoritarian nations where the military are the major institution, one positive outcome of further militarization may be the necessity to educate an otherwise largely illiterate population in order to produce the skills required by the latest weapons technology. Perhaps the only limits on the militarization of authoritarian LDCs will be the inability to borrow, barter, or otherwise pay for their military objectives.

Add the weight of LDC militarization to (a) the prospects of massive global unemployment, (b) the downswing of the predicted fifty-year economic cycle, and (c) the continued lack of well-established global economic and political institutions for coping with such conditions, and the world outlook for the period leading up to 2032 appears dim indeed. The implications for the Democratic party, in its familiar role as the "rescue party," will be profoundly challenging not only at home but globally.

Yet another major strategic—and economic—

development will have emerged by 2032: the arrival of the Pacific Century. The present rise of Japan, South Korea, Taiwan, Singapore, and Hong Kong as thriving industrial and commercial communities has already converted the Pacific Rim into the world's most vital economic and strategic arena. For example, the United States' two-way trade across the Pacific ($136 billion in 1983) surpassed this country's transatlantic trade ($110 billion). With an eye to the future, Americans already have $30 billion invested in Pacific Rim ventures, a 65 percent increase in investment over the previous five years. Joint production and distribution ventures between American and other Pacific Rim countries are increasing in number by leaps and bounds; more than one thousand Japanese companies are already operating in California alone. The Japanese are also the United States' major competitor for similar joint ventures with East Asian companies.

By 2032 Mainland China's modernization program, spurred by a literate people devoted to the work ethic, will have produced a third member in the superpower ranks. The reacquisition of Hong Kong and its market economy, friendly relations with Taiwan, development of a relatively nonideological mixed economy domestically, pacification of the Korean Peninsula, joint ventures with Japan and the United States, massive Chinese enrollments in Western universities and technical schools, and successful family planning programs will combine to elevate Mainland China to developed-country status. With this will come the augmented significance of the Pacific Basin as the strategic center of the world.

Less noticeable but equally important for the Pacific Rim will be the *eastward* internal development of the Soviet Union. In contrast to the internal westward movements that have historically taken place on the European and North American continents, the Soviet Union's version of Horace Greeley's famous counsel will be "Go East, young man." The Soviet frontiers are east of European Russia and expansion into Siberia goes on apace. Anticipating its future as a Pacific Rim nation, the Soviet Union is already establishing its military presence in the Pacific: the claims to Japanese islands in the

Kurils; interest in the Communist movement in the Philippines; alliance with Vietnam and others in Southeast Asia; and military installations along the periphery of the Indian Ocean.

A new and more pragmatic generation of Soviet leaders will also give a great deal of attention to reestablishing friendlier economic, strategic, and cultural ties with their former protégé, the People's Republic of China. The new Soviet pragmatism does not necessarily predict a softening of Soviet totalitarianism and its commitment to the dictatorship of the proletariat; the process of recruiting top leaders, in fact, reinforces hard-line approaches to both domestic and foreign policies. Leaders move up the ranks of the Communist party of the Soviet Union by first being chosen "candidate" members of the party committee to which they are elevated. This probationary status, which may last for several years, assures that no New Generation will upset Old Guard policies.

Coming from the other direction—westward—is the United States. Of the eight United States mutual security treaties now in force, five are with Pacific Rim countries. By 2032 the Japanese attack on Pearl Harbor, the Korean War, and the Vietnam War will be viewed as ancient beginnings of the militarization of the Pacific.

Economic and military competition will bring constant friction and geopolitical adjustment among the Pacific Rim nations. There will be border incidents and minor military engagements. Military expenditures will become burdensome as they will be everywhere. However, the probability of major wars in the Pacific area will be minimal, kept low by a number of military, diplomatic, and economic deterrents.

The military deterrents will be both nuclear and conventional. Mainland China—with the largest army in the world—will have increased its nuclear stockpile and delivery capability to the point of deterrent credibility. Japan, Taiwan, and South Korea—not to mention India and Pakistan—will have the technology for producing and rapidly assembling nuclear bombs. The huge and conservative army of Mainland China, the relatively disarmed condition of Japan, and the security treaties providing an American nuclear and conventional umbrella for U.S. allies will contribute to overall security in the region. Successful economic modernization and growth among the major powers on the Pacific Rim will promote diplomatic rather than military solutions to the inevitable frictions. Occasional military adventures by aberrant and unskilled leaders will be quickly quarantined. In sum, the obsolescence of international warfare will be most appreciated and evident around the Pacific Rim despite the militarization of most of its nations.

Communication and Worldviews

When in 1969 the first televised pictures of Earth were transmitted by the astronauts of the Apollo-Saturn lunar mission, the astronomical and philosophical concepts of the world as humanity's only home were given a dramatic new visual reality. A million words and maps could not communicate a worldview as strikingly as those television pictures. Before, during, and since that event, global communication and transportation links have spread and reinforced popular consciousness of the world as a unit, a single community, and a fragile possession.

A more terrifying reminder of the smallness of Earth has been the growing popular realization that intercontinental ballistic missiles can deliver deadly nuclear warheads from anywhere to anywhere on the planet in half an hour or less. Intercontinental air travel transports persons from one corner of the world to other remote corners in less than a day. Televised conversations between leaders and experts in distantly separated parts of the world are carried into our living rooms, along with views of wars and disasters in progress. Satellites bring together family members and business executives by telephone from different continents. The news media reiterate the comprehensive words "world" and "global." These reminders of our spatial proximity to each other are radically focusing perceptions of the planet as a single entity. Perhaps the ultimate measure of this process of perceptual change is the claim of some automobile manufacturers that they have produced a "world class" car. By 2032 the perceptual and conceptual "miniaturization" of the planet will have become pervasive, reaching even those living in primitive circumstances, relatively untouched by contemporary media or transportation.

Further reinforcing one-world concepts are various ocean, space, and ecological enterprises. Explorations of the ocean floor, concern for the preservation of whales and other sea creatures, preparations for mining the ocean's minerals, debates about the oceans as the common heritage of mankind, proposals to float icebergs to desert regions—these and other widely disseminated references to the water-covered surfaces of the Earth give remote issues a psychological nearness. Similar responses occur as worry about the ionosphere, speculation about life on other planets, proposals for mining the moon, plans for satellite communities, and similar topics are bandied about. Impressions of the oneness of the world are engrained by the growing number of ecological problems that traverse national and even continental lines: pollution of rivers and seas; pollution of the atmosphere; the spread of diseases from nation to nation; deforestation; waste of finite natural resources such as oil; acid rain; radiation from nuclear tests—the global list seems endless. Awareness of these issues leaves no doubt that the planet is a small neighborhood.

Thus, by 2032, speaking of "one world" will no longer have the visionary aura that it had when Wendell Willkie spoke of it in 1940.

Worldviews will undoubtedly emanate soonest from those nations, with the United States and Japan in the lead, that first enter the much-touted postindustrial information era. According to some forecasts, this Information Age will be characterized by an exponential increase in knowledge and transmission of information (already in progress), rapid obsolescence of perceptions of and concepts about the physical and social environment, increasing immediacy and access of communications, increasing individual, organizational, and institutional dependence upon information and communications services, and growing skill and deliberateness in individual and collective decision-making processes.

The effects of these tendencies to think globally in symbolic, conceptual, and informational terms will begin to have far-reaching practical consequences as the time approaches for the Democratic party bicentennial. The economies of several regions and continents will have begun, falteringly in some cases, to function within common markets. A few groups of contiguous nations will have cooperative internal security and national defense arrangements. Multinational industrial, financial, and service corporations will have multiplied manifold. Culture, as manifest in the arts, entertainment, foods, expressive values, and various lifestyles, will be increasingly universalized as international "jet sets" become more numerous and less exclusive. The transnational and global content of popular values and conversation will, of course, be both cause and effect for changes in world political discourse and institutions.

Political

As always, political institutions will be the slowest to respond to the exigencies of a rapidly changing world. But the Madisonian model of constitutional evolution will continue to unfold. Transnational and world problems—unemployment, pollution, terrorism, hunger, commerce, etc.—will continue to give rise to globally organized interest groups, or nongovernmental organizations (NGOs). NGOs will intensify their relationships and involvements with domestic and transnational political parties. Transnational parties will articulate world issues, help affiliated parties gain national and supranational office. As the media become more attentive to the highly visible and dramatic aspects of world politics at the United Nations, the various functional organizations of the UN system and the several regional organizations—the European Communities, the Organization of African States, the Organization of American States, etc.—will begin to operate with greater scope and effectiveness.

Thus, by 2032 the world will know more about its supranational and transnational political and economic organizations and institutions, and perhaps be more sensitive to their limitations and potentialities. A world government will still be considered visionary and a major threat to what may be left of national sovereignty. The concept of world government will be vigorously resisted from many directions: the superpowers—the United States, the Soviet Union, Mainland China—jealous of their leadership status in world affairs; the regional organizations just beginning to feel the magnification of their influence as a consequence of regional cooperation; the more authoritarian of the LDCs, fearful of losing their domestic control.

While most nations will defend their status as sovereigns and as principal actors in world affairs, the daily practical politics of the world will be moving in small increments toward greater interdependence and integration.

—Supranational agencies and bureaucracies, acquiring a vested interest in their own success, will be implementing global agreements and programs with increasing assertiveness and consequences.

—Members of the nuclear tier of the arms race will begin to do something about limiting the military competition among those in the conventional tier. Support for domestic revolutions and state-supported terrorism will diminish drastically as alternative forms of political competition are adopted by less-developed nations.

—Transnational political movements—NGOs and transnational parties—will increasingly influence the identification of world leaders, the language of global ideological debate, and the agenda for world policy making. The transnational parties—a new Communist International, the Socialist International, the Christian Democratic International, the Liberal International, and others—will pursue their objectives in ways familiar to constitutional democracies, namely, by debating global public policies, campaigning for popular support by world opinion, and promoting stronger governmental (national and supranational) institutions to which they may elect their leaders.

This preview of the 2032 era will hardly have the surprise and drama usually depicted in science fiction and futuristic movies. Much that is forecast will seem to be "more of the same," with a few new twists. Nuclear war and other holocausts are not forecast here; otherwise the hopeful outlook of this book would become irrelevant. What *is* anticipated is grounded on tendencies already with us. These forecasts provide an informational setting within which to consider what the United States and its two hundred-year-old Democratic party will be up against in the world of 2032.

THE UNITED STATES IN 2032

During the century from 1932 to 2032, the population of the United States will have more than doubled, from 125 million in the first years of the New Deal to about 305 million at the time of the Democratic party's bicentennial. This doubling will be in sharp contrast to the world's quintupling in population. Further, the average American will be twice as old as the average individual in the hundred less-developed nations of the world. The two trends underscore the differences between Americans (and Europeans and Japanese) and most of the rest of the world, differences in medical care, diet, education, and other life patterns. The differences extend to political institutions and party politics.

Demographics

The 305 million Americans will be distributed across the land differently from the present. The westward migration of the past two centuries will continue, filling the West Coast and Rocky Mountain states. Two states in the Sunbelt—Texas and Florida—will have had dramatic population growth (currently at the rate of 40 percent annually). Population will decline or remain stable in New England, the North Atlantic states, and the North Central region. Small increases will occur in the Upper South.

The implications for United States party politics are profound. The greatest population growth will be in states currently tending to become more Republican, that is, Mountain, West Coast, and Sunbelt states. Recruits or converts to the Republican party in these states plus greater representation in the electoral college and the House of Representatives will present the Democratic party with a serious handicap in national politics, as suggested by the returns in the presidential elections of 1980 and 1984.

Immigration—documented and illegal—will add to the millions. Between 450,000 to 560,000 immigrants annually enter the country legally, an average that is not likely to diminish. Another yearly half million—some predict over one million—will enter as "undocumenteds." The bulk will be Hispanics, significantly influencing the politics of California, Texas, Florida, New York, Illinois, and the District of Columbia. The others, in rising proportions, will be Asians and Pacific islanders. Internal migration, as noted above, will also continue, with an important ethnic aspect; blacks appear to be leaving central cities and moving back to the South in substantial numbers.

As more LDCs adopt democratic institutions and as global transportation becomes more convenient, one type of immigration into the United States is likely to diminish, namely, the brain drain. This refers to LDC citizens who come to the U.S. for advanced training and stay rather than return to the physical and political hardships of their homelands. In the past, American-trained individuals have encountered ideological pressure, jealousy, and, incredibly, unemployment upon their return. Domestic democratization and easy travel between homeland and the U.S. will make it possible for these ambitious individuals to succeed "at home," particularly if they are working for a multinational corporation or in an open political system.

The composition as well as the distribution of rural and urban populations will change markedly. Today, less than 3 percent of the population lives on rural farms, and this tiny percentage is likely to remain for the next couple of generations even as farms become fewer, larger, and more industrialized. The present 1 billion acres of United States farmland will probably increase by half as more acreage is brought into production in practically every state. Others will be only technically rural because of residence in small country towns. In many respects these people will be more suburban than rural, more cottage industry than industrial, more culturally urban than countryside.

With urban growth moving along at a 6 percent clip annually, entire regions will become urbanized, with a megalopolis at their centers and satellite cities all along the main arteries of transportation leading into them. The ethnic composition of central cities will change gradually as Hispanics and young white singles and couples arrive and blacks depart. Renewal of urban cores will gather momentum by the turn of the century and by 2032 will again become important sources of employment and economic activity.

Nearly 12 percent, or 28 million, Americans were 65 or older in 1984. By 2032 this proportion is likely to rise to 20 percent, or 61 million. Life expectancy is currently 84 years for women and 79.5 for men; by 2032, it will be closer to 90 years each, with several thousand active, if not jogging, at 110. Some forecasts anticipate that there will be some 16 million persons over 85, with eleven women for every five men in this age bracket. However, at the rate women are entering the work force, with all its accompanying pressures and health hazards, the gender ratio is likely to even out.

Today, two out of every five Americans are under twenty-five years of age. By 2032, as the nation approaches zero population growth, the proportion of young will decline, reaching one in five under twenty-five. A new wave of baby-boomers, probably born during the prosperity years from 1990 to 2010, may alter the tendency toward fewer youth and more seniors, but the odds seem small in the light of increasingly self-conscious family planning and improved birth-control methods.

The current generation of baby-boomers will continue to appear as a departure from the smoother lines in the population trends. The baby-boomers are persons born between 1946 and 1964. They currently comprise approximately one-third of the population. From 1946 on, the birth rate rose sharply and remained high until 1964, with married women giving birth to two or more children on the average. After 1965, the birth rate dropped and remained below 4 million a year to the present time.

The baby-boom generation is characterized by high education (about one-fourth with college degrees), high interest in family and religion, an inclination toward two-income households, and knowledgeable concern for economic issues and policies. They constitute a large proportion of the food-service and secretarial work force. About one-third of the baby-boomer population have been called "yuppies" (young, upward, mobile professionals—lawyers, scientists, computer specialists, etc.).

A very large proportion of the 1948–1964 baby-boomers will be among the 61 million over sixty-five's in 2032, looking forward to another ten to twenty years of life. With the revolution in medical technology and health care that lies immediately ahead (see below), these elderly boomers are likely to be in vigorous health, perhaps with a few replacement organs in their bodies, and politically as well as socially and economically active.

Economy and Technology

The indications are strong that the American economy will be postindustrial, that is, predominantly informational and service in character. The simplest way to detail this generalization is to indicate what people will be doing for a living in 2032.

Agribusiness, the biggest industry in the nation, will maintain the United States' status as the "bread basket of the world." Genetic engineering and new sources of renewable energy will permit production of new, more nutritious, safer fruits, vegetables, meat, fish, fowl, and synthetic foods. Year-round and indoor agriculture will increasingly be a part of the farming industry, particularly after new methods of coping with soil erosion are perfected. Seafoods of many types, particularly shellfish, will be raised in ocean "farms" under scientifically controlled conditions. Mechanization and robotics will practically eliminate the need for unskilled or semiskilled farm workers.

The oceans and the seas will begin to be cultivated and produce on a relatively large scale by 2032. More than 700 American companies are already planning ventures in mining minerals, aquaculture, transportation, military uses, and recreation. The necessary technologies are presently available or in sight. What will take time are further experimentation, training of personnel, and sizable capital investment.

Solar, wind, and nuclear fusion energy will be sufficiently well developed to begin fulfilling the promise of limitless renewable energy. Adapting equipment such as automobiles, airplanes, furnaces, lighting, etc., to accommodate these energy sources will be a major technological and manufacturing activity. While the United States will remain the principal energy user in the world at twentyfold its present rate, many other nations will be increasing their usage and purchasing conversion equipment, primarily from the United States and Japan.

Care of the environment will become Big Business and then some. More than half a trillion dollars will be spent on air and water purification and pollution control during the 1980s, and this is only a beginning. As industries and other polluters assume greater responsibility for environmental protection, the economics of financing waste disposal and recycling will be resolved in ways that permit new control technologies to be put to use. Polluted lakes and rivers will be systematically cleaned up. Sources of air pollution will diminish. Individualized air and water purification packs will be available as a consumer product.

Grand projects for reforestation and irrigating desert lands in other parts of the world will be underway in large measure as American commercial enterprises. Polymerization (the building up of larger molecules from smaller ones) will produce a flood of alternatives to minerals and similar scarce natural resources.

The present revolution in physics, biochemistry, genetic engineering, organ replacement, pharmaceuticals, and the organization of medicine and health care will cascade along with gathering force. New scientific knowledge about the immune system and reduced use of carcinogenic materials will lead to the near conquest of many types of cancer and greater success in the implantation of organ replacements. The genetic and chemical causes of the aging process and of the predisposition to psychosis will be much more fully understood and controlled. The institutional "storage" of the aging and the mentally ill will be subjected to radical change long before 2032.

In 1965 health care costs constituted about 6.1 percent of the United States' gross national product. By 1983, the costs had risen to nearly 11 percent. The trend will probably carry this to 15-or-more percent by 2032. The *per capita* annual cost of health care in the early 1960s was about $130-$150; in 1984, $1,500 and going up. An American over sixty-five today requires about three times as much in health care as any other citizen except a newborn baby, a tremendous expenditure by 2032 when 61 million Americans will be over sixty-five. The economics of health is and will continue experiencing substantial change over the next thirty to forty years in response to more expensive technologies and therapies, the impact of inflation on a labor-intensive industry, and the growing demand for health services. The industry's response will include more numerous for-profit medical facilities, more out-patient care, more economical and efficient use of facilities, greater emphasis on preventive medicine, new forms of health insurance and financing, rapid growth of paramedical specialties, and other cost-limiting strategies. The public policy debates about health care, particularly as ethical issues regarding the allocation of scarce resources become more salient, will undoubtedly reach white heat well before 2032.

The nation's infrastructure today needs an estimated $550 billion worth of rebuilding: $275 billion for highways, $49 billion for bridges, $110 billion for water systems, and $118 billion for wastewater treatment systems, to mention the principal items only. The need will become serious enough by the turn of the century to compel large-scale investment of public funds, possibly at the $2 trillion level of expenditure. These expenditures may prove to be the public works answer to the unemployment situation that will prevail in the decade prior to 2032. Not included in these figures are the costs— another $40-50 billion—of building or rebuilding mass transit systems in the country's major urban centers, for which plans are in being or under discussion. Who will pay for the construction and maintenance of all this? Users and taxpayers— the former on the basis of ability to pay and actual use, the latter, via general tax funds, for benefits accruing to their communities.

With millions of robots performing the drudgery tasks of industrial production and human services, a twenty-five-hour work week, expanding leisure and entertainment, a much more highly educated labor force, 14 percent structural unemployment along with more severe unemployment in less-developed countries, multinational corporations employing overseas workers, and new forms of unionization and employee participation in the management and finances of productive enterprises, to mention but a few trends, there can be no doubt that the concept of work and the nature of employment and unemployment will be subjected to fundamental review. At issue will be the need to redefine full employment, unemployment, volunteer activity, underemployment, uncompensated but compulsory work, part-time employment, retirement, etc. The debate will be less a matter of conceptual definitions and more a struggle between new types of unions and multinational corporations as employers. As much as 14 percent unemployment (by current definition of the term) will probably be politically tolerable and, in fact, the norm.

Strategy

As suggested earlier, the nuclear tier's arms race will probably decelerate by 2032. With its membership enlarged by nuclear weapons proliferation, the nuclear club will become a multilateral rather than a bipolar set of relationships. Cooperation in the development of defensive space weaponry will assure the maintenance of the Soviet-American duopoly at the nuclear summit.

The arms transfers at the second or conventional tier will present the troublesome dilemmas. Arms manufacture will still be a significant part of the American and other economies. Restrictions on U.S. arms sales will have evolved over the years along specific lines. The exceptions will be approval of transfers to regional organizations for collective security uses under shared control, transfers to treaty allies, transfers to United Nations peace-keeping forces, and transfers to members of a future security association of all major democracies. As noted earlier, most of the transfers will be to Pacific Rim countries, with declining sales to Latin America and the Middle East.

By 2032, most allies will have picked up their full share of the burden of military expenditures. NATO ties will remain strong but at a plateau. NATO itself will probably be reorganized as an alliance between a more strictly European military institution (a European Defense Community) and a North American command consisting of the United States and Canada. Deterrence, security alliances, and a diminution of border disputes and "wars of national liberation" will decrease but hardly halt the pace of arms build-ups. There will be increased interest in collective internal security and national defense arrangements, to which the U.S. will contribute its good offices, training when requested, and weaponry.

Military research and development will increasingly become a double-edged sword. It is nearly impossible to terminate or even control human creativity and inventiveness, particularly when pertinent activities are well financed. Of the $97 billion spent by both industry and government on research and development in the United States in 1984, a third—$32 billion—went into military research. This R & D expenditure represents nearly 3 percent of the gross national product, with one-third for defense. Other industrialized nations spend almost as much, with a difference: less for the military and more for consumer goods, health, energy, and environment. Japan and West Germany, with relatively modest military expenditures, are major competitors of the United States in the latter category of research. On the one hand, research accelerates the qualitative arms race; on the other hand, it fuels a large part of human technological progress.

Communication and Worldviews

As the leading Information Society in the world, the United States will be increasingly alluding to *world* issues and approaching problems as *global*. Ideological and policy campaigns on world policies will be conducted through transnational party affiliations and NGOs at the United Nations, in regional organizations, and in the world press. Pollution will be *world* pollution. Unemployment will be *global* unemployment. Analysis and argument will be transnational and supranational in formulation and objective. As a millenial and missionary society of long standing, worldviews will come easily to Americans.

By 2032, American television, radio, and press will be as pervasive throughout the world as it is domestically today. Even the most totalitarian of nations will have long given up trying to jam these "alien" media. While American television, film, and musical productions will continue to be extremely popular, competition from European and domestic producers will be on the increase. American worldviews, however, will tend to be the principal source of themes that make up the content of global cultural and ideological discussion.

The much-anticipated explosion in American educational technology will have taken place by 2032. Home learning and information centers will be as common as telephones, radios, and television sets. Computer-assisted and computer-delivered instruction will be major supplements to books, classrooms, laboratories, and live teachers. For those who cannot afford the necessary equipment for home study, it will become available in schools, public libraries, and other public institutions.

The learning process in schools and at home will become much more individualized, that is, paced according to the particular needs and capacities of the individual student. Talking computers will be common and especially significant in the instruction of the very young and of illiterates. Adult self-instruction will increase dramatically, particularly as occupations become obsolete, unemployment prevails, and third and fourth careers become common. Computers and other communications technology will make work-at-home feasible and desirable in many fields, particularly the service occupations.

The Information Society will take a biological turn when biochips are perfected, probably around 2010. Biochips, now the subject of intense research, are protein or other living cells that will receive, store, and retrieve data just as silicon chips (integrated circuits) now do. When it becomes possible to "weld" or otherwise incorporate biochips into the body's sensory and central nervous systems, only lack of imagination will limit speculation about the possible implications for human intelligence and experience.

Political

American pragmatism and reformism reflect an acknowledgement of the need for adaptability and change and a willingness to experiment with institutions and programs. Some students of the American political system consider it the most revolutionary in the world; it *does* change. Few know this better than Democrats, who have been reforming and changing their party almost without let-up since 1936 when the national convention two-thirds rule was abolished.

It must be said again: changes in political institutions usually occur at a much slower pace than in other institutions in most societies. This is understandable. Political leaders, in order to avoid surprises or new dilemmas, tend to cling to established ways of public decision making. Scientific knowledge of political processes is still quite primitive, hence it is difficult to predict which reforms will work as intended and which will be counter-productive. Reform and change also require heavy expenditures of reorganizational energy, of which there is a limited supply among overworked politicians. Above all, however, there is the redistribution of power and influence that usually, and often unpredictably, accompanies institutional and procedural reform; astute political leaders are not inclined to risk or squander power and influence.

Several present political tendencies in the United States have been going on long enough to make it probable that they will continue well into the twenty-first century. A sampling follows.

The contraction of the operating function and staffing of the federal government will continue. Increasing numbers of federal functions will devolve to state and local governments and private sector enterprises, along with personnel and costs. This decentralization has been in progress for over a decade, with special impetus during the Nixon and Reagan administrations. As a consequence, state and local public employment has multiplied severalfold, producing a new state-and-local vested interest in governmental service. (A previous similar vested interest arose among national level public servants under the New Deal and Fair Deal.) In lieu of federal operating agencies to implement national policies and programs, the federal role will be to establish nationwide rules and standards, gather nationwide data and other information, and monitor the implementation of programs.

The programs and policies that the federal government will manage directly will tend to be those bearing upon supranational, transnational, or international concerns and responsibilities. Only the federal government can provide the administrative backup for U.S. representatives to the United Nations or other supranational agencies in the UN system. Only the federal government can deal with transnational business, labor, party, and similar organizations. Only the federal government can manage international alliances, membership in regional organizations, and other internation relations.

After the turn of the century, these external activities will expand rapidly. As a consequence, the Defense Department will probably double in administrative personnel, and the State Department will be reorganized to concentrate on support of delegations to supranational agencies while many of its operations will devolve to international divisions in other federal departments, for example, Commerce, Treasury, Labor, and so on.

The operation of the Congress is now a billion dollar enterprise, with no end of functional and administrative growth in sight. In the next decade or two, the usually intractable problems of legislative staffing, congressional workload, committee organization, control of the federal bureaucracy and budget, reconciliation of local, national, and global policies, and congressional party organization will reach crisis proportions. In addition, the influence of Congress as an institution will be subject to serious challenge—one could almost say subversion—from political action committees, single-issue pressure groups, the media, and, above all, the military-industrial complex. Much of this challenge will be crystallized in terms of the funding of election campaigns and lobbying expenditures, although the flow of money will only be symptomatic of a number of institutional pathologies.

In coping with these institutional problems, the Congress will probably adopt some form of public financing of election campaigns for its offices. Congress will also favor a constitutional amendment for a four-year term for members of the House of Representatives, thereby reducing the amount of time and campaign funds needed by party nominees. Reorganization of the committee structure in both houses will take place at least twice before 2032 in attempts to reflect the changing agenda of public issues, sources of power in society, and organization of the federal bureaucracy.

Perhaps the most significant reorganization reforms will pertain to the party leadership mechanisms in the House of Representatives. After years of diffusion of leadership function and influence, it will become clear to the members, particularly the Democrats, that their collective powers have been lost to other national political institutions. Reforms will tend to concentrate rather than diffuse the party leadership's prerogatives, taking especially into account the implications for party grassroots organization. A major motivation for such concentration, and a source of prickly relations with the president, will be the increase in the chief executive's responsibilities as head of state, manager of foreign relations, and world leader.

The presidential office, as distinct from the federal bureaucracy, will continue to expand to the point of itself becoming a relatively oversized bureaucracy. The growth in Office of the President functions and personnel will be one of many justifications for decentralizing federal programs to the states and local communities. The constitutional duties of the president amid complex and difficult global circumstances will contribute to his status and influence as chief diplomat and world leader. Other executive duties—management of the economy, civic education, and other domestic functions—will devolve to others at state and local levels, possibly coordinated by stronger and better-organized national party agencies.

One of the most difficult problems associated with the presidency will be its relationship with the party, the media, and the electorate. These relationships are rife with ambivalence and competitiveness. How should national agencies of the party be coordinated to take into account the interests of the president and both houses of Congress? How should the new affiliations with transnational parties be incorporated into national operations? How should state and local party organization be integrated with the national? Ordinarily, the party in control of the presidency enjoys opportunities—often neglected—to deal with these dilemmas. The out-party sometimes tries but almost invariably fails in reaching for answers. As the influence of the media and the disinterest of the electorate increase, the problems will become critical for presidential politics and party leadership. The invention of solutions and the concession of power in the larger interests of the presidency and party will require a degree of domestic political statesmanship not frequently demonstrated in the twentieth century. If the recent history of Democratic party reforms, with its sequence of trial-and-error panaceas, is any indication of future approaches, the outlook for solutions does not seem promising.

The federal court system will face old and new stresses. Judicial workload will continue its steady rise, with ironclad limits of personnel and time at the top of the pyramid. The nine justices of the Supreme Court can decide only so many full cases (between 150 and 200) in a single annual term. The U.S. district courts, already sagging under an annual load of nearly 200,000 cases, will be augmented and reorganized time and again, either by increasing the number of federal district judges or developing a system of judicial referees or mediators. The latter—third-party mediation or arbitration—will become a major feature of the court system.

The Reagan appointees to the Supreme Court in the 1980s will assure a relatively conservative court well into the twenty-first century: devoted to judicial restraint rather than judicial activism; protective of governmental authority and private property; concerned about family and religious issues; bemused by profound issues of medical ethics and health care; struggling with endless refinements of civil rights legislation; and friendly to damage claims in environmental, industrial, and medical cases. One type of legal issue will grow rapidly with the approach of 2032, namely, domestic cases with substantial implications for United States foreign policy and the American role in world affairs.

Freedom of speech and association in a complex postindustrial society guarantees the exponential increase of organized interest associations. The increase in numbers of domestic pressure groups will be multiplied by the rapid growth of foreign groups and interests seeking to influence the policies and political life of the United States. The sheer numbers of lobbying and other organizations operating in the nation's capital, the capitals of the states, the city councils, the political parties, the media, and the general public will bring near chaos to an already frenetic American politics. At some point early in the twenty-first century it will become apparent that the only agencies capable of coordination and coalitioning the hoards of pressure groups are the political parties, at which time the parties will experience a rise in leadership and public confidence and support.

The party system, of which more later, will begin to recover its strength toward the end of this century. Political leaders dedicated to parties as essential instruments of democracy will respond to the challenges coming from the media, the pressure groups, and foreign sources of influence. These leaders will design statutes and party rules that will better enable them to consult and manage their colleagues and face their own leadership responsibilities. The changing character of the general American electorate and of specific party constituencies will lead to less group coalitioning and more broadly based, nationally directed contact with party rank-and-file workers and voters. This will be accompanied by substantial nationalization of the party organization. A new dimension will be affiliation with and active participation in the affairs of transnational parties, in effect, putting the two major parties directly into world politics.

The purpose of this exercise in futuristics about the world and the United States in the year 2032 has been to sensitize the reader to the probable context—global and national—within which the Democratic party will function over the next two or three generations. The survey has been a rough sample of trends already in being or developments widely anticipated. Alvin Toffler (*Future Shock*) and a host of other professional futurists enumerate the details and the probabilities much more carefully and compellingly. The intent here has been to focus the reader's mind-set on some of the circumstances that will demand the attention and judgment of the Democratic party between now and its bicentennial in 2032. Connecting the party's past with its probable future may, it is hoped, facilitate discussion—more likely, argumentation—about the problems and prospects of tomorrow's Democrats.

TWO

Democrats at the Bicentennial and In the Beginning

A brief swoop of the Time Machine over the Democratic party as it reflects the world and the nation in 2032 will give some basis for comparison with the first 150 years of the party's history.

DEMOCRATIC POLITICS IN 2032

The crowd that will gather, probably in Baltimore, for the Bicentennial Democratic Convention in early September 2032, will be quite unlike the one that met in that same city in 1832.

The nation will have grown from 1832's 14 million living in twenty-four states to more than 300 million in fifty states. The great waves of European immigration at the beginning of the twentieth century will have been followed by somewhat smaller waves from Latin America, Asia, and the Middle East by the end of the century. In the 1970s the party concerned itself with representation of certain social attributes of its constituents: ethnic, sex, age, and income. This concern, with less emphasis on earlier quota-like distributions, will be reflected among the delegations to the 2032 convention.

Of the 4,500 delegates, some 54 percent are likely to be women. When the Democrats nominated Representative Geraldine Ferraro for the vice-presidency in 1984, the party already had a rule calling for a 50-50 gender split on all delegations. The party also had a large share of the nation's feminist activists. The Ferraro nomination made the presidency feasible for women for the first time and stimulated female participation in party activities. By the turn of the century there will probably be more women delegates than convention seats for them, since many women in public office will be attending the presidential nominating event.

More than half the delegates are likely to be over fifty years of age. This will not be surprising in an aging population. During the 1980s the over-50 age group made up some 35 percent of the party's convention delegates, comparable to their proportion in the general population. The age factor will also reflect a development within the party that will be continuing for several decades, namely, the intensification of its internal organization. Long-time party activists will have aged while serving in the party's ranks.

Delegates from Congress, particularly the House of Representatives, will be numerous, with congressional Democrats playing a much greater organizational as well as policy role in party affairs. A high proportion of delegates will be established party officials and elected public officers, in contrast to practice in the 1970s and 1980s.

The delegates will be highly educated, reflecting the

American people at large. About three-fourths of the delegates will be college graduates, many of whom will have gone on into professional or other advanced training. Again, two centuries of national commitment to education will make the difference. The United States, with its bountiful natural resources and its land-grant college system, became the leading agricultural economy in the world by the 1950s. It was the leading industrial society throughout most of the twentieth century and will undoubtedly enter its postindustrial twenty-first century on a high technology binge originating in the genius of its university, industrial, and public research centers. Education will also have provided the infrastructure for conversion of the nation into an Information Society whose main product will be knowledge and whose labor force will be increasingly involved in the production, transmission, and application of knowledge.

With high education will come a greater number of delegates in the professions and the service industries, higher incomes (the average annual income of the delegates will probably be about $100,000), and stronger commitment to policies and ideological postures. The latter circumstance may be reinforced by factional splits over the issue of party membership in one of the major, presumably more ideological transnational political parties: the Liberal International, the Christian Democratic International, or the Social Democratic International.

Particularly fascinating and visible will be the ethnic and nationality composition of the convention. The Democratic party's long history as the party of immigrants and racial minorities will continue into 2032, with a difference in color and shading. The newest immigrants will have come from Latin America, Asia, the Pacific Islands, and the Middle East, and many of the newcomers will find the ladder of upward social mobility in the Democratic party. Meanwhile, the older ethnics—blacks, Jews, Irish, Italians, Poles, and others—will have become affluent and better integrated into American society, inevitably leading to a weakening of their loyalty to the Democratic party. As a consequence, large proportions of the faces at the convention of 2032 will be Hispanic, Asian, and Arabic.

By 2032 the Democratic party will have come out of a long period of wandering in the political desert. In the last decades of the twentieth century the Republicans may well out-organize the Democrats both nationally and at the local level. The Republicans also are likely to capture a major portion of the generation of voters—the baby-boomers—who reached their thirties and forties in the late 1980s. Democrats will probably begin to catch up in the first decade of the twenty-first century, building a national political party machine reminiscent of the great urban organizations of earlier eras.

The major issues confronting the convention's platform committee will include global and domestic unemployment, financing of environmental and national infrastructure reconstruction, ethical issues of national health policy, proposals for new approaches to Pacific region trade, expansion of the technical political aid program to new or emerging democracies, approaches to the advancement of supranational institutional development, new constraints on the flow of money in domestic party politics, and other new formulations of traditional themes.

Baltimore would be the obvious city for the bicentennial celebration. The date may present problems, however. The birthdates were May 21 to 23. With the shortening of the preconvention nominating campaign period and the postconvention general election campaign period, the official national conventions will most likely be held closer to the month of September. The Democratic National Committee probably will decide to have a year-long celebration with the main event in May and a full nominating convention in September.

The bicentennial celebration in May may prove to be an historian's dream. It could be at least a three-day production that will tell much of the story of the nation and its oldest political party. Members of the Democratic National Committee may be the formal delegates, although thousands of other Democrats are likely to be in attendance. The first day may be devoted to the events, personalities, and issues surrounding the Jacksonian convention of 1832. The second day could focus on the New Deal convention of 1932. And the third day could anticipate the national convention of 2032. Every historically significant Democratic hero will be extolled, and those still alive will be featured in an old-fashioned political parade.

All the major intraparty crises could be reviewed in order to draw on the experience of the past for the party's future. Two hundred years of campaign songs, buttons, and leaflets are bound to be reproduced with nostalgic abandon. On the third day all living former Democratic candidates for the presidency and all the current candidates will undoubtedly be brought together in a great show of party diversity and party unity.

The September nominating convention will be no less exciting. Clearly, the Democrats will still be around in 2032.

DEMOCRATIC POLITICS IN 1832

In the beginning . . .

There have been arguments about the birthdate. Some history buffs, using the biological metaphor, set the time of conception as long ago as the late seventeenth century when antiroyalist coalitions in the English Parliament were gathering together the first groupings that could be called modern political parties. During the mid-eighteenth century several of the English colonies in America, particularly Massachusetts, developed competing electioneering organizations commonly known as Country and Court parties; some later Democrats considered themselves descendants of the Country parties.

Country parties were in many respects New World cousins of the Whig party in England: small shopkeepers, craftsmen, and laborers opposing royal policies. Deacon Samuel

Adams and his son, Sam, became the leaders of the Caucus Club of Boston, one of the first urban political machines in the New World. The Caucus Club was the hub of cooperation among Country parties and, later, among the extralegal committees of correspondence that coordinated the American Revolution.

In the Continental Congress that governed the colonies through the Revolution, Sam Adams was the leader of the radical faction responsible for the Declaration of Independence, the Articles of Confederation, and the selection of George Washington to command the revolutionary army. Some Democrats see their party's beginnings in this lineage.

Others claim that June 1791 is the time of birth. During that month two distinguished Virginians, Thomas Jefferson and James Madison, conducted a "botanizing expedition" up the Hudson Valley of New York. The trip brought them in touch with New York's Governor George Clinton and Tammany Hall's Aaron Burr. The "botanical" outcome was the flowering of the first national political coalition between North and South in the new Union. The Jeffersonian party (also known as Madisonians in Congress) was the immediate forebearer of the Democratic-Republicans.

Some cite April 2, 1796, as the date of birth, when the first Democratic-Republican congressional caucus met to improve its collective control over policy making in Congress and to nominate Jefferson for president. The first three Congresses under the new Constitution included many "Hamiltonians" (Federalists) and "Madisonians" (Antifederalists, later Jeffersonians), but disciplined partisan voting did not emerge until the Fourth Congress (1795–1797). In the Fourth, about 65 percent of the Federalists and 74 percent of the Democratic-Republicans voted consistently with their fellow-partisans. The instrument of cohesion and discipline was the party caucus, that is, an informal conference of partisans meeting prior to debate and voting. In 1796 the congressional caucus also became the presidential nominating forum of the Democratic-Republicans. As a consequence, Jefferson became vice-president in the administration of Federalist John Adams. In those days the electoral college made separate decisions on the presidency and the vice-presidency, the latter being the runner-up in the balloting.

The congressional caucus thus became the first national organization of the parties and remained the instrument of presidential nomination and de facto election until 1824 when Andrew Jackson launched a campaign against "King Caucus." In that year's presidential race Jackson won a plurality of the popular and electoral college votes. Since an absolute majority of the electoral votes was necessary for election, the final choice had to be made in the House of Representatives, where a coalition of John Quincy Adams and Henry Clay supporters elected Adams. For the next four years General Jackson and his managers mobilized state parties and voters on an unprecedented national scale to assure his eventual election in 1828.

The first Democratic-Republican national convention in May of 1832 is the preferred birth date for several reasons. The convention was national; delegates came from every state but one. It convened in response to a formal call by the legislature of New Hampshire, which was controlled by Jacksonians. The convention created rules, procedures, and a permanent organization. Later, when the party's name was changed, it was done casually at the third national convention; on May 6, 1840, the platform that was adopted simply referred to itself as principles of "the Democratic Party of the Union."

National nominating conventions were new and popular in 1832. The Anti-Masons met in Baltimore in September 1831, with thirteen states represented. The gathering was not only the first of the national conventions but also a training ground for future major-party leaders—New York's Thurlow Weed, who later was a leading figure in Whig and Republican politics, and Massachusett's Benjamin F. Hallett, who served in 1848 as the first Democratic national party chairman. The Anti-Masons adopted two precedent-setting procedures: (a) nomination by a special majority (three-fourths of the delegates), and (b) calls for future conventions to originate from the party's national committee only.

The National Republicans, led by Henry Clay, also met in Baltimore in December 1831, with 157 delegates from seventeen states.

THE FOUNDING NATIONAL CONVENTION

The largest and most contentious early convention was run by the Democratic-Republicans five months later. The coalition supporting Andrew Jackson was an uneasy one. Jacksonian merchants, laborers, and small farmers in the Northeast favored a protective tariff and opposed large public expenditures for internal improvements in the West. Southern plantation-owners wanted tariffs reduced and the right to nullify tariffs and other laws with which they disagreed; Vice President John C. Calhoun, a leading states' righter, was their champion. Western frontiersmen, divided in their support of Jackson and Henry Clay, sought cheap land, low interest rates, and improved transportation to the West. Several of these objectives were mutually exclusive.

To bring together and hold the support of these many constituencies, Jackson surrounded himself with a unique (at that time) inner circle of political advisers, the Kitchen Cabinet. The Kitchen Cabinet was led by Senator Martin Van Buren of New York, the "Little Magician." Van Buren was renowned for his political wizardry, which was generally made possible by his organizing talents. The Kitchen Cabinet included the Jacksonian managers in Congress, the president's private secretary, the editor of the administration's official newspaper, the leader of the Jacksonian party in New Hampshire (who was also the creator of the Jacksonian system of patronage distribution), and others. Constituency coalitions, state party organizations, press communications, and national party strategies were the work and the achievement of the Kitchen Cabinet.

President Jackson's renomination was taken for granted. The convention simply endorsed the nominations he had already received from various state legislatures. The choice for second place was in dispute, mainly between Calhoun and Van Buren supporters, although there were several other well-known contenders.

Jackson was particularly grateful to Van Buren. This and the hostility of Vice President Calhoun were the driving forces behind the divisions of the 1832 national convention. The contest was further complicated by the demands of the various regional constituencies.

The call from New Hampshire's legislature requested each state party to send a delegation equal to the size of its vote in the electoral college. This brought a total of 270-280 delegates (not including the District of Columbia, which was later allowed to cast a vote). Delegates were selected in a variety of ways: by state legislative caucuses, state party conventions, local party meetings in cities and counties, and even by self-appointment. Some of the delegations were sent with instructions on how to vote.

Eager to demonstrate party unity, the Jackson managers followed the Anti-Mason precedent. They were able to have the convention adopt the requirements of a special majority—the two-thirds rule—to nominate. The rules also required unit voting by delegations. The unit rule stated that the entire vote of a state delegation was to be cast for the candidate of the majority in that delegation, thereby negating the political influence of any minority. Van Buren was nominated on the first ballot with 208 votes to 75 for others. The two-thirds and unit rules were destined to become twin albatrosses during most of the ensuing century.

A platform—usually referred to as an "address to the nation"—was left unwritten, various versions prepared later by state organizations in response to local conditions.

As might be expected, the delegates to the first Democratic National Convention were all males, white (with a handful of mixed ethnic background, primarily Indian), in their thirties, and, for the most part, elected public officials (many were members of Congress coming from nearby Washington, D.C.) or employed under local party patronage systems. Their factional differences related principally to their support of different regional leaders. Policy issues were divisive, but dealt with by avoiding the preparation of a platform.

With the Kitchen Cabinet thoroughly in command of the convention's activities, there was ample time for the delegates to enjoy the pleasures offered by the City of Baltimore.

THE GESTATION PERIOD

The Democratic party of the United States is one of the oldest human organizations surviving. Only the Catholic Church and a very few nation-states are older. Even its opponents and enemies will acknowledge that the Democratic party has been a major influence upon the development of the United States and a vital component of America's distinctive political party system.

The Democratic party did not spring into existence spontaneously. Political parties first appeared as a distinct form of political collaboration among the members of the English Parliament during the latter part of the seventeenth century. By the middle of the eighteenth century the two major voting alignments in Parliament were known as Whigs and Tories. The principal prize for the party with the most parliamentary votes was control of the English cabinet, itself a novel instrument of governance introduced by Robert Walpole during the period 1721–1742. The leaders of colonial America were themselves often divided along Whig and Tory lines.

Political parties in the colonies developed with an important difference. The Country and Court parties of that day formed their separate coalitions in the colonial legislatures in a manner comparable to Parliament's Whigs and Tories. In addition, these parties competed for the support of qualified voters among the colonial citizenry. Although popular suffrage was usually restricted to white male property-holders and exercised in elections of members of the lower houses of colonial legislatures, the voters as well as their representatives were early divided along partisan lines. By the 1750s, to a degree not yet known in the mother country, caucusing to nominate candidates and electioneering to solicit the support of voters were a familiar part of the colonial political scene.

The Country party was the more activist of the parties. Its energetic center was initially the Caucus Club of Boston, led by Deacon Samuel Adams and his son, Sam. Similar clubs, soon to be known as "patriotic societies," were established in other colonies, all with the principal objective of capturing seats in the colonial legislatures. Perhaps the most significant consequence of the British Stamp Act of 1765 was the landslide election of Country party candidates to the Massachusetts House of Representatives, placing the party and Sam Adams in control of that legislature. As clerk of the House, Adams was able to promote the organization of patriotic societies in other colonies.

These patriotic societies and Country parties gained control of other colonial legislatures as well as their legislative committees of correspondence. The latter were standing committees whose duty it was to report local official activities and decisions to the assemblies of the other colonies, hence a channel of colonial communication that would prove vital for the mobilization of the Revolution. The committees of correspondence have been referred to as "the Party of the Revolution." The committee of correspondence of the New York legislature on May 23, 1774, issued the call to convene the First Continental Congress.

The Declaration of Independence, the Articles of Confederation, and the commissioning of George Washington as the commander of the Continental Army were the work of the Continental Congress, heavily influenced by the negotiating talents of Sam Adams, now in the role of leader of the radical faction of the Congress. The Congress prior to independence split into three factions: loyalists wishing to remain under royal rule; conservatives seeking some new constitutional arrangement within the English system; and radicals urging complete independence.

As the new nation fumbled along under its Articles of Confederation, the conservatives tended to become "nationalists," who made the case for converting the confederation into a more centralized system and were the prime movers in calling the Constitutional Convention that designed a new federal government. Their opponents were known as Antifederalists, many of whom had previously been the radicals of the Continental Congress and who later became leaders of the Jeffersonian Democratic-Republicans.

Thus, by the time the new Republic inaugurated its first president, George Washington, in 1789, its citizens and political leaders were already divided into self-conscious and fairly well-organized interest groups, factions, and parties. James Madison, in his *Federalist* Number 10, worried about the possible detrimental consequences of these interests and factions. Nonetheless, the principal constituencies of the political parties were in place. The colonial Court parties, the loyalists and conservatives of the Continental Congress, the nationalists of the confederation, and the Federalists of the first years of the Republic represented one lineage. The Country parties, the radicals of the Continental Congress, the Antifederalists of the confederation, and the Jeffersonian Democratic-Republicans were the other.

THE EARLY CONSTITUENCIES

The constituencies inherited by the Federalists included land speculators, large planters, importers, merchants, ship builders, fishing interests, bankers, manufacturers, artisans, and officer veterans. The latter were extremely well organized throughout the colonies as the Society of the Cincinnati and provided the Federalists with a powerful grassroots machine.

Ironically, the Federalists denied that they were a political party and abjured overt organizing activity. In general, these groups were a creditor class, eager to maintain the face value of all debts and prevent the devaluation of the currency. Their masterful spokesman was Alexander Hamilton, President Washington's secretary of the treasury. Most of these constituents resided along the eastern seaboard, primarily concentrated in New England.

Quite another set of constituency groups made up the coalitions of the Country parties and the later Democratic-Republicans. From the earliest colonial days small farmers, hunters, and cattle-raisers who could not afford the more desirable land on the eastern seaboard migrated westward toward the frontiers. These frontiersmen became politically embittered because they were almost never adequately defended by colonial militia against Indian raids and were almost always underrepresented in the colonial legislatures.

Over 90 percent of the colonial labor force was engaged in farming, and typically this constituency became a debtor class. As such, farmers favored easy credit and a depreciating currency. On these economic grounds alone, they dissented from Federalist policies and developed strong antibank attitudes. Their opposition also had nationality origins, for a major proportion were in America because they or their families had been Scotch-Irish, Welsh, and English dissenters of one kind or another. Often these constituencies were joined by enlisted veterans of the Revolution and the small but increasing numbers of urban laborers. The Society of St. Tammany, better known in later years as Tammany Hall, began as an organization of former enlisted men. They and other urban patriotic societies became the grassroots organization of the Jeffersonians.

Components of these two coalitions have survived for more than two centuries, with, of course, important lapses during periods of party disintegration or realignment. Today's party coalitions cannot be understood without knowledge of this early electorate.

JEFFERSONIANS ORGANIZE AND PREVAIL

The Jeffersonian patriotic societies and other local political clubs were the first "loyal opposition," and, as such, were initially intent upon returning a Democratic-Republican (more commonly, simply Republican) majority to the House of Representatives in 1793. By 1800 Republicans were so well organized that they backed themselves into a constitutional crisis in that year's presidential election. Under the original electoral college procedure, each elector was to vote for two persons. The person with an absolute majority of the electoral votes became president and the runner-up vice-president. In this way, Federalist John Adams became president and Republican Thomas Jefferson became vice president in 1796. In 1800 the Republican congressional caucus nominated Jefferson (a Southerner) and Aaron Burr (a Northerner) as their national slate.

When the electors were chosen, everyone who voted for Jefferson also voted for Burr, creating a tie for the presidency. The choice was then made by the House of Representatives, with each of the sixteen states having a single vote. Jefferson received eight votes (with nine required to elect), Burr six, and two state delegations remained tied. Finally, Hamilton, Jefferson's old adversary, asked several of his Federalist colleagues in the tied delegations to shift from Burr to Jefferson. By this strange twist of fate, this Federalist archfoe of the Republican party was responsible for bringing into the presidency the first of the Jeffersonian "Virginia Dynasty" (Jefferson, Madison, and Monroe) which held that office until 1824.

Despite Hamilton's efforts to build a Federalist party organization, fewer and fewer Federalists were elected to public office over the next two decades. Most Federalist leaders would neither raise a finger to organize themselves as a party nor even acknowledge that they were a political party. Extremist Federalists in New England openly supported the British in the War of 1812, earning great popular disdain.

Western "War Hawks," under the leadership of Congressman Henry Clay of Kentucky, favored American resistance to the British; they let no one forget Federalist "treason." Consequently, by 1816 the Federalists were no more. Politicians North, South, and West were all Jeffersonian Republicans. It was the one-party Era of Good Feeling. The bad feelings manifested themselves mainly in the form of regional issues and competing regional leaderships.

New constituencies brought new issues. The British blockade from 1812 to 1815 sent New England capital from ship-building and shipping into new manufacturing enterprises; hence, protective tariffs became an issue. Manufacturing increased the number of urban workers and craftsmen; hence, wages, working conditions, and cheap slave labor grew in saliency. Cheap land stimulated internal migration to the West; hence, roads and canals became essential for linking up the agricultural West with the industrial East. Revival of trade with the English, particularly the English textile mills, led to a widespread surge in cotton planting in the South, implemented by slave labor; slavery and the plantation system became national issues.

By 1824 the Union consisted of twenty-four states, with forty-eight members in the United States Senate, 213 in the House of Representatives, and 261 in the electoral college. The Democratic-Republican party was essentially a collection of personal factions: Speaker Henry Clay's War Hawks from the West; Daniel Webster's and John Quincy Adams' post-Federalist remnants from New England; John Calhoun's states' righters from the South; William H. Crawford's "Richmond Junto" seeking a successor to the Virginia Dynasty; and Martin Van Buren's "Albany Regency" committed to an alliance with Crawford and to winning elections. These personal factions tended from time to time to coalesce around a policy question that had opposing nationalist or states' rights answers: Should the central government do it (build roads and canals, provide agricultural credit, etc.) and, if so, how much local autonomy would be lost?

As the end of the Monroe administration approached,

these factions had to face the problem of choosing his successor. When the 231 Republicans in both houses of Congress were surveyed in February 1824 by a special party committee, 78 percent deemed it "inexpedient" to hold the usual nominating caucus. In the absence of this party coordinating institution, it was every man for himself.

JACKSON AND THE NEW PRESIDENTIAL ELECTORATE

It was a time of far-reaching change in the political and economic life of the nation. The Panic of 1819 severely affected farmers and workers throughout the country. Their embitterment was deepened by widespread land purchase frauds in the West. At the same time the politically impotent unpropertied citizenry was being given the vote as restrictive suffrage requirements were removed in state after state. Tens of thousands of newly enfranchised voters were now able to express their displeasure at the ballot box. They could do this by supporting a new national leader, General Andrew Jackson, hero of the battle against the British at New Orleans in 1815, who was giving voice to the plaints of these unhappy constituencies and serving as a political link among them.

Aside from the advantage of his own charismatic personality, Jackson was fortunate in having at his disposal the skills and wisdom of a small group of Tennessee politicians— the "Nashville Junto"—whose organizing talents and devotion to him were exceptional. These men converted Jackson's military fame into political alliances across the nation, particularly between the western frontier farmers and the labor interests in the eastern cities.

The Jacksonian demands were for easy credit, better wages, and state and local self-rule. The Jacksonians took aim at all the old Jeffersonian villains: the banks, the federal government, the seats of financial and commercial power in New

England, and the elitism of Adams, Calhoun, Webster, and Clay. The center of presidential politics was about to leave the halls of Congress and locate itself in the electorate. Among those anticipating this shift was Senator Van Buren of New York, whose Albany Regency was a powerful network of alliances with political colleagues in nearby states.

The presidential election of 1824 hastened the changes of this period. Jackson, with 42 percent of the popular vote and 38 percent of the electoral college, led runner-up Adams by a substantial margin. Trailing far behind were Clay and Crawford. With no candidate receiving an absolute majority, the election went to the House of Representatives. There, Clay, sitting as speaker, withdrew in favor of Adams. Jackson, blaming his defeat on King Caucus, had his campaign theme for the next four years.

This election put Crawford and the Virginia Dynasty tradition to rest. Van Buren was now free to form a coalition with the Jacksonian forces. Farmers and workers would yet have their president.

As the suffrage was extended during the 1820s, party organizational activity at the local level intensified. Ward and county committees were created in cities, townships, and rural areas as never before. Political rallies, campaign literature, delegate selection to local and state party conventions, fund-raising, preparation of voting lists (there was as yet no registration procedure), surveys of voter leanings, and the printing of ballots (there were as yet no officially printed ballots) became the familiar tasks of party politicians.

On January 13, 1827, looking toward the upcoming presidential race, Senator Van Buren suggested for the first time the convening of a national nominating convention to concert the effort against President Adams. The convention idea was shelved until 1832. It also proved to be unnecessary. Jackson won in a landslide by a margin of 140,000 popular votes, which converted to a 178 to 83 electoral college vote. A dramatic increase in voter turnout, by 300 percent in some places, made the difference.

Jackson was the first president to be elected by the people, that is, with the least intervention by Congress, congressional caucuses, or state legislatures in the selection of presidential electors. Ninety-five percent of the electors were now chosen by popular vote. Nearly half of the electoral votes were contested in two-party states. New suffrage laws and intensive party organization more than doubled the voter turnout. Jackson, Van Buren, and their colleagues understood the new presidential electorate and its distinct mandate. They proceeded to change the nature of the presidency, develop a presidential system of government, and convert the array of personal and regional factions into a national party system.

Soon added to those of the farmer-labor coalition that elected Jackson were the competing regional demands noted earlier. The post-Federalist Jacksonians in the Northeast wanted protective tariffs for their infant manufacturing enterprises and, as prospering commercial centers, they were opposed to heavy taxes for internal improvements that would benefit the distant frontiersmen of the West. Western Jacksonians wanted not only road, canal, and other internal improvements but also cheap land, low interest rates, and more militia to deal with the Indians. Southern Jacksonians, with Vice President Calhoun as one of their principal spokesmen, wanted lower tariffs on the imported goods they needed for their economy and, more provocatively, the right to nullify federal laws deemed detrimental to their interests. These were the constituency interests that would contest each other within the Democratic party for the next three decades.

The task for Jackson and his Kitchen Cabinet was to minimize the political damage of the factional conflicts and find the common ground on which they could unite. This meant trimming away those party leaders who were least reasonable and loyal, even if this meant losing some voter support. It meant picking a unifying "enemy" against which to rally the rank-and-file.

Calhoun was shoved aside by the two-thirds rule at the first Democratic-Republican national convention in 1832 and replaced on the ticket by Van Buren. Meanwhile, the Adams-

Webster elite in the Northeast, forming a natural coalition with westerner Clay, nominated Clay for president.

The chosen "enemy" for uniting the Jacksonians was the National Bank, whose many branches literally constituted a Clay campaign organization. When the bank's charter renewal was passed by Congress, Jackson returned the bill with a smashing veto message that aligned the bank with the "rich and powerful" against the "humble members of society." The phrasing would echo across many Democratic generations.

The humble members of society who were most gratified by the bank veto—the Scotch-Irish frontier farmers from Illinois to Tennessee—were dedicated supporters of their fellow-countryman, the Scotch-Irish conqueror of the hated British at New Orleans. German farmers were another anti-English, antiaristocracy Jacksonian constituency excited by the veto. Yet another group were the immigrant Irish who had been flooding into Boston and New York for over a decade and had been mobilized into political clubs such as Tammany Hall from the moment they arrived. The Irish would play a major role in the Democratic party for generations to come, initially, as a magnet for later arrivals from Ireland, then, as managers of the party, and, eventually, in the presidency of the United States.

In the election, the Jackson-Van Buren ticket significantly increased Democratic pluralities in every state except Vermont, Pennsylvania, and Kentucky.

FROM JACKSONIAN UNITY TO DEMOCRATIC DIVISION

Along with the sweeping majorities came the seeds of party division. Now replaced by Van Buren, Vice President Calhoun returned to his native South Carolina to refurbish his political fortunes. His first move was to provide the

Nullifiers of South Carolina with a formula for combatting the protectionist tariff policies of the Jackson administration. A special state convention of Nullifiers issued an Ordinance of Nullification which stated that any federal law considered unconstitutional—in this case, the tariffs of 1828 and 1832—could be declared by a state to be null, void, and unenforcible. On the very same day, President Jackson issued a proclamation to the effect that the national government was sovereign and indivisible and, further, that no state could leave the Union. Jackson then submitted a Force Bill to Congress authorizing military measures if necessary to preserve federal interests in South Carolina. Thus was written the scenario played out by Abraham Lincoln three decades later.

The opposition denounced "King Andrew" in response to Jackson's actions against the National Bank and South Carolina's states' righters but could not get their own forces together. Anti-Masons and National Republicans went off in several directions, one of which led to the formation of the Whig party. "Whig" was chosen as the party name to emphasize the "King" in King Andrew and to remind the voters of the British Whig struggles against King George III.

As the Jackson administration drew to a close, it could look back to substantial achievements. Jackson was the first president to reach that office by mobilizing the electorate through party organization, hence the first to enjoy a clear popular mandate and the right to consider himself the leader of his party. He was the beneficiary as well as promoter of the extension of the suffrage. The Democratic party was incorporated under his direction. His policy themes sought to align the poor against the rich, the debtor against the creditor, and the national government against the states' righters. He passed this heritage along to his successor, Vice President Van Buren.

The 1836 Democratic national convention revealed the deep fissures in the Jacksonian coalition. Pro-Calhoun Nullifiers and pro-Jackson Unionists in South Carolina reflected factional hostilities more serious than the tariff issue. Abolitionists in the Northeast were beginning to organize against the immoral institution of slavery, threatening the entire southern plantation economy and its expansion westward. While Van Buren's nomination for president was pro forma— after all, "Old Hickory" was still in the presidency—it was impossible to agree on a vice-presidential nominee. Van Buren's Albany Regency and the Virginia Dynasty's Richmond Junto, both headquarters for regional factions, had been going their separate ways for some time. Richard M. Johnson became Van Buren's running-mate. Virginia, that is, the Junto, split off to nominate John Tyler for vice president on someone else's ticket.

Van Buren's presidency was burdened from the outset by economic disaster and increasing extremism on the slavery issue. Jackson had withdrawn public funds from the National Bank and distributed them among state banks. Each state bank had its own notions about extending credit and the worth of its paper currency. This severely unsettled farm credit arrangements. The situation was confounded by land spec- ulation associated with the building of canals to the West and by crop failures. When the Panic of 1837 hit, Van Buren was unable to marshal the votes in Congress for an independent treasury to coordinate the nation's monetary needs. Nor could he get very much else accomplished to combat the depression that plagued his administration. Disenchanted, workingmen formed their own political party and farmers began to support the Whigs.

On December 12, 1837, Congressman John Quincy Adams, former president and crusty legislator, introduced a petition calling for the abolition of slavery in the District of Columbia. The abolitionist camel was poking its nose under the tent. In protest, Southern congressmen walked out of the House of Representatives. The Adams petition was roundly defeated, but that hardly settled the matter. It did, however, settle Van Buren's political future.

Another move made in the Senate originated with Cal- houn. It took the form of a series of resolutions declaring that the right to possess slave property was a local matter guar- anteed under the Constitution but leaving the question of slavery in the District of Columbia and the territories in the hands of Congress. Submitting to pressure from the Southerners, President Van Buren agreed that slavery was a local issue and denied that Congress could intervene anywhere— District of Columbia, territories, or the states.

By 1840 the Whigs pulled themselves together to nominate General William Henry Harrison ("Old Tippecanoe") as the Whig version of "Old Hickory." Virginian John Tyler was his running-mate. The national convention that renominated Van Buren was also the one that changed the Party's name from Democratic-Republican to Democratic. The Harrison-Tyler slate beat Van Buren in what was the first of a series of close presidential elections. The margin was 147,000 votes of the 2,404,000 cast.

So close a defeat could be considered "honorable." Undaunted, Van Buren actively assumed the role of titular leader of his party, the first Democratic presidential nominee to do so. From his home, Van Buren urged his fellow-partisans to build party organization. He assisted many candidates in local and congressional elections. He paved the way, whenever possible, for his own renomination in 1844. His work was suddenly frustrated by President Harrison's death and the elevation of a hostile ex-Democrat, John Tyler, to the presidency.

THE "FOUNDING" CONSTITUENCIES

By the mid-1800s there could be little doubt who would make up the Democratic party's clientele. The Democrats would be the party of the common man, broadly defined. In the colonies and during the early days of the Republic, "common man" included the frontier settler, the small farmer, the unskilled laborer, the craftsman, the enlisted soldier, the immigrant, the English dissenter, the debtor, the poor, and the disenfranchised. From the outset, these constituencies were where the discontented, the angry, and the resigned could most often be found.

When it could overcome its inertia, this Democratic clientele could follow a charismatic leader—a Jefferson or a Jackson—willing to represent its many interests. When Democratic leaders could reconcile competing constituency interests, form an enthusiastic coalition, and organize the grassroots thoroughly (for Democrats have always been the most difficult to organize), these leaders could bring vitality to public offices, change in the direction of public affairs, and greater justice and opportunity to the common man.

These generalizations were already becoming political truisms by the 1840s when the declining fortunes of Martin Van Buren symbolized the beginning of an era of party self-destruction. The principal issue was slave property and the political power that depended on its practice. Half of the Democratic party saw slaves as people, as common men and women. The other half saw slaves as property, a special form of labor, and the essential foundation of a regional economy. Democratic leaders were able to put off the day of reckoning on this issue for more than twenty years. But when that day arrived, the party split irreparably and the nation sank into civil war.

THREE

The Torments of Division, 1844 to 1876

The Jacksonian unity gave way to sectional and factional disunity within the party after 1840. Yet, for two decades, the party's leaders were able to maintain the appearance of consensus. In doing so, they invented the Dark Horse, northern nominees with southern principles, and other devices of compromise. At last, in 1860, despite the fragmentation of opposition parties, the Democrats succumbed to their own factional strife and did not recover until the 1870s.

The slavery debate was articulated in moral and religious terms, but the concerns of the principal constituencies were economic and political: How to defend the survival of the plantation economy? How to maintain regional influence at the nation's capital? The questions at every level divided the Democrats, with no third force to moderate the confrontation.

DARK HORSES AND DOUGHFACES

Tyler's party affiliation—a Richmond Junto Democrat elected on a Whig ticket—was by now ambiguous and debatable. His principal adversaries were Henry Clay, a Whig, and Martin Van Buren, a Democrat. On the Democratic side, he had an ally in Senator Robert J. Walker, the "Wizard of Mississippi," who had become the spokesman for the Southwest in congressional politics. In large measure, Tyler represented the cotton-growing plantation interests of the South and the cotton-mill Whigs of New England; hence he was a moderate on the issue of slavery. Walker favored westward expansion, particularly into Texas, and the possible creation of several new proslavery states. Texas had declared its independence from Mexico in 1836 and was in the process of seeking admission to the Union.

It was Walker who masterminded the seven-ballot stalemate in the 1844 Democratic convention that denied renomination to Van Buren and produced the first "dark horse" nominee for president, Governor James K. Polk of Tennessee. It was Walker who managed the Polk campaign. Walker arranged for President Tyler's withdrawal from the race upon assurances from Jackson and Polk that Tyler's 150,000 "friends" (read: patronage appointees) would be "respected." Walker won the support of the Calhoun press for the Democratic ticket. Walker was the one who issued two versions of the platform, one in the South, favoring the extension of slavery into Texas, and another in the North, restricting slavery to those states in which it was already practiced. In sum, Walker, with Tyler's tacit approval, achieved the nomination and election of Polk and the defeat of Clay, the latter in his third try for the presidency. Clay's defeat was particularly gratifying to both Walker and Tyler.

The Polk administration was Democratic to the hilt. Hoping to unite the party, Polk brought some of its most powerful leaders into his cabinet: Walker into Treasury; James Buchanan of Pennsylvania as secretary of state; William L. Marcy of New York into War; John Y. Mason of Virginia as attorney-general, and Cave Johnson of Tennessee as postmaster-general. Johnson was patronage manager, with more than 14,000 postmasterships to distribute. Polk made the unprecedented vow to serve only a single term, gratuitously making himself a "lame duck" president from his first day in office. The inevitable leadership competition within the cabinet embittered and exhausted him, and he survived only a few months after leaving office.

Congress voted to annex Texas in 1845. To this end, and with the enthusiastic encouragement of the South, Polk ordered General Zachary Taylor to recover territory that had been settled by Mexicans in a disputed border area of Texas. Taylor did so and became a national hero for the deed, earning him the Whig nomination for president in 1848.

The military engagement soon led Congress to declare war against the hapless Mexicans. The ensuing peace treaty of 1848 settled all border disputes relating to Texas and ceded to the U.S. the lands that eventually became the states of California, Arizona, New Mexico, Nevada, Utah, and part of Colorado. The United States paid Mexico $15 million, a bargain price that made Jefferson's purchase of Louisiana seem extravagant. Some politicians, however, were shamelessly greedy; Secretary of State Buchanan, for example, advocated annexing all of Mexico.

The cotton-growing slaveholders of the South were ecstatic over the prospect of extending the plantation system westward. (They were even more joyous about the invention of the sewing machine in 1846. The machine was also good news for New England mill owners and urban garment-workers.) Others who rejoiced over the conquest included those who shared in the more than $100 million spent on military supplies and those who dashed to California to partake in the gold discoveries of 1848.

At home, farmers were happy with the establishment of an independent treasury, which took public funds out of the hated private banks and stabilized the credit supply. Commerce and the import-export trade prospered sufficiently to enable Secretary Walker to write legislation starting a process of tariff reduction, thereby fulfilling a promise to Calhoun. A settlement with the British brought Oregon under American jurisdiction, feeding the country's expansionist appetite. The times were good. The pace of economic and social change was fast.

As always, change was accompanied by anxiety and anger. Revolution and hard times in Europe brought waves of Irish and other immigrants to the eastern seaboard causing local workingmen, already upset by the threat of slave labor moving north and west from the South, to become politically active in the interest of free labor. From the mid-1830s to the mid-1840s the minuscule Liberty party spread the abolitionist and workingmen's message.

These ideological and theological issues became practical political ones with the acquisition of new territories. Would cotton or wheat be the main crop when the new lands were tilled? Would slavery be allowed in the new states coming into the Union? How would the new West affect the traditional balance of power between North and South in the Senate, the House of Representatives, and the electoral college, not to mention the Democratic national conventions?

One answer was succinctly stated by Congressman David Wilmot, a Pennsylvania Democrat. The Wilmot Proviso, introduced as an amendment to an appropriation bill, simply banned slavery in all territories acquired from Mexico. The proviso triggered a political explosion. It was promptly endorsed by ten free-state legislatures, passed by the House, but rejected by the Senate. The Wilmot Proviso became a litmus test of pro- and antislavery sentiment among party leaders.

Some Democrats were called "Barnburners" for their

willingness, like the proverbial Dutch farmer, to burn the barn (the nation) in order to rid it of rats (slavery). Barnburners returned the compliment, calling their factional adversaries "Hunkers" for hungering so much to hold public office as to be willing to join hands with slaveholders. Polk administration patronage was carefully channeled to Hunkers, in the case of New York, to Secretary Marcy's Hunkers. By 1848, former president Van Buren, supporting the Wilmot Proviso, led New York's substantial Barnburner faction into the new Free Soil party. This defection cost the Democrats the presidential election that year. Eight years later the Free Soilers and northern Whigs formed the core of another new party, the Republicans.

Democrats were playing hard-ball politics with each other and the rough game spread north, south, and west. From 1848 to 1860 national leaders of the party did their best to straddle, reconcile, and resolve the Barnburner-Hunker, North-South, slavery-abolitionist divisions. Democratic presidential nominees personified the effort. Lewis Cass (1848), Franklin Pierce (1852), and James Buchanan (1856) were "northern men with southern principles," or, in less elegant language, "doughfaces."

Most of the partisan political action during the 1850s took place in Congress and in covered wagons. Westward migration and slavery, with all their attendant issues, dominated debate and policy. Talk of secession became serious among Democrats and Whigs in the South. California requested admission as a free state. New Mexico readied itself for territorial government. Abolitionists again demanded the end of slave trade in the District of Columbia. Southern slaveholders were insisting upon a more stringent national fugitive slave law, that is, requiring the return of escaped slaves. The voices of the oratorical giants of the day—Calhoun, Clay, Webster, Benton, Cass, Douglas, Seward and others—resounded in the halls of Congress.

President Zachary Taylor recommended admission of California and New Mexico into the Union under conditions that would allow each to make its own decision whether or not to permit slavery. Since the legislatures of both territories were antislavery, their admission would have tipped the balance of power in Congress in favor of the free states. Northern Democrats and northern Whigs did little to assuage the outrage of southern Democrats and southern Whigs. As the conflict heated up, Henry Clay came forth with the Compromise of 1850.

The Compromise gave the North a free California and the abolition of slave trade in the District of Columbia. For the South the Compromise would leave the slavery question to some future local resolution in the territories of New Mexico and Utah and would tighten federal enforcement of the fugitive slave laws. President Taylor's unexpected death left a leadership void among the Whigs, who split bitterly and permanently on the Compromise proposal. It took Illinois Senator Stephen A. Douglas' best efforts to carry Clay's plan successfully through Congress. Elsewhere, the political damage was profound.

PARTY DISINTEGRATION AND SCATTERED CONSTITUENCIES

The Whig party never recovered and, by the end of the decade, had been replaced by the Republicans as the second major party. Democrats were divided as never before. In some localities "Union" party was placed on ballots in lieu of the Democratic party name as a way of demonstrating support of the Compromise of 1850. (President Abraham Lincoln, running for reelection in 1864, would make good use of the Union party name.) At the 1852 Democratic national convention, still operating under its two-thirds nominating rule, it required forty-nine ballots to break a three-way deadlock and nominate another "dark horse," General Franklin Pierce. The three deadlocking candidates were James Buchanan, supported by the South, Stephen Douglas, representing the predominantly antislavery Northwest, and Lewis Cass, trying for the presidency a second time on a local-option policy for deciding each state's slavery law.

The Pierce administration was largely paralyzed by the North-South contest. Moderates on the slavery issue were thoroughly frustrated by extremists. The question of railroad routes to the West precipitated unexpected violence. Jefferson Davis, Pierce's secretary of war and a Southerner, urged the building of a southern railroad route as a matter of national defense. Senator Douglas, backed by Chicago business and real estate interests, sought a northern route through Chicago. In time, Douglas was willing to settle for a central route through the Platte region of Kansas and Nebraska. To accomplish this, Douglas introduced legislation to organize the Nebraska territory, in which he avoided all reference to the slavery question.

Attempting to be even-handed, Congress passed the Kansas-Nebraska Act authorizing two territories. Within months local civil war raged in "Bleeding Kansas." Reminiscent of the Party of the Revolution in the 1770s, northern Democrats, Whigs, Know-Nothings (a nativistic party), and Free Soilers promptly encouraged and organized a mass migration aimed at saving at least Kansas from slavery. Southerners inaugurated their own mass movement. Violence followed.

The events thrust the doughface president and the Little Giant from Illinois out of the presidential running and gave the 1856 Democratic nomination to James Buchanan. His running-mate was John C. Breckinridge, a youthful Southerner. The ticket meant another safe four years for slavery. The election results reinforced this impression. Fourteen of the fifteen slave states gave Buchanan their electoral votes whereas only five of the sixteen free states supported him.

The situation deteriorated during the Buchanan administration. The Supreme Court handed down the Dred Scott decision recognizing slaves as property and ruling that Congress had no right to discriminate against property, slave or otherwise, simply because that property happened to be in a territory. This proslavery development was accompanied by the LeCompton Constitution crisis. As Kansas prepared for statehood, a draft constitution was written at LeCompton, Kansas. It was expected that this constitution would forbid slavery. Instead, through a political ruse, it protected slave property already in the territory.

The House of Representatives rejected the LeCompton Constitution. During this debate, Senator Douglas established himself as the leading spokesman of the antislavery wing of the Democratic party. Later, in a series of debates with Republican Congressman Abraham Lincoln, Douglas asserted his Freeport Doctrine denying that Congress had the power to force slavery upon a territory against the will of its people. Lincoln and others in the new Republican party were more absolute, assuming a strong antislavery posture.

With slavery as the most salient issue of the decade, which were the constituencies that were at first being scattered and polarized? In the North, small farmers saw their wheat and corn crops competing with the southern cotton, tobacco, and sugar crops for such public largesse as improved transportation and protective tariffs. Northern railroad, real estate, and commercial interests urged Democratic politicians to facilitate northern transportation links to the West Coast and its gold mines. Northern workingmen were increasingly hostile to the newly arrived Irish and took on a nativistic tone that eventually led them to the Know-Nothing—and, later, to the Republican—party. Meanwhile, Irish and German immigrants were being naturalized and integrated into Democratic city machines. In sum, Democrats in the North were becoming an aggregation of certain kinds of farmers, businessmen, and workers.

Democrats in the South were of a strikingly different stripe. The cotton, tobacco, and sugar crops were grown by large and small planters, each with different attitudes about slavery and the economy. The large planters, mainly Whigs, were far more paternalistic and protective of their slave property and more influential among the business, professional, and political elites of the region. Their social and financial relationships outside the South and their intense commitment to the Constitution inclined them to moderation and compromise on most political issues. In contrast, the small planters and the poor nonplanter whites held strong views about slaves and immigrants. The increasingly high price of slaves in the 1850s, the growing intrusiveness of northern abolitionists and workingmen's organizations into the affairs of the South, and suspected papal influence on Irish Catholic immigrants inflamed some of the basest racism and nativism with which a southern politician would ever have to deal. In the South, Democratic politicians, inheritors of the back country populism of the early days of the Republic, were not reticent about doing so.

By 1860 the Buchanan doughfaces and the Douglas moderates were no match for the extremists of the abolitionist North or the proslavery populists of the South. Although the Douglas forces controlled the national nominating convention meeting in Charleston, they won the platform fight by only one vote and clearly did not have the two-thirds needed to nominate. The southern delegates from five states walked out to conduct their own Constitutional Democratic National Convention and subsequently nominated Vice President Breckinridge to lead their ticket. The remaining Democrats adjourned to meet again six weeks later in Baltimore, where they nominated Douglas.

Here was an extreme example of Democrats defeating themselves. The nation also lost, for the Democrats had been the only major party able to hold the unruly sections together for more than a decade. Despite the high degree of party organization throughout the 1830s and 1840s, the nation's party institutions were not yet stable enough to cope with the bitter ideological, economic, and cultural differences of the period. Even before Lincoln assumed the presidency in March, seven southern states, on February 8, 1861, established the Confederate States of America. The secession crisis was in full swing.

CIVIL WAR OVERCOMES ELECTORAL POLITICS

Confederate leaders had every military reason to believe that their cause would prevail. Among the state militia only New York and Massachusetts in the North and Virginia and Louisiana in the South had substantial forces in military readiness. The federal army of some 16,000 officers and men was spread all over the country: 4,300 in Oregon and California, 6,000 in New Mexico and Texas, 2,900 in the Midwest and Great Plains, 1,200 along the Atlantic coast and Canadian border. The latter made up fifteen companies, hardly a defense force for the nation's capital. In addition, the president of the Confederacy, Jefferson Davis, had been Buchanan's secretary of war, and the members of the federal army's general staff were nearly all Southerners who resigned to join the secession.

On April 12 Fort Sumter was attacked, galvanizing public opinion in the North against the secessionists. President Lincoln ordered General Winfield Scott into action and called up 75,000 state militia to suppress the "insurrection." Lincoln then called Congress into special session for July 4. Congress was, perhaps in name only, overwhelmingly Republican. The Senate had thirty-one Republicans, ten Democrats, and eight from other parties. The House had 105 Republicans, forty-three Democrats, and thirty others. The Republicans, however, were of two kinds: the radical populists from states such as Michigan, Minnesota, Wisconsin, and Iowa, plus a few from New England, and the moderates from older two-party states such as Illinois, Indiana, and Ohio. The Radicals, with an exaggerated conception of parliamentary government and congressional supremacy, harried Lincoln's management of the war effort from beginning to end. Later, the Radicals nearly succeeded in removing President Andrew Johnson from office, designed a vengeful Southern Reconstruction program after the Civil War, and dominated the administration of President Grant . . . all with far-reaching consequences for the Democratic party over most of the next century.

During the months that he was president-elect (November to March), Lincoln let it be known that he expected the secession movement to be suppressed within the South itself, that there was no reason to compromise the integrity of the Union, and that the federal government should act with restraint, if at all. The firing on Fort Sumter changed all that.

Party politics was hardly adjourned during the Civil War. When Winfield Scott, a Whig turned Republican, lost the battle of Bull Run, Lincoln promptly gave command of the federal forces to George B. McClellan, a Democrat, who had saved West Virginia for the Union. The Radicals, highly sensitive to the party implications of successful generalship, demanded that Lincoln appoint only Republican generals to the highest commands. However, as Lincoln well knew, there were some eighty Democrats among the 120 generals of the federal army in 1861, and McClellan was one of the most skillful and best known among them.

With the departure of the South from the Union, the Democrats were deprived of some one hundred reliable electoral college votes: fully half of the party's popular vote had been in the southern states. The party's future now rested upon three clusters of competitive two-party states: New York and New Jersey in the East; Ohio, Illinois, and Indiana in the Midwest; and California and Oregon in the West. New York (thirty-five electoral votes) and Ohio (twenty-three votes) were the largest, and, not surprisingly, became the opposing centers of the wartime factional conflicts between "War Democrats" and "Peace Democrats." The war-peace division became another hallmark of Democratic factional politics for generations to come.

Prior to 1861 the western and eastern wings of the party had been held together in large measure by Senator Douglas of Illinois and Democratic National Chairman August Belmont, a wealthy New York banker. When Douglas died suddenly in 1861, the manager of the Douglas presidential campaign, Ohio Congressman Clement L. Vallandigham, tried to step into the midwestern leadership role by devoting much time to designing a compromise for the North-South sectional conflict. His plan: an electoral college majority within *each* of the nation's four sections in order to elect a president. Further, secession would be a legal right, but only with the consent of all the state legislatures of a section. When his plan failed to attract support, Vallandigham gave his attention to other party issues in his region.

The Midwest had important commercial and cultural ties with most of the nearby southern states. Many of its citizens were either reluctant supporters or downright opponents of the Unionist war effort; most hoped, with Vallandigham, that there would be a stalemate and a peace without victory. By 1863 large numbers of Peace Democrats had organized themselves into secret societies, with such names as Knight of the Golden Circle, and most had military subsidiaries, with some 340,000 of their members trained for military action. The Republicans tagged these Peace Democrats as "Copperheads," after the venomous snake of the same name. For their part, War Democrats in the region established clubs called "Loyal Leagues."

When Vallandigham lost his race for reelection to the House in 1862, the Ohio Democratic state convention nominated him for governor. Defiantly, he delivered two "disloyal" antiwar campaign addresses and was arrested for treasonous conduct. Denied a writ of habeas corpus under the president's war powers, he was tried and convicted by a military court. The Vallandigham campaign held the rapt attention of all sections of the country and the Confederacy. Lincoln commuted the sentence and instructed the military authorities to send Vallandigham into exile in the Confederate states, subject to imprisonment if he returned. Vallandigham subsequently campaigned for governor from a headquarters in Canada. His overwhelming defeat began a decline in the fortunes of the Peace Democrats. Vallandigham himself remained perhaps the most interesting and aggressive of the party's leaders for the next half dozen years.

In New York and elsewhere in the Northeast, National Chairman Belmont mobilized the War Democrats in support of Lincoln's conduct of the war. Belmont, with strong business and family ties in Europe, prevailed on the British and the French to refrain from unduly helping the Confederacy. He offered Lincoln several constructive proposals for a negotiated peace, some of which Lincoln later adopted in his own postwar reconstruction plan.

"UNION" REPUBLICANS AND "UNION" DEMOCRATS

Lincoln issued his Emancipation Proclamation in September 1862 as a war measure aimed at dividing the South and intensifying abolitionist support in the North. Nevertheless, the midterm election returns, as they almost always are, proved unfavorable to his incumbent administration. Radical Republicans were emboldened and more critical of the president and his advisers.

Lincoln became convinced that he could only find sufficient support for the war through a coalition of War Democrats and conservative Republicans. The term "Union" began to replace "Republican" in many localities. Administration patronage—jobs and contracts—began to flow to Unionist leaders, organizations, and places. Eventually the Republican National Committee referred to itself as the Union National Committee. This became an opportunity for the Radicals to capture full control of the former, which they did. Meanwhile, New York Republican and Democratic leaders began to discuss an immediate reconstruction of the parties. Republicans attending the Union National Convention in 1864 renominated Lincoln and added Andrew Johnson, a War Democrat, to the national ticket.

On the Democratic side, Clement Vallandigham of Ohio, Governor Horatio Seymour of New York, and General George B. McClellan, now former commander of the Union armies, were the available candidates for president. Draft riots ended Seymour's prospects. War Democrats, led by Samuel J. Tilden of New York, vetoed Vallandigham. The mantle fell to McClellan, a lackluster campaigner.

Lincoln's real opposition came from the Radical Republicans, who continued to berate him in such documents as the Wade-Davis Manifesto reminding him that Congress was the supreme branch of government. The Lincoln-Johnson Union ticket was bolstered in early September by the news of General Sherman's victorious march into Atlanta.

The Civil War shook loose party constituencies and coalitions as never before. The world had never seen so bloody and prolonged a fratricide. The huge Union army needed to be clothed, fed, supplied weaponry, transported, and provided with medical care. Large contracts were let to clothing and shoe manufacturers, producers and packers of meats, grain, and other foods, munitions-makers, railroads, and pharmaceutical firms. The industrialization of America was begun, and unprecedented profits brought a grateful new constituency to the Republican party. Bankers were pleased to purchase war bonds at discount, with high interest assured. Railroads were busy and subsidized. Import duties were raised to new heights of protection for domestic producers, and Republicans acquired a taste for high tariffs. Free 160-acre parcels of public land were offered migrants to the West under the Homestead Act. Notwithstanding Lincoln's and the Radicals' populist and abolitionist origins, in a single administration and during a war economy, the Republican party was converted to a coalition of the new industrial and financial interests of the country.

Left for the Democrats was the native labor force, suffering a raging inflation, military service, and competition from the growing use of foreign contract labor intended to promote immigration. When the time came to vote, these and the homesteaders were the constituents who gave Andrew Johnson their support. During the postwar occupation of the South, the normally Democratic small planters and poor workingmen were, of course, unable to vote for anyone.

RECONSTRUCTION BY AND FOR RADICAL REPUBLICANS

Elected to the Senate in 1864 were thirty-four Republicans, eleven Democrats, and five "Administration Republicans." In the House were 135 Republicans, forty-one Democrats, and eight "Administration Republicans." Absent were the twenty-two senators and fifty-eight congressmen from the eleven states that went into the Confederacy. In party terms, the Radicals controlled Congress, congressional Democrats were at less than half their prewar strength, and Lincoln's Presidential Reconstruction Plan, forgiving and feasible, faced a hostile legislature.

When southern states sent senators and representatives to Congress at the end of hostilities, the Radicals moved quickly and decisively. Their control of Congress, the electoral college, and the nation was in jeopardy. They refused to seat the Southerners (mostly Democrats), put together their own repressive Congressional Plan for reconstruction, and, after Lincoln's assassination, embarked upon a campaign of vituperation against President Johnson. The Radicals then proceeded to capture Union party organizations throughout the country and wave the "bloody shirt" (blame for the Civil War) against the Democrats. This left Unionist Johnson and many Democrats without a political party organization.

The Democratic situation was pitiable. War Democrats in Congress had been helping Republicans pass legislation and had been coopted by the Unionists (nee Republicans). With Unionist clubs and party organization being refurbished as Republican by the Radicals, Democrats had practically no organization of their own. Nor could they follow the partyless and beaten Johnson. The only ray of hope was the fact that, even without the South, Democrats polled 45 percent of the major-party vote for president in 1864.

The midterm election of 1866 gave the Radicals two-thirds of the seats in Congress, enough to overcome any presidential vetoes—and to impeach a president, though the

Senate Radicals were one short for conviction. The pretext for the impeachment was Johnson's removal of Secretary of War Stanton in December 1867 without the advice-and-consent of the Senate as required by the recently enacted Tenure of Office Act. With the vice-presidency vacant since Johnson's succession to the presidency, the next in line for the presidency was "Bluff Ben" Wade, presiding officer of the Senate and one of the original Radical leaders. It was a bold and, for many, a frightening ploy.

The Radicals turned to General Ulysses S. Grant, hero of the Civil War, as the "front man" for their new Republicanism. The irony was that Grant had been an antebellum Democrat, Lincoln's commander of the Union armies, and Johnson's secretary of war. Some Democratic managers did make an effort to recruit the war leader. Had they been successful, the party would undoubtedly have been spared the factionalism into which it soon sank and the "bloody shirt" image of rebellion that Republicans hung over it for the next two decades.

Virtually leaderless since the loss of Stephen A. Douglas, many Democrats wondered how they would ever put the pieces of the party back together again. National adversity once again helped. A postwar business depression brought demands, particularly from farmers, for cheap money and easy credit. Farmers organized the National Grange in 1867 to look after their political interests; membership grew rapidly. The Knights of Labor was founded in 1869 and operated as a secret order until the mid-1870s when its membership suddenly spurted to a million. In new shapes, the old farmer-labor constituencies were once again rebuilding their ties to the Democratic party.

At the same time local Democratic machines continued their large task of Americanizing vast numbers of new immigrants and calming the anxieties of older workers. The latter was not easy. Older workers felt increasingly threatened by the competition of the new arrivals, that is, immigrants and black freedmen from the South. The birth of another constituency was taking place in the far-off Wyoming Territory when in December 1869, the territorial legislature enacted the first women's suffrage law.

The end of the Civil War and the dominance of the Radical Republicans also brought on a major transformation in that party. The war had spawned innumerable millionaires, new mass production industries, and relatively modern financial institutions such as the stock market. Beyond the Mississippi River lay a vast and munificent land: mines whose gold, silver, and other metals had yet to be exploited; plains that would some day provide the wheat and cattle that would make the nation the bread-basket and meat supplier of the world; forests sufficient to provide a cabin or a mansion for every American family as well as fleets of ships and libraries full of newspapers and books. Industrialists, merchants, and financiers, always ready to deal with a winner, flocked to the new Republican party. Grant's was the best-financed presidential campaign to that date.

One Democrat, George H. Pendleton of Ohio, responded to the farmers' plight with a proposal to pay all government and other bondholders with cheap money, that is, greenbacks issued by the Treasury. This inflationary "Ohio idea" quickly elevated Pendleton into the ranks of potential presidential candidates in 1868. It also unsettled eastern banking interests and Democratic "sound money" defenders.

Frustration marked the efforts of the party's national politicians at every turn. McClellan was abroad, and not missed. Johnson was destroyed by the impeachment proceedings. Pendleton was locked in a bitter feud with Vallandigham for control of the Ohio organization. New York Governor Horatio Seymour, over the protest of State Democratic Chairman Samuel J. Tilden, took himself out of what seemed a hopeless race against a popular military hero. Most frustrating of all was the sight of Radical leaders eloping with General Grant, whose deference to wealth and professional politicians made for a quick and easy courtship.

Robert J. Walker, now an aging Wizard of Mississippi, suggested the availability of a popular but politically inexperienced Union general, Winfield Scott Hancock, for the party's presidential nomination. A sound-money Midwesterner, Senator Thomas A. Hendricks, was proposed by others on grounds that inflation and currency questions were the political issues of the day.

The Hancock and Hendricks candidacies were stalemated for twenty-two ballots at the party's national convention. In a surprise maneuver, Ohio gave its vote to Seymour, and was quickly followed by New York. The New York governor became the reluctant sound money nominee, for whom the convention wrote a greenback platform (which he later disavowed). The platform gratuitously condemned black suffrage. The vice-presidential candidate, Francis P. Blair, Jr., having urged the removal of the army from the South so that the whites could reorganize themselves, was another cross for the ticket to bear. Some southern Democrats at the convention were obviously still fighting the Civil War, making the party all the more vulnerable to the Republican "bloody shirt" campaign.

THE TILDEN INTERREGNUM

What did emerge from the 1868 campaign was a new leader in the national affairs of the party: Samuel J. Tilden. A New York corporation lawyer who had accumulated substantial wealth in sometimes questionable stock market dealings, Tilden had been active in local and state politics since the 1830s and would remain a major actor in the party's national affairs until the mid-1880s. Cultured, aloof, and frequently in poor health, Tilden never attracted a popular following, but his talents and resources were thoroughly appreciated by the party's managers. He was a party organizer in the Van Buren tradition and a politician's politician. As Democratic state chairman and as Seymour's campaign manager in 1868, Tilden aggressively promoted the New York governor's interests. His principal achievement that year was to supplement the tattered official party machinery with a vigorous new organization: The Order of the Union Democracy.

There was no winning against Grant. At this time Republicans locked New England solidly into the Republican column. Republicans dominated the relatively competitive states of the Corn Belt: Ohio, Indiana, and Illinois. King Corn became for Republicans what King Cotton has been for Democrats. Although Grant carried most of the electoral college, one happy fact remained: this time the Democrats received 47 percent of the major-party popular vote.

The Radicals running the Grant administration were now variously known as "The Directory" (reminiscent of the French Revolution's dictatorial oligarchy) and the "Stalwart Cabal." The tariff was kept excessively high. The South was kept excessively oppressed. The Union Pacific Railroad, the first transcontinental line and a source of national excitement and pride, was completed at the beginning of Grant's administration, and Republicans took full political credit for the achievement.

Republican moderates, including Horace Greeley, publisher of the *New York Tribune*, found themselves completely excluded from the president's circle. These moderates were unable to win a hearing for a more tolerant southern policy and a program of civil service reform that would reduce the outrageous patronage corruption rampant throughout the country. By 1871 they departed to form the Liberal Republican party.

In New York, Democrats were deeply concerned about the growing influence of the Tweed Ring. Tammany Boss William Marcy Tweed, master organizer of new immigrants, shrewd manipulator of job and contract patronage, and unabashedly corrupt, dominated both city and state governments. Press exposures generated an anti-Tweed movement, and Samuel J. Tilden jumped in to lead it. Dramatic public investigations and law suits that eventually put Tweed in jail also put Tilden into the governorship and among the small number of Democratic presidential candidates. Reform was the slogan of the day.

Horatio Seymour had retired from politics. Tilden was wary of expending himself against a still popular president seeking a second term. Southern Democrats had not yet fully returned to the fold, and those who had were something of an embarrassment. Could an alliance in 1872 with the new Liberal Republican party (as with the Unionists under Lincoln) produce a victory that could be shared or, in defeat, dilute the stigma of being a loser? Could the Liberal Republicans later be absorbed by the greater electoral mass of the Democratic party?

The way was paved for Democratic endorsement of a Liberal Republican nominee, generally expected to be from among such acceptable moderates as Supreme Court Justice David Davis or Charles Francis Adams. The nominee turned out to be Horace Greeley, erstwhile Radical Republican, a fire-eating assailant of most things Democratic, and a friend of the more vociferous Southern Democrats. Greeley's nomination was a big and bitter pill, a source of division in the party, and a disaster on Election day.

Organizationally, however, the outcome was positive. Southern Democrats became once again full-scale participators in the party's national affairs. Large numbers of Republican liberals stayed with the Democrats. The reform issue was blazened onto the national political agenda. Tilden, as governor in 1874 and conqueror of the corrupt Canal Ring in 1875, moved into full control of the national party machinery and was the front-runner for the presidential nomination in 1876.

The nation's Panic of 1873 provided the economic setting. Congress refused to deal with the currency shortage created by the rapidly expanding economy. Hoping to succeed where the Grange, the Liberal Republicans, and the independent farmers' parties had failed, the Greenback party was formed in 1876 and found a ready constituency in many parts of the South and the Northwest. The Democratic soft-money and hard-money factions were alive and kicking more than ever. Reform—creating a civil service and public accountability in the granting of public contracts—was the issue around which most Democrats, with the exception of Tammany Hall, could unite and upon which Tilden had a solid record.

Tilden organized his own campaign even more thoroughly than he had Seymour's: a campaign organization separate from the regular party's; a private advertising agency for some functions; and a strong fundraising effort, to which Tilden contributed some unspecified portion of his own fortune. October local elections in Ohio, Indiana, and West Virginia predicted a Democratic sweep in November. The November presidential returns did in fact give Tilden 250,000 more popular votes than Rutherford Hayes and, at first glance, a 203-166 vote margin in the electoral college. However, returns from Louisiana (eight votes), South Carolina (seven votes), Florida (four votes), and Oregon (one vote) were tardy and of questionable validity. With 185 votes needed to elect, Democrats could only be certain of 184.

PARTY POLITICS INSTEAD OF CIVIL WAR

The political mood was ugly. The Stalwart Cabal had waved the "bloody shirt" with particular nastiness during the campaign. As postwar militiaman and voter, the Negro had been the principal pillar of Republican state governments in the occupied South, inviting a virulent racism in the form of such subterranean groups as the Ku Klux Klan and anti-Republican rifle clubs. Carpetbaggers and scalawags exploited anyone they could in the South. Balloting was often bloody, making it necessary for President Grant to send in federal troops. The period from Election Day (November) to Inaugural Day (March) was so intense as to raise fears of a second civil war.

The Democratic majority in Congress established a special fifteen-member Electoral Commission to determine which sets of disputed state returns should be accepted. The Senate selected three Republicans and two Democrats to serve, the

House chose three Democrats and two Republicans, and the Supreme Court added two Democratic and two Republican justices. These in turn chose the fifteenth "nonpartisan" member: Justice David Davis, Lincoln's close colleague.

The commission made 8-to-7 decisions in favor of Hayes on each set of returns. What had been a Democratic "compromise" produced a Republican president. The trade-off was a policy of troop withdrawal and general conciliation in the South under a Hayes administration as well as the appointment of southern Democrats to important federal posts in the South.

Sadly, it was too late for conciliation. Racism and the Democratic party were as one in the "Solid South" for most of the next century.

The election of 1876 did bring the two major national parties electorally abreast of each other for the next two decades, much as in the 1830s and 1840s. This time, however, the national organizations were buttressed by and often beholden to substantial state and local machines. Tilden's organizational work at the national level provided a strong and flexible institution for reconciling Democratic intraparty differences. The party experienced another near victory in 1880 and did not return to the presidency until 1884 when it did so with Tilden's protégé, Grover Cleveland.

In retrospect, the four decades from the mid-1840s to the mid-1880s saw the Democratic party sink into deep ideological division, with many ambivalences about loyalty to party or nation, a dearth of leadership, and constituencies that were confused or excessively hostile to each other. It required nearly half a century for the party to travel from the Jacksonian coalition to that of Tilden and Cleveland. The close major-party national contests of the 1840s did not return until the 1880s. Slavery, Civil War, and Reconstruction were happily past, but other political stresses lay ahead as the nation expanded westward, industrialized, and became a world power.

FOUR

The Pendulum of Faction, 1880 to 1932

During the final quarter of the nineteenth century the nation felt growing pains of many kinds. Poverty, populism, and racism cut down most efforts to reintegrate the South into the normal life of the nation. Mass migration westward brought in new states, altered the balance of power in Congress and the electoral college, changed the United States into a continental community, and put the Pacific Ocean and the Far East onto the political agenda. Postwar corporate enterprise continued to burgeon. The tiny national military force was occupied in maintaining order in the South, fighting Indians in the West, and, in the Spanish-American War, invading foreign shores. State militia were used to break up labor strikes. Machine politics, sharp campaign practices, election frauds, the dunning of public appointees for campaign contributions, and purchased legislatures were "normal."

While the reform issue made for a righteous politics, it was the currency issues that evoked the religious fervor. On the face of it, the nation's new and plentiful silver supply, mined in the Mountain States, seemed a good supplement to the short supply of gold and paper currency in the expanding, money hungry economy. The Bland-Allison Bimetallism Bill, enacted by a Democratic Congress, said as much, but the bill was vetoed by Hayes. The silver issue joined the tariff issue as top debate themes within and between the parties. The silver question was how to get more money into circulation. The tariff issue, in a time of growing treasury surpluses, revolved around how to get some of that extra money out of the government's hands.

MANUFACTURED CONSTITUENCIES: THE SOUTH AND THE POPULISTS

Although the Tilden forces controlled the national party, Tilden himself never fully recovered from his 1876 defeat. He was ambiguous about his presidential intentions in 1880—he was neither running nor retiring. The New York delegation chose to interpret his situation as retirement. The national convention went for General Winfield Scott Hancock who had straddled the soft-money and hard-money question success-fully and had said hardly a word on most other issues.

Hancock's campaign management lacked the firm hand of Tilden and the funds needed for a winning enterprise. On the other hand, it enjoyed, uneasily, the vigorous support of Tammany Hall (happy to be rid of Tilden). The popular vote divided 48.3 percent for James A. Garfield to 48.2 percent for

Hancock. The Democratic managers charged that twenty thousand Republican votes had been cast illegally in New York alone. Hancock went to his grave believing he had been defrauded. President Garfield also went to his grave, but only two months after inauguration, the victim of an assassin's bullets. Succeeding him was his vice president, Chester A. Arthur, a New York Stalwart and machine politician of questionable political purity.

President Arthur discontinued Hayes' policy of appointing conservative southern Democrats to federal positions. Instead, the jobs went to Republicans loyal to the president, thereby assuring their support in succeeding Republican national conventions. The southern Republican party for decades thereafter consisted of a tiny coterie of federal jobholders.

The Democrats were free to construct their own aberration: a South solidly Democratic and a party organization run by demagogues exploiting the poor white backlash against the excesses of black Republicanism during Reconstruction. Through poll taxes and at gun-point, black citizens were denied access to the southern ballot box. The terror of the Ku Klux Klan spread, and racist rhetoric became the winning formula among Democratic politicians.

With Hancock retired and Tilden a recluse, the latter's younger colleagues regained the initiative in national politics. New York's Governor Grover Cleveland endeared himself to Tilden by seeking his counsel frequently and by embarking upon a noisy public quarrel with the leaders of Tammany Hall. A bachelor and political loner, Cleveland welcomed the endorsement of the Tilden team but was careful to bring other factional leaders—at this time, chiefly tariff protectionists and tariff reductionists—into his tent. Readily nominated, Cleveland launched a hard-hitting election campaign that included an attack on Republican James G. Blaine's personal integrity (unethical association with railroad promoters while he was Speaker of the House). Blaine's managers responded in kind (charging that Cleveland had fathered an illegitimate son). The election was so close that both parties claimed victory.

In the end, Cleveland carried New York by a mere 1,200 votes, and with it, the electoral college.

The Democrats, after twenty-four years in the wilderness, once again controlled the White House, 50,000 federal postmaster appointments, and a federal treasury spilling over with custom revenues. The federal patronage had become too much for any political party to handle; each appointment left one or more disappointed office-seekers. The tariff was less a source of revenue than the occasion for building and rebuilding logrolling coalitions. In addition, the rising flow of silver from western mines was becoming a threat to the stability of the nation's monetary system.

A treasury surplus is a temptation that no normal politician can ignore. Congress went on a spending binge that included veterans' pensions, appropriations for rivers and harbors, and, in lesser amounts, aid to education. President Cleveland took a more quixotic approach; he called for tariff reduction to reduce the Treasury surplus. This was the sole topic of his Annual Message of 1887. It was hardly a welcome message for the protectionist alliance between business and labor, as subsequently demonstrated at the polls. Benjamin Harrison and a Republican Congress carried the next national election. Two years later the supremely protectionist McKinley Tariff was enacted.

Out of office in 1889, Cleveland became a corporation lawyer in New York, made some money in the stock market, and soaked up the views of corporate, financial, and commercial leaders. He became a sound money man, quite removed from the agrarian depression that was worsening in the West and South. Because Cleveland lost to Harrison in another squeaky close contest in 1888, he was the most likely candidate for the Democratic nomination in 1896. Realizing that a Cleveland-Harrison rerun was a choice between Tweedledum and Tweedledee, labor, farmers, single-taxers, women's groups, prohibitionists, and other radical or reform groups met to found the Populist party.

Benjamin Harrison's administration dealt with a number of issues in ways that polarized factions in both parties and energized a populist third-party response. He endorsed the protectionist McKinley Tariff, and tariff reductionists united to fight. He supported the Sherman Silver Purchase Act which swamped the Treasury with silver and led to a run on the Treasury's gold reserve, to the delight of agrarian interests. He approved passage of the Sherman Anti-Trust Act as a gesture to labor and consumer interests seeking to constrain monopolistic business enterprises, only to earn the hostility of business. With the South going solidly Democratic by denying the ballot to blacks, Harrison simply watched as the Force Bill (a federally protected ballot box), introduced by Henry Cabot Lodge of Massachusetts, was filibustered to its grave in the Senate. He did nothing to cope with the severe agrarian depression.

As Populists organized during the 1890 midterm congressional elections, many Democratic and independent candidates pledged support of Populist programs such as bimetallism (free coinage of both silver and gold) and easier farm credit. Some Democrats even ran on the Populist ticket. While Democrats swept the congressional elections in general, the populist vote was impressively large. In several states it seemed as though the Populists would take over the Democratic party's agrarian constituencies lock, stock, and barrel.

The trend was accelerated in 1891 when Grover Cleveland declared unqualifiedly that free coinage of silver was a "dangerous and reckless experiment." Labor, now becoming increasingly unionized by the recently founded American Federation of Labor under the leadership of Samuel Gompers, was distrustful of Cleveland's Wall Street friends and angered by President Harrison's use of state militia to break the Homestead strike of 1892. Blocked out of both major-party national tickets, labor, silverites, and western and southern farmers proceeded to select their own nominee for president under the Populist banner.

Both major parties pursued the same dangerous strategy in the 1892 presidential contest. Where Democrats were a minority in the West, they endorsed the Populist ticket as a way of knocking states out of the Harrison column. Where

Republicans were a minority, mainly in the South, they endorsed the Populist ticket to deny states to Cleveland. Cleveland won 5,554,000 votes to Harrison's 5,191,000. Another million votes went to the Populist nominee, James Weaver.

Since Populist alliances with local Democrats had been so numerous, it was inevitable that Populist and silverite leaders would be a major force in the Democratic party in the coming years. This became immediately true in Congress where great pro-silver speeches were made by Representatives William Jennings Bryan and Richard P. Bland and Senators James K. Jones, George Vest, and Henry M. Teller. The congressional silverites soon played Achilles' heel to the second Cleveland administration, undermining Cleveland's tariff proposals and providing little or no help as the administration tried to cope with the Panic of 1893. Meanwhile, Populism was attracting growing support from all lower-income groups.

The depression hit labor as well as farmers. When Pullman railway workers went on strike in Chicago in 1894, Cleveland followed Harrison's example in the 1892 Homestead strike. To the shock of many Democratic leaders, Cleveland broke the strike by dispatching federal troops to the scene. Elsewhere, the farm crisis worsened and the currency issue sharpened. The congressional elections of 1894 returned 284 Republicans and a mere 104 Democrats.

SILVER AND INTERPARTY COALITIONS

As 1896 approached, sound-money, gold-standard men continued to make up the majority on the Republican side, although that party's free-silver minority was loud, powerful, and ready to defect. Among Democrats the split was right down the middle on the bimetallism issue and 2-to-1 opposed to Cleveland as president and as a third-term candidate. By convention time it was evident that the party's nominee would be drawn from the free-silver leadership. But which one?

Front-runners were Richard P. Bland and Horace Boies, whose supporters stalemated each other. Every silverite's second or third choice, it turned out, was thirty-six-year-old William Jennings Bryan.

Bryan understood the presidential nominating process as few others did. He had a silver tongue as well as a silver program. He was the first potential nominee to be present on the floor of the convention with a major opportunity to address it. His speech would have been a precedent-setter even if it had not been a masterpiece of oratory and symbolism. He was in complete agreement with the majority's platform favoring a silver-gold ratio of 16-to-1 in currency value and condemning "government by injunction," a reference to Cleveland's handling of the Pullman strike. The Boy Orator's platform address concluded with the ringing phrases:

> We shall answer their [Republicans'] demands for a gold standard by saying to them, you shall not press down upon the brow of labor this crown of thorns. You shall not crucify mankind upon a cross of gold.

As Bryan had predicted the prior evening to a visiting delegation, he received the nomination on the fifth ballot.

Bryan's unenviable assignment was to defeat a gold-standard, protectionist Republican, William McKinley, without the help of the gold-standard Democrats, who, Cleveland among them, bolted the party. All that kept President Cleveland from making a campaign tour for the Gold Democrats' ticket was his need to conduct legislative business with Congress. The situation led the party to build a complex coalition of Silver Republicans, Populists, and the National Silver party. Each of these parties had a stubborn antifusion faction. Coordinating the campaigns of all four parties was barely achieved by the end of September. "Popocrat" disorganization was a favorite topic for ridicule in the Republican press.

In contrast, Republican National Chairman Mark Hanna, a multimillionaire whose managerial talents were legendary, conducted an extraordinary campaign for Governor William

McKinley. Speakers, campaign literature, and fundraising were organized as never before in national party history. Hanna introduced the modern era in presidential campaigning, a model that Democrats were unable to emulate until James A. Farley ran Franklin D. Roosevelt's campaigns more than three decades later. If anything, Democrats spent most of the nine national elections between 1896 and 1932 defeating themselves.

Bryan could not dodge much of the blame laid on the Democratic party for the Panic of 1893, the bank failures, the railroad receiverships, the unemployment, the currency shortage, the farm crisis, the labor turmoil, and other economic and social ills of the day. Working-class voters joined the silk-stocking crowd in a broad shift to the Republican party in 1896. The shift was reinforced by the happy discovery of new gold deposits in the Klondike and a bumper wheat harvest during the fall campaign. Almost magically, prosperity returned to the nation at the very outset of McKinley's first term.

The career of William Jennings Bryan in the Democratic party encompassed three presidential nominations and an out-party titular leadership grasped with the same vigor as evinced by Martin Van Buren and Samuel J. Tilden before him. The national leadership of the Democratic party retired almost en masse after the election, enabling Bryan to make himself a full-time titular leader. He wrote a book about his *First Battle* (implying that there would be others), traveled over a 93,000-mile lecture circuit to expound on the currency, trusts, and imperialism, and encouraged the development of local party clubs. Complicating Bryan's organizational efforts were factional struggles in many Democratic state organizations across the country, leadership changes in the Populist and Silver Republican parties, the decision of Gold Democrats to return to the regular party, and the emergence of new and well-organized pressure groups representing bimetallists, anti-imperialists, antitrusters, prohibitionists, and others. Democrats in Congress were little more than a squabbling minority, not exactly certain what constituencies they represented.

Cooperation with the Populists helped the Democratic party among the western electorate but drove midwestern and eastern voters into Republican arms. Labor was wary of the inflationist consequences of a free-silver program and worried about the competition from cheap foreign labor that could occur under a free trade doctrine. Eastern farmers worried about what might happen to their produce if urban workers went broke. Bryan, who had been nicknamed the Peerless Leader, sought to reassure labor by promising restraints on the excesses of monopoly capital. To farmers he promised government assistance in maintaining farm prices and access to low-interest credit. Foreign policy, hardly a big issue with rank-and-file Democrats, became prominent as a consequence of the country's gains in the Spanish-American War of 1898: the Philippines, Puerto Rico, and other distant territories. Bryan condemned imperialism at a time when a chauvinistic nation had hardly begun to digest its feast of new possessions.

Bryan was unable to keep this multiparty coalition intact in 1900. One Populist faction, joined by many Silver Republicans, held a separate national convention, at which it bid for the Democratic party's vice-presidential nomination. As a consequence, the Democratic vice-presidential selection became a comedy of machinations.

The Democratic election campaign lacked direction, enthusiasm, and sophistication. The presidential electorate was polarized between the two sets of one-party states: fifteen overwhelmingly Democratic states, mostly in the South, and fifteen safe Republican states. Of the fifteen remaining states, only ten could be considered relatively competitive. Democrats were out-organized and out-financed in nearly all. Republicans elected their McKinley-Roosevelt ticket.

Progressivism: "Radical" Stances for the New Constituencies

President McKinley was assassinated in September 1901, and his rambunctious, highly political vice president, Theodore Roosevelt, succeeded him. In an era of rapid economic, political, and international change, this turned out to be bad news for Democrats. Unlike McKinley, Roosevelt was an extremely adaptable politician, willing to ride the wave of progressivism that was gathering force in the nation. The "Radical" or progressive policies that William Jennings Bryan popularized were picked up by Roosevelt one by one: regulation of banking; the break-up of monopolistic trusts; the provision of pensions and other benefits for labor; tariff reduction; government inspection of food and drug products to safeguard consumers; direct popular election of United States senators; conservation of natural resources. It all added up to a progressivist program of government intervention to protect specific constituencies. It was an historic irony that Bryan prepared public opinion for Theodore Roosevelt, who in turn paved the way for Woodrow Wilson's policies. A generation later, a second Roosevelt, Franklin D., picked up the progressivist approach where Wilson had left it.

At forty, Bryan had the unpleasant distinction of being the first presidential nominee to suffer electoral defeat twice consecutively. He hardly viewed this as the occasion for retirement from leadership of the Democratic party. "I am not a candidate for any office," he said in 1901; "however, I would not enter into a bond never to become a candidate." He published a weekly newspaper, the *Commoner*, wrote *The Second Battle*, and lectured interminably, with increasingly religious content.

The *Commoner* became the forum for Bryan's advocacy of a federal income tax, direct election of senators, independence for the Philippines, prohibition of the sale of liquor, women's suffrage, a Department of Labor in the cabinet, public reporting of election campaign expenditures, and the various demands of agrarian and labor interest groups. Both Roosevelt and Bryan were dedicated to political parties as indispensable instruments of popular sovereignty and urged that public funds be used for the legitimate expenses of parties, on the same grounds that had allowed for governmental printing of ballots in earlier years.

Bryan took himself out of the presidential race in 1904 and was unable to help William Randolph Hearst's candidacy against a coalition of eastern Democratic machines. The nominee, a little known New York judge, Alton B. Parker, was thoroughly committed to the gold standard, alienating the diminishing Democratic electorate in the West. His wealthy supporters were a perfect target for President Roosevelt's anti-monopoly tirades, frightening off much of what remained of the party's support among labor.

The Democrats did not recover from the Theodore Roosevelt landslide until the Franklin D. Roosevelt landslide of 1932. Only thirteen states from the Solid South and a few Border states voted Democratic. The South was to be the electoral center of the party for the next third of a century. The South's influence was further assured by the seniority system in Congress, which placed repeatedly reelected Southerners into the powerful chairmanships of committees.

Bryan prepared for a third nomination, occasionally acknowledging that President Roosevelt was looking more and more like a progressive. Bryan's own radicalism was apparently moderating sufficiently to bring into his fold a number of the "bosses" who were then thoroughly in command of state or urban Democratic machines: Tom Taggart, leader of the Indiana organization and chairman of the Democratic National Committee; Roger Sullivan, undisputed boss of Chicago; Charles Murphy of Tammany Hall; Arthur P. Gorman of Maryland; and others.

To remind everyone that he was still an opponent of bosses, whether machine or corporate, Bryan publicly questioned Roger Sullivan's close relations with the corporate world. To confirm further his progressivism, Bryan took the trouble in 1906 to assert before a Madison Square Garden crowd that *ultimately* the railroads would become public property. This was over half a century before Amtrak.

Renominated, Bryan was again defeated, and, as before, he refused to retire. He conducted himself as though 1912 would bring him another nomination.

The Taft administration very quickly ran into difficulties. Building a navy and other defense forces was a troublesome new activity for this new world power. Administering overseas territories was proving expensive and strenuous. Reform of corrupt city governments was becoming urgent. Monopolies were being attacked everywhere, including the House of Representatives, where a Democratic minority, with the help of progressive Republicans, sheared Speaker "Uncle Joe" Cannon of his near-dictatorial powers. Congressman Champ Clark of Missouri led the successful revolt and soon after became speaker and presidential timber.

The institutional consequence of the rules change was to disperse congressional power from the speaker to committee chairmen, who were themselves entrenched by the seniority system. This eventually led to a durable coalition of conservative Republicans and southern Democrats as well as to deep divisions within each of the major parties.

CONSTITUENCIES REWARDED—THE WILSONIAN PROGRAM

Progressives in both the Democratic and Republican parties made large gains in the 1910 midterm elections. This emboldened the two "retired" titular leaders once again to exercise their progressivism. Roosevelt berated Taft for failing to help the progressives against Speaker Cannon and dedicated himself to Taft's defeat for reelection. Although there were a great many candidates, including himself, for the 1912 Democratic nomination, Bryan eventually proclaimed that the real choice was between Speaker Clark and the new governor of New Jersey (and former president of Princeton University), Woodrow Wilson.

Bryan played the 1912 Democratic convention like a master musician. He flushed out the size of the progressive delegation vote by becoming a candidate for the temporary chairmanship against conservative Alton B. Parker and losing, 579–508. Clark's delegations split their votes, suggesting indecisiveness among the Speaker's support. Wilson's delegates went solidly for Bryan. In the balloting for the nomination, there was a stalemate among the four major candidates. Bryan's supporters voted for Clark at first but shifted to Wilson on the fourteenth ballot. This started a cautious shift toward Wilson, who was nominated on the forty-sixth ballot.

Meanwhile, Theodore Roosevelt was busy running for president as the nominee of the new Progressive party. In the election, Wilson's 6,286,000 plurality was less than the combined total for Roosevelt and Taft but sufficient to carry forty-two states in the electoral college. Roosevelt had at the same time defeated Taft and kept Wilson from becoming a majority president.

The new Democratic administration brought into office leaders and policy themes that persisted into the New Deal era. A university president and political scientist, Woodrow Wilson thought and wrote extensively about the institutional development of the national government and the party system. He was an enthusiastic admirer of the British parliamentary system and, much as did Alexander Hamilton, tried to function as though the American presidential system was parliamentary in character. This seemed feasible during his first two years in office because House Democrats had, in 1910, reactivated the party caucus for the purpose of legislative management. Thus, the congressional structure, Democratic votes, and the usual political honeymoon enjoyed by new administrations were in place at the beginning of Wilson's term to help implement his lengthy progressive program.

Wilson sent Congress a barrage of bills and messages and often stationed himself in the President's Room just off the Senate chamber in order to guide the process. The major pieces of legislation responded to the party's constituencies. Monetary and banking reforms were adopted in the Owen-Glass Federal Reserve Act over the objection of the banking industry. The Clayton Anti-Trust Act, exempting labor and farm organizations, tackled the malpractices of numerous industrial monopolies. The Newlands Act improved the arbitration system available to railway labor. Federal farm loan banks were established for the agrarian interest. Contrary to all expectations, a basic revision of the tariff was legislated. It was a virtuoso performance, interrupted by the end of the session and the beginning of World War I in Europe.

The war set aside domestic issues and brought foreign affairs to the fore. The country was divided over its attachments to the contending powers in Europe, but, for some time, benefited from trade with both sides. It eventually became a poor choice between German atrocities and the British blockade. As secretary of state, Bryan exerted himself to bring about a negotiated settlement, but resigned in June 1915, frustrated with the European contestants and doubtful of the neutrality of his president.

On the Republican side, conservatives were defeating progressives in off-year elections, reducing the prospect that Roosevelt would make another race. The opposing wings of the Republican party found a compromise candidate in Supreme Court Justice Charles E. Hughes. Republican unity presented a serious challenge for Wilson, who had by now thoroughly alienated the business and Democratic machine leaders who had originally supported him. Wilson placed his confidence in the Solid South, western farmers, urban labor (particularly the American Federation of Labor), small business, and the increasingly self-conscious and consumer-conscious middle class. (The following year Wilson became the first president to address an annual convention of the American Federation of Labor.) Wilson won by the few thousand votes that carried California, where progressivism was having a heyday.

Although "He kept us out of war" had been the principal Democratic campaign theme, Wilson, soon after inauguration, recommended that Congress declare war against the Central Powers. Unwilling, on principle, to select a bipartisn war cabinet, Wilson nevertheless brought numerous leading Republicans into his second administration, e.g., William Howard Taft, Herbert Hoover, Robert S. Brookings, and others. The war surrounded Wilson with an aura of national unity, and he demanded or assumed near dictatorial wartime executive powers. The latter tendency eventually aroused congressional ire and institutional defenses. In Whig-like fashion, Republicans took up the antiexecutive cudgels and decided to campaign vigorously for a Republican Congress in 1918.

Despite the historical certainty that the party incumbent in the presidency loses congressional seats in the midterm elections of a first term, and more so in the midterm of a second administration, Wilson put his personal reputation on the line by campaigning intensively for a Democratic Congress. This terminated the brief wartime political consensus. Andrew Johnson (re-elected as president, a second midterm election leader of a successful war effort), failed in such a campaign effort in 1866, a lesson not lost on succeeding presidents. Under substantially different circumstances. Wilson's 1918 midterm campaign was an historic first. It was motivated by his sense of parliamentary obligation, his tendency to "go to the people," his concern for the imminent peace treaty negotiations, and his personal vendetta with Republican Senator Henry Cabot Lodge of Massachusetts.

Wilson's attacks on the Republicans were met by equally strident Republican counterattacks. When Republicans captured majorities in both houses on Election Day, the principal victim was the Paris Peace Conference scheduled to begin on January 12, 1919. Wilson's plan for a League of Nations and his negotiating strength were considerably weakened by the election outcome. Lodge's hostility to Wilson and the League concept was additionally debilitating. On March 7, 1919, the Republican national chairman, Will Hays, in effect launched the 1920 presidential campaign on the issue of national interest versus the League of Nations. The Democratic National Committee took the bait and promptly proclaimed the League of Nations to be the paramount issue before the country.

To overcome the handicap of being a lame-duck president, Wilson encouraged speculation that he might seek an unprecedented third term. On September 3, 1919, he also embarked upon an extended tour of the country to defend the peace treaty and the League covenant. On September 28, he suffered a paralyzing stroke and was compelled to remain inside the confines of the White House. His illness and his unwillingness to negotiate with a Republican Congress about the provisions of the treaty led to its defeat, 53 to 38, in the Senate.

PARTY-WRECKING, DEMOCRATIC-STYLE

William Jennings Bryan, ever ready to exploit the party's divisions, came out against Wilson. Bryan Leagues were revived. Wilson let it be known that his interest in a third term was real, a way to take the League issue to the country. A split nominating convention seemed inevitable. The two-thirds rule, now providing the Solid South with complete veto power and almost guaranteeing deadlocked conventions, came under widespread discussion among Democratic leaders. Other candidates most prominently mentioned were William Gibbs McAdoo, Wilson's former secretary of the treasury and now son-in-law, Governor James M. Cox of the "weather-vane" state of Ohio, Governor Alfred E. Smith, a favorite son of New York and numerous urban machine bosses, and John W. Davis, ambassador to England.

It was a party-destroying national convention. State and local bosses opposed Wilsonians. Populists and progressives opposed conservatives. "Drys" on liquor prohibition were opposed by "Wets." Wilson's silence on his health and his availability added to the uncertainty. Of the twenty-four names put in nomination, only four—McAdoo, Cox, Smith, and A. Mitchell Palmer, Wilson's red-baiting attorney-general—maintained their delegate strength. Wilson's name was much discussed as a way of uniting the party but was never submitted. Cox defeated McAdoo on the forty-fourth ballot. Wilson's under-secretary of the navy and an associate of Governor Smith, Franklin D. Roosevelt, was chosen by acclamation for the vice-presidential place on the ticket.

As soon as Cox agreed to make the League *the* issue of

the campaign, the big-city Democratic organizations cut themselves loose from the national effort, going so far as to have separate ballots printed for presidential electors. The League of Nations was, after all, a radically new "foreign entanglement" for a nation still attentive to George Washington's warning against such entanglements. Besides, ethnic voters—Italians, Germans, Irish—were upset by treaty provisions that seemed unjust to their countries of origin.

The Nineteenth Amendment providing women's suffrage went into effect on August 26, 1920. The first women to turn out to the polls came from the better-educated, wealthier, more Republican constituencies, helping to build Warren Harding's landslide. Republicans gained a 59-37 margin in the Senate and 296-235 in the House. Republicans would be in charge for the next dozen years.

The Democratic party now faced the problem of irreconcilable factional leaders and constituencies. The younger generation of Wilsonians was cast against an older generation of party professionals. In the South, there were moderate and conservative congressional leaders and fiery populists, the latter bringing in religious fundamentalism and a determined commitment to prohibiting the sale and use of alcoholic beverages. Creeping up from outside the party was a rejuvenated Ku Klux Klan, revived by the patriotic fervor of the war, fear of the influx of millions of immigrants, and resistance to Negro advancement. By 1923, Klan membership was in the millions and the organization's leaders controlled senators, congressmen, and other public officials of both parties in nearly a third of the states.

The nation in general turned inward to assume an isolationist stance in world affairs. Farmers remained debt-ridden. White supremacy policies and tactics were bringing bloodshed to the South. Prohibition gave organized crime a major place in the nation's lifestyle. The business boom of 1919–1920 became the depression of 1920–1921. Over two million workers were unemployed. Unions, when not on strike, were struggling to organize those who had work. In 1923 the nation was stunned by the revelation that members of the Harding cabinet were implicated in bribes involving leases for the private exploitation of public oil reserve lands at Teapot Dome. Several suicides and the death of the president himself gave the scandal particular impact.

Calvin Coolidge assumed the presidency and promptly suffered several legislative defeats at the hands of a conservative Republic cabal in the Senate. Progressives who, with Theodore Roosevelt, remained outside the two major parties after the 1912–1916 period prepared to nominate Robert LaFollette in 1924, hoping to attract Republican progressives. Among Democrats, William Gibbs McAdoo, who never disavowed the overt support he was receiving from the Ku Klux Klan, was the best organized for a presidential race.

There was no way that McAdoo could be acceptable to the big-city coalition that controlled the convention votes of New York, Illinois, Indiana, Pennsylvania, Ohio, and several other states. Their man was Al Smith, and Smith's preconvention manager was Franklin D. Roosevelt, just returning from his battle with infantile paralysis. The Smith forces were intent upon making the Klan the major issue at the convention. Smith was the urban, Catholic, Wet from the North determined to beat back McAdoo's rural, Protestant, Dry following, mainly in the Democratic South.

The convention was bizarre. A motion to condemn the Klan by name was defeated by a vote of 543 3/20 to 542 7/20. Nearly twenty candidates received votes on the first ballot. On the 69th ballot, McAdoo reached his greatest strength: 530 votes. On the 93rd ballot Franklin Roosevelt announced that Smith would withdraw his name immediately upon the withdrawal of McAdoo. John W. Davis was given the worthless nomination on the 103rd ballot. The election was another landslide for the Republicans. McAdoo and Smith supporters began preparing for 1928.

The LaFollette Progressives as well as progressives in each of the major parties also began to pull themselves together immediately after the election. Agrarian and labor distress was mounting in contrast to the business prosperity apparent everywhere. A farm depression persisted throughout the

1920s. Unemployment was high. Prohibition and crime were becoming intolerable. In December 1924, Franklin Roosevelt took it upon himself to write to three thousand Democratic leaders urging upon them a midterm conference on matters of party organizational improvement. Such a conference never occurred in 1926, but the concept eventually was implemented in 1974. Instead, the McAdoo-Smith confrontation began.

Governor Smith took his campaign directly to the South. He advocated that the national convention be held there but at the same time threatened a strong fight to abolish the two-thirds rule so long cherished by the South. By summer 1927 McAdoo announced his withdrawal from the race, favorite son candidates fell by the wayside, and the 1928 nomination was Smith's, the first Catholic to receive major-party nomination for president.

BRINGING OUT THE NEW CITIZENS

Voter turnout is normally low in years of economic prosperity. The election of 1928 brought out the highest increase in popular vote over an immediately preceding election since 1856, with the exception of 1920 when woman suffrage went into effect. The vote for Smith pulled the Democratic party's percentage of the total popular vote up from 29 percent in 1924 to 41 percent in 1928. The Protestant South was no longer solid; Florida, Texas, Virginia, and North Carolina went to Herbert Hoover. Smith doubled the Democratic vote in states where Progressives had been strongest in 1924. In the large urban states Smith drew large numbers of workers and immigrants voting for the first time.

A new generation of professional political analysts, sensitive to socioeconomic attributes and group behavior, gave close attention to the 1928 election. They found, for example, that the urban support for Smith and the agrarian support for Hoover did not have as great an impact on the outcome as was usually claimed. Nor did the voter's foreign parentage. What did make the difference were: the Wet-Dry issue, the recentness of the immigrant's arrival in this country, and the issue of the influence of the Catholic Church on Smith. Being Catholic, Wet, and popular among recent immigrants may not have helped Al Smith in 1928 but did pull these constituencies into the Democratic party for the long term.

In New York, where Smith had asked Franklin Roosevelt to make the gubernatorial race, Roosevelt won by a close margin and almost automatically was seen as a presidential candidate. Both men, seeing the need for a full-time national organization for the party, urged this project on National Chairman John J. Raskob of General Motors Corporation and a long-time friend of Smith. Raskob willingly paid the bills for such an organization, expecting that it would eventually be influential in Smith's renomination and election.

Roosevelt's landslide reelection victory in New York in 1930 in the midst of the worsening economic depression, the mounting resistance of southern Democratic leaders to Smith-Raskob control of the national committee headquarters, the return of control of the House of Representatives to the Democrats for the first time in over a decade, and the assignment of New York Democratic State Committee Chairman James A. Farley to the management of Roosevelt's preconvention campaign combined to pave the way for Roosevelt's challenge of his old friend's candidacy. Al Smith never forgave FDR.

By convention time, Roosevelt had a majority of the delegates pledged to him but fell short of the necessary two-thirds. For exactly one century the two-thirds rule had dominated and shaped the fortunes of the Democratic party. The Roosevelt managers, forgetting that a major part of their candidate's support came from the principal beneficiaries of the rule, that is, the South, sought to have it abolished right then and there. Southern protest was quick in coming and effective in having the rule issue referred to committee for future study. Roosevelt obtained the needed two-thirds when he agreed with William Gibbs McAdoo, now leader of the California delegation and close ally of Speaker John Nance Garner of Texas, that Garner have second place on the ticket.

The Democrats of 1932—contentious as always, intent upon sweeping back into national office, and led by a consummate politician—completely forgot to celebrate their party's centennial on May 21.

FIVE

The New Deal Coalition and Its Reincarnations, 1932 to 1968

The Great Depression meant a 45 percent unemployment rate among factory workers, an 86 percent decline in residential building between 1929 and 1932, and a 75 percent drop in steel production over the same period. More than a third of the nation's banks were failing. Farm foreclosures were rampant as harvests lay rotting. Nations, including the scrupulous British, were defaulting on their debts. Hunger and destitution were everywhere, in the United States and throughout the world.

Most Americans became a citizenry united in despair. Out of this misery, Franklin Delano Roosevelt's New Deal brought together a coalition of constituencies that prevailed through a half century of wars, recessions, civil rights demonstrations, moon landings, and other high political drama. As the nation's majority party during this period, the Democrats were thoroughly tested, frequently torn, and remarkably successful in guiding the nation to leadership of the free world and toward the twenty-first century in its domestic development. If anything, Democrats became overly hesitant about straying from the New Deal coalition. By 1968, there was some question about the capacity of the coalition to revitalize itself.

ROOSEVELT'S CONSTITUENCY BUILDING
AND PARTY MANAGEMENT

In May 1932, a "Bonus Expeditionary Force," representing 800,000 veterans, staged a protest march in Washington, demanding increased veteran benefits. Displaying a remarkable lack of political sensitivity, President Hoover authorized his secretary of war to disperse the bonus marchers. The task was given to General Douglas MacArthur, who performed it with relish. The event ignited an angry populism. Republican progressives who had been jumping onto the Democratic campaign train were happy that they had. Blaming the depression on Hoover and condemning the Republicans for serving only the rich, Roosevelt promised a New Deal for the Common Man.

The Common Man responded with his vote. Roosevelt received 7 million more votes than Hoover of the 39 million cast. Norman Thomas, a Socialist with many programs that later found their way into New Deal legislation, received a million votes. Two-thirds of the seats in Congress were won by Democrats: sixty in the Senate, 310 in the House. For the first time ever, only two-fifths of the Senate Democrats and one-third of the House Democrats were from the South, drastically reducing that region's bargaining and veto powers in national politics.

Franklin D. Roosevelt's New Deal gave the Democratic party an auspicious and historic start into its second century. It began an era in which the United States became a world power, the federal government grew many times over in function and size, and Democrats, for decades, were clearly the nation's majority party. The New Deal coalition returned FDR to the White House an unprecedented and unrepeatable four times, kept Harry Truman's Fair Deal in place for seven years, was reenergized during the John F. Kennedy and Lyndon B. Johnson years, and, a shadow of its original self, helped Jimmy Carter and Walter Mondale in their efforts to lead the party and the nation.

The coalition that initially brought FDR to the presidency was made up primarily of Old Wilsonians, progressives of various origins, regional leaders, and machine bosses. It was hardly a durable combination and floated in different directions on the electorate's tidal wave rejection of the Republicans. Wilsonians became New Dealers. Progressives became Democrats. The South was outvoted within the party and the Congress, and itself was soon no longer solid. Machines and their bosses melted away, one at a time, as the federal government took on the functions, if not the appearance, of the beneficent precinct captain. Once elected, Roosevelt helped supportive constituencies—labor, farmers, etc.—to reconstitute themselves and then encouraged them to help rebuild the Democratic party. The result was the New Deal, an historic masterpiece of coalition-building.

The legislative achievements of the first New Deal Congress set new and enduring pathways in national policy. While reminiscent of Wilson's first Congress, no session of Congress had ever worked so hard and so fast. There was truly an atmosphere of crisis and near revolution. New Deal measures, often ill-conceived and poorly drafted, poured into the congressional hopper. The roster of statutes was as large and varied as the complex industrial society that the United States had become. Famous "alphabet agencies" were created one after the other. Hardly a constituency escaped Roosevelt's notice and treatment.

The Agricultural Adjustment Act (AAA) introduced price supports for farm products and crop reduction procedures for farm surpluses. An emergency farm mortgage financing plan was thrown together to dam up the flood of foreclosures. Confidence in the stock market was restored by securities exchange legislation that clarified rules and responsibilities of brokers and traders. The National Industrial Recovery Act (NIRA) provided for organized labor's right of collective bargaining, over $3 billion in public works, and the preparation of codes of fair competition aimed at reviving stagnant industries.

The Civilian Conservation Corps (CCC) took hundreds of thousands of young men off the bread lines and into projects for conserving the nation's natural resources. The Federal Emergency Relief Administration (FERA) was created to give immediate aid to the starving and homeless. A Public Works Administration (PWA) dispensed money for jobs on community projects. A Civil Works Administration gave short-term employment to 4 million persons on 180,000 projects within a matter of weeks. An Emergency Banking Act arranged to safeguard bank deposits and improve the currency supply. The Tennessee Valley Authority was established as a grand experiment in regional planning. Looking forward to the repeal of the Eighteenth Amendment (Prohibition), an amendment to the Volstead Act permitted the sale of light beer and wine.

The country had never seen anything like it! The electorate expressed its gratitude quite clearly. The midterm congressional election of 1934 was the first in United States history in which the party of an incumbent administration gained rather than lost seats in Congress: sixty-nine Democrats in the Senate, 319 in the House. Southern Democrats were suddenly aware that they were a minority in the party that they had so recently dominated. This diminished status was further weakened at the 1936 national convention, where the two-thirds rule was at last repealed.

Between 1934 and 1936 Roosevelt cemented the group

and electoral coalition that, in several revivals and resurrections, remained the basis of Democratic victories for most of the next half century. Ethnic and nationality minorities, a substantial number of whom were the recent immigrants attracted to politics by Al Smith, were thoroughly mobilized by Jim Farley, now national chairman, and most of the big-city machines. Catholics, Jews, and northern blacks became the staunchest of Democrats, the latter voting 76 percent Democratic in 1936.

Facilitated by the collective bargaining provisions (Section 7A) of the NIRA, trade union organizing activity and membership increased by leaps and bounds. The American Federation of Labor was enthusiastic about helping its political friends; union labor voted 80 percent Democratic. Dr. Francis E. Townsend's program for old-age pensions brought millions of neglected elderly citizens to the polls, and the New Deal response was the Social Security System. Millions of poor farmers and rural citizens, rescued by Roosevelt's agricultural programs, left Republican ranks to vote Democratic, and farm organizations could do nothing but follow. Turning to the universities for advice and personnel, Roosevelt recruited the intellectual community into government to an unprecedented extent. Thus, by 1936, rural domination of national politics ended and leadership was assumed by constituencies that were mainly urban: unions, ethnic minorities, city machines, intellectuals, consumer-oriented business enterprise, the elderly, the small farmers—in sum, the New Deal coalition.

During the 1936 campaign, *Literary Digest* magazine, employing faulty survey procedures, forecast a victory for Alf Landon. Farley, relying on time-honored party intelligence procedures, forecast a Roosevelt landslide. Roosevelt carried every state except Maine and Vermont. Encouraged by such popular support, Roosevelt was determined to take on a hostile Supreme Court.

The Court, six of whose members were over seventy years of age, had been invalidating a number of key New Deal measures. Without serious consultation with Democratic leaders in Congress, Roosevelt proposed adding an additional judge to any federal court in which a sitting judge, having reached the retirement age of seventy, did not retire.

FDR paid an unexpectedly high price in party prestige as a consequence of this court-packing plan. The non-New Dealers in the party, particularly from the South, saw an opportunity to remind the president that there were three *separate* branches of government and a southern interest still alive within the party. The Republicans decided to let the Democrats fight it out among themselves. This opposition and the close leadership fight that followed the sudden death of Majority Leader Joseph T. Robinson of Arkansas doomed the court plan, Roosevelt's first major legislative defeat. Other defeats followed: a wages-and-hours bill and an administrative reorganization bill. Party leaders seemed to be acting on the assumption that Roosevelt was a lame-duck president.

THE LABOR CONSTITUENTS REORGANIZE THEMSELVES

Significant developments were occurring in the American labor movement at this time. Despite the battle over the court-packing plan, the Supreme Court in 1937 upheld the constitutionality of the National Labor Relations Act in five cases. This had important implications for the organizational structure of unions. The American Federation of Labor's 1920 membership of 4 million had declined to 2.5 million by 1932. New mass production industries could no longer be organized along the craft lines of the older unions. In 1934 the AFL leadership approved in principle the organization of industrial unions among radio, automobile, and rubber workers.

Unhappy with the modest support given to industrial, or "vertical," organizing activity, John L. Lewis, president of the United Mine Workers, brought together the leaders of eight AFL unions to form the Committee for Industrial Organization. In 1936 these and two other unions were suspended from the AFL, renamed themselves the Congress of Industrial

Organizations, and proceeded to organize aggressively. Engaging in spectacular sit-down strikes, they won industry-wide automobile and steel contracts the following year. Before long, the CIO turned to party politics, door-bell ringing for Democrats where the party itself had weak organization.

One of the unwritten rules of American politics has been that, in a federal system, national leaders should never intervene in state and local contests between fellow-partisans, certainly not overtly. In practice, this meant "stay out of the party's primaries." During 1938, Roosevelt considered a plan to intervene in certain Democratic primary elections to support liberals against hostile conservatives. Jim Farley opposed the idea as destructive of party unity and an infraction of his own required neutrality as party chairman. Nevertheless, Roosevelt publicly expressed his support of the primary election opponents of Senator Walter George of Georgia, Senator Millard Tydings of Maryland, and Representative John J. O'Connor of New York. George and Tydings won despite the president's opposition; only O'Connor lost. The failure of the "purge" was yet another blow to Roosevelt's prestige.

Elsewhere in the world Stalin, Hitler, and Mussolini had by 1937 established their totalitarian regimes and were planning moves beyond their own borders. Having conquered Manchuria in 1931, the Japanese once again invaded China in 1937. Other nations looked on helplessly. In Europe during 1938 Hitler annexed Austria and the Sudetenland region of Czechoslovakia. The following year Hitler annexed all of Czechoslovakia. At the same time Germany concluded a non-aggression pact with the Soviet Union. Within days, Germany invaded Poland. Great Britain and France declared war against Germany.

World War II started up a new phase of Roosevelt's New Deal leadership. A recession burdened the United States economy in 1938 and required new economic strategies. The question of Roosevelt's ambition for an unprecedented third term became a lively one, with Jim Farley and Cordell Hull mentioned as available successors.

As Germany swept through Denmark, Norway, Belgium, and Holland, Roosevelt called Congress into special session to modify the Neutrality Act of 1936 so that all aid short of war could be extended to Great Britain and France. What Congress passed was a cash-and-carry plan whereby combatants could buy United States goods on a cash basis for delivery on their own ships. Shortly after, Roosevelt proposed, and Congress approved, a lend-lease arrangement for providing essential war supplies to Great Britain. The nation was taking sides in the war, gearing up its defense industries, coming out of its recession, and positioning Roosevelt for his new role as a great war leader.

GLOBAL LEADERSHIP IN A THIRD TERM

Despite the intense opposition of southern and isolationist leaders concerning a third term, Roosevelt kept the country titillated over his intentions. In June 1939, his confidante and secretary of commerce, Harry Hopkins, began to advocate a third term. Vice President Garner and Postmaster General Farley objected and eventually allowed their own names to go before the 1940 convention in order to record a protest. In choosing Secretary of Agriculture Henry Wallace for the vice-presidential spot, Roosevelt dispensed with the principle of ticket-balancing (North-South, liberal-conservative, etc.) and chose an ardent supporter from his own wing of the party. FDR felt that Wallace would help in the farm states and energize his strong support in the CIO. On Election Day, Roosevelt defeated Wendell Willkie by a 5 million-vote margin and later enjoyed referring to the outcome as "close."

The war against the Axis now consumed the attention of Roosevelt and the entire country. By May 1941, the president declared an unlimited national emergency. In August, he and Prime Minister Winston Churchill enunciated the Atlantic Charter in which eight principles were offered as a basis for peace: no territorial aggrandizement by the U.S. or Britain; territorial changes only through self-determination; the right of all peoples to choose their own form of government; free international trade; worldwide cooperation to secure improved labor standards and social security; freedom from fear and want; freedom of the seas; and arms reduction, particularly disarming of aggressor nations. The propriety of these presidential actions was bitterly debated in Congress and countless other forums.

On December 7, 1941, the Japanese attacked Pearl Harbor and thoroughly united the American people. Congress declared war against the Axis. With the Pacific fleet battered, it was impossible to help Douglas MacArthur and his American and Philippine troops at Corregidor. Elsewhere, the United States became "the arsenal of democracy," with supply lines stretching around the Arctic Ocean to the Soviet Union, across the South Atlantic to the British in North Africa, and directly across the North Atlantic to the British Isles.

Roosevelt called on the nation and its allies to conduct "total war" until Fascist and Nazi tyranny had been completely destroyed. Upward of $400 billion was spent for the war effort. The United States produced nearly 300,000 combat planes, over 80,000 tanks, and some 45 million bombs before the end of the war. A secret Manhattan Project, costing over $2 billion, successfully achieved nuclear fission and ushered in the Atomic Era. By 1944, the Allies were able to launch attacks against the German lines in Italy, mount a new offensive in Russia, and land an invasion of France. In the Pacific, MacArthur began his promised return to the Philippines.

Congress gave Roosevelt everything he needed to carry the war to a successful conclusion. Some, however, recalled the greed, inefficiencies, and dishonesties in the handling of public funds in previous wars and pondered the prospect of some future accounting of the Democratic party for its performance in this one. Senator Harry S. Truman of Missouri was particularly concerned. In February 1941, he recommended the creation of a special "watch-dog" committee to flush out waste and corruption without embarrassing Roosevelt's leadership. In the several years of its operation, the Truman Committee was conservatively credited with saving the federal government some $15 billion. FDR and the Congress were universally grateful. When southern leaders refused to go along with Henry Wallace's renomination at the 1944 national convention, Roosevelt, nominated for a fourth term, turned to Truman as a compromise choice for the second spot.

Between 1940 and 1944 Wendell Willkie did his utmost to serve as leader of the loyal opposition. But he was never fully acceptable to Republican conservatives: a former Democrat, too liberal, too internationalist, too eager to bring blacks and sharecroppers into the Republican party. After losing in the Wisconsin primary and lacking encouragement from significant Republican quarters, Willkie withdrew, making way for Governor Thomas E. Dewey of New York, the eventual Republican standard-bearer. Dewey put together an election campaign that posed a real threat to the Roosevelt-Truman ticket. He pitched his appeals, for example, to industrial labor, blacks, and lower-income voters by promising postwar full employment and more generous social security. Even though a more even electoral balance was returning to national politics, Dewey's appeals fell on the ears of solid Democratic constituencies who had quite other images of the Republican party.

Distracted by the requirements of the war and showing physical strain, Roosevelt did not give much attention to the campaign until his famous address to a Teamsters Union convention in which he berated the Republicans for libelous statements not only about himself and his administration, which he fully expected, but also about his dog, Fala. The humor and spirit of this single speech lifted the morale of the party and the campaign out of their doldrums. And Republican Thomas E. Dewey's fortunes started to decline.

The campaign was the first in which the organizing talents of the CIO's Political Action Committee, under Sidney Hillman's ("Clear it with Sidney") leadership, came into full view. Organized labor went all-out for Roosevelt-Truman.

Another component of the New Deal coalition began to receive special attention in the 1944 campaign, namely, the black electorate. Mechanization of southern agriculture and the labor shortage in northern war plants started an internal migration during the war years that placed over a million southern blacks in northern communities. Democratic city organizations, such as Kelley's in Chicago, enlisted the new residents and offered them a role in the nation's politics that they had been denied for generations. Even though the Democratic platform avoided all mention of betterment for blacks, Roosevelt emphasized the need in one of his speeches. These efforts brought out a northern black "swing vote" that later multiplied in importance when black soldiers settled in the North after the war and the civil rights movement began its crusade. National Chairman Robert Hannegan went to great lengths to mobilize state and local party leaders to register not only blacks but also war workers and migratory workers. He also pressed for simplification of absentee ballot laws to enable persons on military duty to vote.

One small incident during the campaign had potentially significant implication for the party system. In conversation with Governor Pinchot, Wendell Willkie, cast aside by Republican conservatives, suggested that the time seemed right for a new line-up of the nation's parties. Willkie was ready to encourage a coalition of liberals drawn from both parties, leaving the conservatives in each party to join together if they wished. Pinchot communicated these observations to Roosevelt, who concurred completely. FDR sent his friend, Judge Sam Rosenman, to a secret meeting with Willkie in New York City on July 5, and plans were made for a Roosevelt-Willkie meeting after election day. By election day Willkie was dead, and five months later so was Roosevelt. The time had not arrived for a liberal-conservative polarization of the two major parties.

THE CIVIL RIGHTS CONSTITUENTS
REORGANIZE THEMSELVES

In the eighty-two days during which he served as vice president, Harry Truman was an unofficial acting president. Roosevelt was away from Washington most of the time, at the Yalta Conference or resting in Warm Springs, where he died on April 15, 1945. To a nation that had come to think of Roosevelt as its permanent leader, the loss was traumatic and his replacement—an average American, by all appearances—not reassuring.

Despite his "down home" style, Truman was a talented politician. Anyone who could be friendly with the Pendergast machine in Missouri and remain independent of it had to be politically talented. As his administration unfolded, it was evident that Truman was qualified to carry the country to the victorious conclusion of a global war, build the foundation of a world organization, and direct the reconversion of the nation from its wartime economy to a free and stable peace economy.

The Germans surrendered, unconditionally, within a month of his tenure. While attending the Potsdam Conference in July to coordinate Pacific strategy and lay the groundwork for peace negotiations, Truman received news of the first successful detonation of an atom bomb. He ordered use of the new weapon against Hiroshima and Nagasaki. On August 14, the Japanese surrendered, unconditionally.

What followed was a boiling period of postwar change in the domestic life of the United States and its reluctant assumption of its new role as the leading and most unscathed power in the world. Without Roosevelt and without war, farmers, workers, businessmen, ethnic groups, and others scrambled to protect their New Deal and wartime gains. Truman bravely enunciated his Fair Deal program in his message of September 6, 1945. It was the beginning of the end of his brief political honeymoon.

Labor, particularly the miners and the railroad brotherhoods, went on strike to end the wage ceilings that had been imposed during the war. Truman countered with a plan to "draft labor" which brought the labor movement down on his head. The strikes ended, and Truman dropped his draft plan. Labor and Truman needed each other for confrontations with less-friendly adversaries. When the Republican Eightieth Congress wrote the punitive Taft-Hartley Act, labor's cries and Truman's veto were to no avail. Truman's support of the Full Employment Act of 1946, making the federal government explicitly responsible for dealing with depressions and unemployment, further endeared him to labor.

To investigate the deepening troubles in the field of civil rights, Truman appointed a Committee on Civil Rights. This move caused political apoplexy among southern leaders. When the committee rendered its controversial report in October 1947, Truman sent a bill to Congress implementing many of its recommendations. Thus began the great Democratic battle over civil rights. Southern governors sent a delegation, headed by J. Strom Thurmond of South Carolina, to Washington to air their complaints. Over fifty southern Democratic members of the House issued a manifesto condemning Truman's civil rights program. Southern leaders discussed openly their plans to deprive Truman of the electoral college votes of their states if he became the party's nominee in 1948.

Traditional wisdom and some scientific data suggest that Republicans tend to be more concerned about and responsive to issues of American foreign policy. However, it is also true that an assertive presidential foreign policy style—strong leadership, bold programs, humanitarian postures, etc.—may exert great influence on the voters in both major parties. In any case, Truman's moves in world affairs brought him stable and strong bipartisan popular support. His appointment of General George C. Marshall as secretary of state was widely applauded. Although the concept was Truman's, he asked Marshall to propose emergency economic and technical assistance to the battered nations of Europe and the needy newly emerging nations of the world, that is, the Marshall Plan.

Aware that the United States was a habitual disarmer after each of its wars, including World War II, Truman convinced the nation to reverse field and rearm itself for its new role as the first nuclear power and the principal protector of the infant United Nations. His Truman Doctrine of aid to Greece and Turkey, both threatened by Communist takeovers, reflected a policy of containment of Communism. Truman also was responsible for the United States' leading role in the creation of the North Atlantic Treaty Organization in 1949.

As spring 1948 approached, the question of Truman's renomination for a full term in his own right began to be debated. Upon the resignation of General Dwight D. Eisenhower as army chief of staff in February to become president of Columbia University, Senator Richard Russell of Georgia, a spokesman for the southern wing of the party, suggested that the hero of World War II be the 1948 Democratic nominee. Concerned about the effect of the Palestine crisis and the civil rights controversy upon Jewish and black constituencies, liberals and organization Democrats joined forces to "dump Truman" in favor of a more appealing candidate. Senator Russell was surprised to find himself with such strange bed-fellows. In his memoirs Truman put the situation succinctly:

> In 1948, I was in a position to control the nomination. When I had made up my mind to run, those in the party who turned against me could do nothing to prevent it. For this reason, Thurmond and Wallace had to bolt the Democratic party and stir up their own following. If Eisenhower had gone after the Democratic nomination, there would have been a four-way split in the party, but otherwise, the situation would have remained unchanged.

Eisenhower waited for a better time: 1952. Thurmond became the Dixiecrat nominee, benefiting from changes in the laws of Virginia, Mississippi, Louisiana, South Carolina, and Alabama that prevented Truman's name and the regular national party symbol from appearing on their ballots. Former Vice President Wallace, Truman's secretary of commerce until 1946, was fired from that position for his strong pro-Soviet statements at a time when containment of the Soviet Union was the administration's policy. The far-left Progressive Citizens of America created a Progressive party to nominate Wallace for president. More moderate New Dealers organized the more enduring Americans for Democratic Action (ADA) to help liberals find their way in the political confusion and to do battle with the Southerners at the Democratic national convention.

NEW TESTS OF PARTY LOYALTY

The national convention faced two fundamental issues that were intimately related and that would shape the future character of the party. The procedural issue was party loyalty. The substantive issue was civil rights. Incorporated in the credentials of the Mississippi delegation was a provision forbidding its delegates to bind the Mississippi Democratic party to the support of any nominee favoring Truman's civil rights program. In the credentials committee, northern liberals, led by ADA, presented a minority report demanding that the Mississippi delegation be denied its seats on grounds that no national party could afford such dubious loyalty. The minority report lost but received 503 recorded votes; 618 constituted a convention majority. The loyalty issue would come up again in 1952, explosively.

Encouraged, the Southerners on the rules committee proposed reinstatement of the two-thirds nominating rule. The immediate object was to deny renomination to Truman. The long-term goal was to return the South to its former glory days as a powerful wing of the party. The convention rejected the proposal on a voice vote. One century of internecine strife caused by the rule was more than the party needed.

The substantive issue was the civil rights plank. The platform committee wrote a relatively moderate plank. Southerners on the committee offered three separate minority reports, each designed to water down the plank. A much stronger plank was presented by Minneapolis Mayor Hubert H. Humphrey and former Representative Andrew J. Biemiller of Wisconsin. Humphrey's dramatic speech and his handling of floor tactics put over this strong plank, 651 1/2 to 582 1/2. It was a watershed achievement for the emerging civil rights movement, Humphrey's career, and a party that had been tongue-tied for more than a century regarding the rights of its black constituents.

Truman's renomination was relatively perfunctory; his election was not. The Dixiecrat and Progressive defections seemed certain to draw off large segments of the Democratic vote at the same time that their departure unburdened the party of its extremist wings. Thomas E. Dewey's well-financed and skilfully run campaign was an improved version of the New York governor's 1944 effort. Public opinion polls, still in their technical infancy, consistently showed Dewey leading by a 49-44 margin. What was not measurable was Truman's handling of his favorite role as an underdog.

The presidential campaign train covered 31,700 miles. Truman delivered 356 prepared and two hundred extemporaneous speeches, most addressed to labor, farmers, blacks, and consumers. The AFL and the CIO, still furious about the Taft-Hartley legislation, fervently supported the president. Truman's civil rights attitudes, no longer in doubt, brought out black voters in pivotal cities. Truman relished "giving hell" to the "do-nothing [Republican] Eightieth Congress" for inaction on farm prices and cost-of-living problems. To the surprise of nearly everyone, Truman received 2 million more votes than Dewey in the 48 million cast. Thurmond and Wallace received slightly more than a million votes each, the former denying Truman only thirty-nine electoral votes. The mandate was close but solid.

Truman was determined to give careful attention to matters of party loyalty and party organization. Shortly after inauguration day, Democratic National Chairman Howard McGrath told reporters that he had proposed to the president a policy of awarding patronage only on the basis of "the appointee's record and an estimate of his future value to the party." He added that a Democrat who did not go along with the party's nominee or platform had no "future value" to the party. Truman himself referred to the platform as "the law of the Democratic party." Asked whether he would consider congressional voting on repeal of the Taft-Hartley law as one of the tests of party loyalty, Truman replied that he certainly would. In his view, an impending political decision becomes a "party matter" if the president wishes it to be so.

Pursuing this line, McGrath did not invite members of the national committee from Mississippi or Louisiana to the national committee meeting to choose his successor, explaining that those state organizations had left the party through their actions in the convention and the campaign. This was challenged in the national committee's credential committee along with a case from South Carolina. All five Dixiecrats were removed from the national committee rolls. That same evening, Truman dined with the national committee members and invited all dissidents to return to the party as "loyal Democrats." But this was not the end of the matter.

World tensions were mounting and affecting the domestic politics of the United States. The Berlin airlift, the establishment of NATO and its heavy burden on the American taxpayer, the retreat of Chiang Kai-shek's army to Formosa, the detonation of the Soviet Union's first atom bomb, the Truman Doctrine, the Marshall Plan, the Point Four program of technical aid, the Judith Coplin and Alger Hiss espionage cases, and, most tragically, the Korean War—all kept the Truman administration in a constant state of crisis and fed the public impression that the Communists were closing in on America.

Party attention focused on these developments with special intensity. Americans "rallied around the flag" during the Berlin airlift, and this may have helped the incumbent president in his reelection bid. NATO was debated as another "entangling alignment" with European powers. The China Lobby charged Truman with having "lost China." The high costs of the Truman Doctrine, the Marshall Plan, and Point Four began the annual cycle of congressional debate over foreign aid. The Coplin and Hiss cases inspired the Communist witch-hunts of Senator Joseph McCarthy, ushering in the McCarthy Era. The United States entry into the Korean War as a "police action" within the framework of the Security Council of the United Nations cost this nation 50,000 lives and tens of billions of dollars. It also cost Truman any prospect of seeking a second full term in 1952.

The issues all showed up at the national convention. Southern Democrats united again behind the regional candidacy of Senator Richard Russell. Senator Estes Kefauver of

Tennessee, whose dramatic investigations into organized crime held the nation rapt, enthralled the liberals, and undermined a number of city political machines, traveled the presidential primary route with precedent-setting success. President Truman had his own candidate: the liberal and articulate governor of Illinois, Adlai E. Stevenson. The decision favored Stevenson on the third ballot.

With ADA again in the lead, northern liberals designed a loyalty pledge for delegates, committing them to do their utmost to have the party's ticket and symbol on the ballot in their respective states. Along with a loyalty pledge, the convention adopted a strong civil rights plank.

The 1952 election witnessed several significant changes in the party's electorate. The Eisenhower candidacy, together with the loyalty pledge and civil rights plank on the Democratic side, offered southern conservatives, nearly all of whom were white, an opportunity once again, as in 1928, to break their Democratic "habit." Presidential Republicans, that is, Southerners who voted Republican at the top of the ticket but Democratic locally, became a persisting feature of the region's politics. The civil rights movement was still a dozen years away from registering enough southern blacks to make a political difference.

THE LOYAL OPPOSITION: LEADERSHIP WITHOUT CONSTITUENCIES

Thirty-two years after their first vote in a presidential election, women finally turned out in equal numbers with men and favored Eisenhower by a substantial margin, at least 5 percentage points more so than men. Blacks were 15 percentage points more Democratic than they had been in 1948 but not yet as fully committed as they became in 1964 and thereafter. Union members began to slip away from the Democratic fold, by more than 10 percentage points. Farmers, who voted 2-to-1 for Truman, went Republican in that same ratio. At the professional and business end of the occupational scale, however, Stevenson was able to attract an impressive number. The very young and the very old were carried off by Eisenhower. The Democratic hold on Catholics and Jews also weakened.

The tradition of war-hero nominees worked for the Republicans. After all, Eisenhower was credited with bringing World War II to a successful conclusion, and now there was the Korean War that the Democrats did not seem to know how to conclude. Furthermore, the American people were quite exhausted from all the activism of the Roosevelt-Truman era. Time for some calm.

Good Democrat that he was, Adlai Stevenson did not remain calm. He began to assume the role of titular leader and leader of the loyal opposition.

> In our country this role is a very ambiguous one. . . . The titular head has no clear and defined authority within his party. He has no party office, no staff, no funds, nor is there any system of consultation whereby he may be advised of party policy and through which he may help to shape that policy . . . Yet he is generally deemed the leading spokesman of his party.

As we shall soon see, Stevenson and National Committee Chairman Paul M. Butler did their best to overcome these out-party difficulties. By 1954, however, when Democrats regained control of both houses of Congress, they ran into personal as well as institutional obstacles that were all but insurmountable. Sam Rayburn of Texas became speaker and his protégé, Lyndon B. Johnson, also of Texas, became majority leader of the Senate. Rarely has the Congress been led by two such talented politicians working as a team. The Rayburn-Johnson legislative strategy was known as "responsibility in opposition." They carefully showed public respect for the hero-president and just as carefully took policy initiatives that would build a Democrat record that contrasted with the Eisenhower administration's "politics of postponement." There simply was no solid institutional base from which Stevenson could demand the attention and cooperation of these two fellow-partisans. Besides, Johnson's name was frequently mentioned for the 1956 presidential nomination.

In July 1955, Johnson suffered a heart attack. Shortly after visiting the Johnson ranch to wish the patient well, Stevenson announced his own candidacy. As he did so, President Eisenhower suffered a heart attack. Suddenly a half dozen Democratic star players—Estes Kefauver, Averell Harriman, G. Mennen Williams, Hubert H. Humphrey, and others— became candidates for president. Stevenson had a fight on his hands, at least until Eisenhower's subsequent recovery and renomination, whereupon the nomination was Stevenson's almost by default.

In a novel move at the national convention, Stevenson threw open the selection of a vice-presidential running mate. The front-runners were Kefauver, Humphrey, Albert Gore, and John F. Kennedy. The balloting was exciting and filled with surprises, not the least of which was the extent of southern support for a Catholic, Kennedy. Johnson was widely credited for this development. In the end, the convention chose Kefauver.

After his second defeat at the hands of Eisenhower, Stevenson joined National Chairman Butler in an effort to put together an Advisory Council of about twenty leading Democrats, both in and out of office at national, state, and local levels, to "advance efforts in behalf of Democratic programs and principles." Once again, Rayburn and Johnson declined participation. As a consequence, the Advisory Council became a voice of liberal Democrats from the Northeast, the upper Midwest, and the Far West. Senators Humphrey and Paul Douglas, the latter from Illinois, took the lead. In the interest of civil rights legislation, the council supported a full-scale assault on the filibuster rule in the Senate. A number of task force committees prepared statements in several policy fields, and some twenty-three statements were eventually issued by the Advisory Council.

An economic recession in 1958 brought oversized Democratic majorities into both houses of Congress. The Senate became a hotbed of Democratic presidential aspirants: Johnson, Humphrey, Kennedy, Stuart Symington of Missouri, and others. The outsider was Stevenson. As majority leader, Johnson was able to give each an opportunity to "show off" to his particular constituencies, LBJ always joining each on stage for the applause. Humphrey, with civil rights groups and legislation in mind, made the case against the filibuster rule. The rule remained, but, with Johnson's help, a compromise produced the first civil rights legislation in eighty-five years. Kennedy, on behalf of labor, initiated a minimum wage bill and another designed to eliminate union racketeering. Symington presented the Democratic critique of the defense policies of the military expert in the White House.

In 1957 the American people were startled by Sputniks I and II, the first man-made satellites placed in orbit around the earth by those "backward peasant people" in the Soviet Union. Reversing the Eisenhower program of economy in defense spending, the Democratic Congress initiated educational and research-and-development appropriations that ultimately carried the United States from the Atomic Era into the Space Age.

Although Stevenson consistently ran neck-and-neck with Kennedy in the opinion polls, he refused to become an active candidate for 1960. In contrast, Kennedy campaigned from primary to primary, demonstrating to all, particularly such big-city leaders as Richard Daley of Chicago, that his Catholic religion was no obstacle to victory. By convention time, the contest was reduced to Kennedy versus Johnson. This pair became the party's ticket against Vice President Richard M. Nixon.

New technologies were importantly exploited by both sides during the campaign. Jet airplanes enabled the nominees to criss-cross the nation within hours. Television permitted the novelty of four debates between Kennedy and Nixon. Robert Kennedy, his brother's campaign manager, employed newly developed mathematical models of the electorate in order to select issues on which to campaign and to determine how to handle the question of Kennedy's religion. In a special session of Congress prior to the election (arranged, of course, by the Rayburn-Johnson team), Kennedy could be observed leading the fight for legislation on minimum wage, care for the aged, public housing, and similar measures. Locked into a passive role as presiding officer of the Senate, Vice President Nixon could do little more than watch the action.

NEW FRONTIER, GREAT SOCIETY, AND CHANGING DEMOGRAPHY

Kennedy won the election by 100,000 votes in the more than 68 million cast. The critical returns came from Illinois, or, more specifically, Chicago, where the Daley machine apparently performed miracles of election administration. Nixon received a larger vote than Eisenhower had in six southern states, confirming the growing size of presidential Republicans in that region. However, the results were close in nearly all of the fifty states, indicating that the United States once again had a closely competitive two-party system.

In one respect or another, John F. Kennedy's New Frontier and Lyndon B. Johnson's Great Society were reincarnations of the New Deal coalition of organized labor, blacks, nationality minorities, Catholics, Jews, intellectuals, and, to a much lesser degree, poor farmers. In changing proportions, these continued to be the electoral pillars upon which Kennedy and Johnson rested their domestic policies and bids for office.

Organized labor in the 1960s reached a plateau in membership growth, with many members earning enough to be considered middle class. This trend was accompanied by ethnic tensions arising from the influx of blacks into the industrially employed labor force. Blacks were increasingly politically self-aware, voting en bloc in the North and courageous enough to register and vote against racist politicians in the South. Among the nationality constituencies, the Irish drift away from the party was temporarily halted by the presence of the Kennedys. Italians, Poles, and Hispanics remained overwhelmingly Democratic. Jews also continued to be loyal to the party of Smith, Roosevelt, and Truman, although increasingly uneasy about the Democratic succession of a Catholic, a Texan, and a born-again Christian in the White House. The decline in the support of poor farmers was easy to explain with trend charts; agribusinesses were rapidly displacing small farmers in the nation's economy.

There were important changes in national demography. Blacks were moving to the cities in growing numbers, becoming the new urban majority. Industries and retirees were moving to the South, changing the economic and political environment there. Senior citizens, that is, the over sixty-five population, were becoming more numerous, and disproportionately active in politics. Youth, particularly in the cities and the universities, were experimenting with lifestyles and demanding the vote for eighteen-year-olds. Themselves young and assertive, the Kennedy brothers—Jack, Robert, Edward (Ted)—and their families, comfortably led the nation's march toward the New Frontier.

The Kennedy legislative program initially consisted of some three hundred items, of which sixteen received special attention. Among these: the Peace Corps, designed to give American youth an opportunity to help the people of less-fortunate countries; the Alliance for Progress, aimed at raising Latin American living standards and cementing friendship with them; unemployment compensation and minimum-wage legislation for labor; intensified implementation of civil rights legislation, particularly with respect to voting rights; creation of a fair employment practices commission; legislation on school and housing desegregation; more aid to education; hospital insurance for the aged; tax cuts for lower income groups. There was something for most Democratic constituencies.

In the international field, there was a succession of crises that tested the mettle of the young president. The civil war in Vietnam was intensifying, and American arms-length support of the Diem regime began to turn into wholesale involvement. The Bay of Pigs attempt to overthrow the Castro regime in Cuba was a military catastrophe and a political embarrassment. Soviet emplacement of nuclear missiles in Cuba, when discovered, led to a nuclear face-down between the superpowers and an American naval "quarantine" of Cuban waters.

The pace of racial integration—at the ballot box, in the public schools and the universities, on public transportation, in residential housing, in employment—stirred racial tensions that reached crisis proportions during the summer of 1963. Governor George C. Wallace of Alabama took his stand against integration at the doorway of the University of Alabama and promptly became presidential timber. Police used dogs and firehoses to disperse black demonstrators in Birmingham. It was a time of black rioting, bombings, and federal troop movements.

Despite the turmoil, polls showed Kennedy's popularity reaching new heights, with biggest gains among blacks and young males, steady support from Jews, Poles, and unskilled workers, but increasing vulnerability among Italians and Irish. He was mainly faulted for his handling of farm problems and for the increase in federal spending.

RIOTS, ASSASSINATIONS, AND VIETNAM

In early preparation for 1964, Kennedy began to tour states and communities where Democratic factional divisions needed mending. During one such trip to Dallas, on November 22, 1963, Kennedy was assassinated. The trauma was projected to millions by television, from the funeral to the bizarre murder of the suspected assassin directly in front of the TV cameras.

As president, Johnson not only endorsed the Kennedy

legislative program, he also used his masterful skills as a congressional broker to move much of that program and his own important additions to it on toward passage. Taxes were cut. An elaborate antipoverty program was inaugurated. A 1964 Civil Rights Bill, floor-managed by Majority Whip Hubert Humphrey, was passed at the end of a seventy-five day filibuster.

When elected to his own presidential term, Johnson carried forward his own massive Great Society program despite continuing large-scale domestic civil strife. Medicare, a program for health insurance for the elderly that was first proposed by Truman, was finally passed. A landmark Elementary and Secondary Education Act sent funds into school programs for low-income neighborhoods and other much-needed educational projects. Programs of job training for the unskilled, economic aid for Appalachia and other depressed areas, low-cost housing for minorities, and higher social security benefits were other features of the Great Society program.

Black political participation, other than ghetto demonstrations and riots, continued to increase. The 1965 Voting Rights Act suspended literacy tests in low-turnout districts and authorized the attorney general to appoint registration examiners. Reverend Martin Luther King, Jr., led a civil rights march from Selma to Montgomery, Alabama, protected by federal troops. In 1967 Thurgood Marshall was the first black appointed to the Supreme Court bench. Carl B. Stokes of Cleveland and Richard G. Hatcher of Gary, both Democrats, were the first blacks to be elected mayors of major cities. On the less-peaceful side were the Watts riots of August 1965, killing thirty-five and causing some $200 million in property damage. Again, during summer 1967, rioting broke out in Newark, Detroit, and other cities in which dozens died and thousands were left homeless.

Returning to the politics of the 1964 Democratic national convention, Johnson's nomination was a foregone conclusion. Leading candidates for the vice-presidential slot were Hubert Humphrey and Attorney General Robert F. Kennedy. Strain between the Kennedys and Johnson was a poorly kept secret among Washingtonians, and this was confirmed when the president issued a statement that members of his cabinet would not be among those considered for the ticket. Kennedy resigned, moved to New York, and was soon after elected United States senator from that state.

Seating contests in the Mississippi, Alabama, and Georgia delegations raised difficult questions of party status (who is a bona fide Democrat?) and party loyalty. Johnson called upon Humphrey to mediate the disputes, which he did with much success. Humphrey also received the vice-presidential nomination to the applause of labor, blacks, and several ethnic and religious minorities.

Factions in the Republican convention were less conciliatory. Goldwater's strongly ideological followers offended the Rockefeller moderates, who apparently stayed home on election day. The Johnson-Humphrey landslide was accompanied by large Democratic majorities in both houses of Congress. With such support, Johnson was able to duplicate the flurry of law-making that marked the first hundred days of the New Deal.

Foreign policy and party management, however, were the fatal Johnson weaknesses. The conflict in Vietnam began on the periphery of the Korean War. Presidents Truman and Eisenhower had sent financial aid to bolster the French and subsequently Ngo Dinh Diem against the Communists led by Ho Chi Minh. Kennedy sent advisers and helicopter pilots. And soon military escalation took over.

By 1966 there were 380,000 United States troops in Vietnam and more on the way. American casualties began to reach into many homes and military budgets were becoming awesome. American leaders—Senators George McGovern, Eugene McCarthy, and, later, Robert Kennedy, for example—and public opinion began to see unnecessary and costly entrapment in someone else's civil war. The American Left and Democratic liberals began to mix civil rights and antiwar demonstrations, as exemplified by the changing themes of Martin Luther King. Using a carrot-and-stick approach, Johnson tried to use air strikes against North Vietnam as a means of bringing the adversaries to the negotiating table. As frustration and casualties went up, Johnson's political fortunes went down.

Another Johnson anomaly was his attitude toward the Democratic party. Accustomed to the *intra*party politics of a one-party state, Texas, and devoted to "consensus politics" in his congressional experience, Johnson had come to rely more on personal brokerage among group leaders than party mobilization of the electorate. He was the consummate behind-the-scenes manager, hence the secretive and somewhat elitist style that frequently alienated the press and the public. To the consternation of many, including George Meany, president of the AFL-CIO, Johnson dropped the Kennedy voter registration drive and decimated the staff of the party's national headquarters. Hubert Humphrey later (1969–1972) tried to put the pieces back together again, without much success. George McGovern (1972–1976) was not interested. Jimmy Carter (1976–1980), like Johnson, from a one-party state, dealt with the party as just another petitioning interest group. It was a bad period for party organization.

SIX

Dwindling Constituencies, Diminishing Party, 1968 and After

The presidency eluded the Democratic party for most of the years following Johnson's departure. The political activists who cut their eye teeth in the civil rights and anti-Vietnam movements and the political newcomers from the feminist, New Left, and related movements were determined to make

133

their place in the party. Older party regulars, labor leaders, and minority spokespersons were not willing to give up their places. The weapons of battle were often reform of the party's rules of representation and decision-making. The clashes were severe. Elections were lost. Constituencies began to shrink in absolute size and degrees of party support. Although positive organizational changes were occurring locally, the national party often seemed to be in the grip of a centrifugal force.

RULES THAT REMOVE THE REGULARS

In 1967 and 1968, the country was shaken by summer riots in about 125 cities, a Tet offensive against Saigon, mounting American casualties in the war, and the assassination of Martin Luther King on April 4, 1968. In the Democratic party, the New Deal-Fair Deal coalition was unraveling visibly. Governor George Wallace was preparing to lead a "backlash" of southern and blue-collar Democrats who were unhappy with the racial changes and tensions in the South and the cities. Senator Eugene McCarthy of Minnesota, Vice President Humphrey's home state, announced his intention to run as an antiwar spokesman against a Johnson renomination. Senator Robert Kennedy, reluctant to challenge an incumbent president but losing his own supporters to McCarthy, finally announced his candidacy on March 17. Two weeks later, ad libbing at the conclusion of a statement calling a halt to the bombing of North Vietnam, Johnson withdrew his name from the race.

As the California presidential primary approached, Humphrey had won 1,279 dependable delegate votes, Kennedy 713, and McCarthy 280. Kennedy took California, but, as he announced his victory, an assassin took his life. Despair consumed the Democratic party and its nominating process. Kennedy delegates tried to draft Ted Kennedy, who declined. They then turned to George McGovern as the antiwar candidate.

Between 10,000-15,000 antiwar demonstrators clashed with Chicago police outside the convention hall, live on TV, and thoroughly scarred the Humphrey nomination inside. The delegates, too, were in an angry mood about the state of the nation and the archaic rules of the party. Two reform commissions were created: one to change the rules on delegate selection, chaired by Senator McGovern; the other to change the rules on the conduct of the convention, chaired by Representative James G. O'Hara of Michigan.

The campaign was arduous, largely because formerly cohesive constituencies were factionalizing in ways that were nearly impossible to mend. George Wallace's nomination by the new American Independent party attracted southern whites, small businessmen, blue-collar workers, more recent immigrants, and anyone who wished to join the white "backlash." The labor movement was split in other ways: older leaders who were centrist were up against younger leaders with an affinity for the New Left. The ethnic minorities and the civil rights movement were split, the latter between older leaders and the new black nationalists who were giving civil rights a religious or revolutionary twist. Ethnicity was "in" and the Italians, the Irish, the Poles, and others were systematically looking for attention. Liberals were split on the war issue.

New national committee and campaign organizations had to be put together, for which Humphrey enlisted a Kennedy stalwart, Lawrence O'Brien. Humphrey, unsuccessfully, tried to disengage himself from Johnson's handling of the Vietnam War; the antiwar groups would not be appeased. In September the polls showed Humphrey 15 percentage points behind Nixon. On election day, however, he trailed Nixon by only four-tenths of a point—one half million votes out of 72 million; some 13.5 percent of the voters had been drawn off by Wallace.

Humphrey went home to teach in Minnesota, where he campaigned for a return to the Senate. Johnson retired to his ranch. The 1970 midterm election found Lawrence O'Brien back in the national committee trying to pay off its large debt and to mediate the disagreements among the Humphrey, Kennedy, McCarthy, and southern factions.

The congressional election returns were positive but not encouraging: two seats lost in the Senate, but still holding a majority; nine additional seats won in the House. One large change, edging along for some time, was the liberalization of the House. Over the previous two decades the number of liberal nonsouthern Democrats had been increasing, many of them replacing conservative Republicans. Concomitantly, conservative southern Democrats were being replaced by liberal or moderate Republicans; twenty-seven southern seats were held by Republicans in 1970 where there had been only two in 1946.

Democratic factions found something new to fight over when the McGovern Commission made its report on the national convention delegate selection process. Hoping to give better representation to the party's new constituencies, the commission recommended that state parties take "affirmative" steps to encourage "minority" participation and to provide "reasonable representation" for them on the delegations. More specifically, "minority" meant blacks, women, youth, and Hispanics. "Reasonable" meant proportional to the group's presence in the state's population.

Blacks were voting in great numbers. The women's movement was in full swing. Youth (eighteen-year-olds and older) had just been given the vote in the Twenty-Sixth Amendment, adding 11 million to the category of potential first voters. The Hispanic electorate was increasing in several ways: by births, immigration, and internal migration from Spanish-speaking territories such as Puerto Rico. Older interests in the party, minority or otherwise, called the rule a "quota system." The criteria of representation would be debated for some time.

In January 1971, long before any of the others, Senator McGovern announced his candidacy for president, hoping to combine these new constituencies with his antiwar supporters into a winning coalition. He expressed his intention to enter as many primaries as possible, and he began raising funds through a massive mail solicitation. Humphrey and Edmund Muskie announced in due course and were the front-runners. Ted Kennedy's name persisted among the top three, although a personal tragedy took him out of the race.

McGovern won primary after primary, including California's entire block of 271 votes. The new delegate-selection procedures led to an overwhelming number of seating contests before the convention's credentials committee: twenty-three cases from fifteen states. The critical contest concerned California, which the convention majority settled in McGovern's favor. The McGovernites were able to unseat a great many party regulars, particularly labor and big-city machine delegations. The Reverend Jesse Jackson, a colleague of the late Martin Luther King, unseated the delegation led by Chicago Mayor Richard Daley.

After McGovern won the nomination, George Meany and the AFL-CIO withheld their usual endorsement and the Daley organization in Chicago attended almost exclusively to local races. Only 44 percent of the young (18-to-25-year-olds), always a low-turnout constituency, voted, splitting 50-48 for McGovern and Nixon, respectively. McGovern carried only Massachusetts and the District of Columbia. The Nixon-Agnew landslide was exceeded only by those of Franklin D. Roosevelt in 1932 and Lyndon Johnson in 1964. It was a disinterested electorate, only 54.7 percent of whom troubled to vote.

THE MIDTERM CONVENTION AND THE PARTY PROS

An unusual thing happened during the campaign. On June 17, 1972, seven burglars broke into the offices of the Democratic National Committee at the Watergate building, and were caught, arrested, tried, and convicted. President Nixon responded to allegations of a connection between the burglary and the Republican campaign by denying any White

House involvement. Somewhat later, two *Washington Post* reporters, in a stunning bit of investigative reporting, began to publish stories linking the Watergate incident to the White House. On February 7, 1973, the Senate set up a Select Committee to Investigate the 1972 Campaign, under the chairmanship of Sam Ervin of North Carolina. The televised hearings held the country spellbound, particularly as witnesses began to confess to illegal deeds. During the hearings, it was also learned that records had been destroyed and tapes of telephone conversations were being withheld by the president.

The Watergate investigation was not all. On August 2, 1973, the United States attorney of Baltimore notified Vice President Spiro Agnew that he was being investigated for extortion, bribery, and income tax violations. On October 10, Agnew resigned from office and pleaded no contest to the felony of income tax evasion. Two days later the popular Republican minority leader of the House, Gerald R. Ford, was appointed vice president by Nixon, the first under the provisions of the Twenty-Fifth Amendment.

Meanwhile, the House Judiciary Committee was actively considering impeachment proceedings against the president himself. On July 30, 1974, the committee voted to recommend three articles of impeachment. On August 9, Nixon resigned, the first president to do so, and was succeeded by Gerald Ford, the first president not chosen in any way by the electoral college. On September 9, Ford named Nelson Rockefeller as vice president.

Democrats could have rejoiced over the Republican woes if they had had their own affairs in order and if the world had been in less turmoil. In the first place, the Agnew and Nixon resignations sent citizen trust-in-government attitudes to a dangerous low in public opinion polls, threatening the stability of American civic life. Leaders of all persuasions saw little profit in such disenchantment. As for Democrats, their work was cut out for them: repair the damage of 1972 and unite for 1976. In the world at large, Communist military activity in Vietnam, Cambodia, and Laos was escalating, war broke out between Israel and the Arabs in the Middle East, and the Arab-dominated Organization of Petroleum Exporting Countries (OPEC) levied an oil embargo that caused a national fuel crisis in the United States.

The 1972 Democratic convention had issued a call for a midterm convention of the party, and the first of these was held in Kansas City on December 6–8, 1974. The gathering drafted a party charter, using most of the recommendations of the McGovern (now McGovern-Fraser) and O'Hara commissions. Most of the delegates were on their best behavior, greeting each other warmly and stretching to agree about most issues.

Such harmony can be stressful for Democrats, and the usual noisy debates did occur, boiling down to a choice between representative democracy (for those constituencies already supportive of the party) and participatory democracy (for those minorities yet to be drawn into the party). National Chairmen Robert Strauss negotiated several compromises on the rules. The convention's public policy statements put the party on record for price controls to cope with inflation, a jobs program for rising unemployment, and a mandatory energy conservation and development program to help deal with oil embargoes and sharp increases in fuel costs.

Candidate-talk abounded. Governor George Wallace, still paralyzed from an assassination attempt, was back at his desk and ready for another presidential campaign. Hubert Humphrey, a two-time loser, was silent about his plans. His protégé, Senator Walter F. Mondale of Minnesota, announced his candidacy but withdrew before the midterm convention. Representative Morris K. Udall, a bona fide liberal of long standing, made an early entry. A few days after the midterm convention, the governor of Georgia, Jimmy Carter, opened his campaign by announcing that he would enter all state primaries and seek delegates in nonprimary states. As 1975 progressed, a host of others joined the fray.

It looked like a Democratic season. North Vietnamese

armies were overrunning South Vietnam, and a Democratic Congress refused President Ford's request for more emergency aid for that enterprise. All Americans and over 100,000 Vietnamese were evacuated. Communist forces were sweeping to victory in Cambodia and Laos. United States unemployment reached 9.2 percent. United States cities were facing a critical shortage of cash and an inability to repay short-term debts. President Ford made this a partisan issue by refusing federal aid to New York City's Democratic administration. California's Governor Ronald Reagan prepared to contest the Republican nomination against President Ford.

Many of the Democratic candidates were burdened by political liabilities of one sort or another: previous defeats; previous errors of political judgment; limited support, etc. In so dispersed a field and against so many wounded warriors, the little-known but appealing governor of Georgia made remarkable headway along the primary election road. Carter was particularly strong in the South and among blacks, who viewed him as a neighbor rather than as a liberal advocate. In choosing Hubert Humphrey's colleague, Walter F. Mondale, for second place on the ticket, Carter acquired an experienced Washington hand and assured himself of the support of the loyal Humphrey following—labor, blacks, nationality minorities, and small farmers.

A NEW SPIRIT OR THE GHOST OF THE NEW DEAL?

The Carter vote, in many respects, seemed to be a shadow of the old New Deal coalition. In other ways, it was a revival. Organized labor was able to deliver 59 percent of the blue-collar workers and 62 percent of all union members to Carter. Seventy percent of registered blacks went to the polls, a turnout 12 percent higher than in 1972; 94 percent cast their ballot for Carter. What Al Smith did to bring the newly registered immigrants into the electoral process Carter apparently did for recently registered southern black citizens. Eugene McCarthy's third-party candidacy cost Carter four states with twenty-six electoral votes. In postelection polls, an unusual number of Democratic voters cited Mondale's presence on the ticket as a major factor in giving their support.

President Carter urged a New Spirit upon the nation— a return to spirituality, reconciliation, and traditional values. Neither the title nor the message took hold. It was a time of transition in the world, the nation, and the Democratic party, and rough waters lay ahead for this former naval officer.

Is it the whim of a numerologist, the figment of a mystic's mind, or a historical coincidence that 1776, 1876, and 1976 appear to be years of fundamental redirection in the politics of the American community? The case is easily made for 1776, the year of the Declaration of Independence, and 1876, the year of the Hayes-Tilden crisis and the beginning of an end to the bitter Reconstruction era. But what of 1976?

The Bicentennial Year of American independence did indeed have all the earmarks of a fundamental national redirection. For the first time in over two generations the United States was not engaged in a hot or cold war, was not suffering a depression or a recession, and was not tearing itself apart with ghetto riots at the base or Watergates at the pinnacle. In 1976 the nation elected a president from the Old South, the first since the days of the Virginia dynasty. Social change and political crosscurrents pressed upon the president, the world, and the nation and were evidence of a transition in progress.

Absent from the push-and-pull of the opening year of the nation's third century was the civic cohesiveness generated by some overriding crisis of war or economic depression or the unifying magnetism of a charismatic leader. President Carter personified the times and, often bravely, articulated its dilemmas. Carter was himself a bundle of anomalies, a Wilsonian moralist who was at the same time a seasoned political tactician and propagandist. His approach to the Democratic party was similarly anomalous.

As a Georgia Democrat, Carter had little concern for party organization, having spent most of his political life campaigning in the primaries against other Democrats. In one-party Georgia, it was the primary election that counted. Thus, Gerald Ford was Carter's first serious Republican opponent and the 1976 presidential campaign was the first in which Carter had to rely upon the organized support of his party. Once elected, Carter again needed his party's support in Congress, where Democrats held an oversized majority in both houses. Carter found congressional Democrats divided, dispersed, and unresponsive, yet his own management of party affairs was routine and minimal. Both the president and the electorate (more than a third of whom called themselves Independents rather than Democrats or Republicans) seemed to agree that political parties were an archaic distraction from the business of politics. As a consequence, the Democratic party was perceived as just another claimant for presidential resources rather than a vital instrument of consensus-building and political action.

The latter impression was reinforced during the party's second midterm conference, conducted in Memphis on December 9–11, 1978. As though the administration were something apart from the party, the president brought with him most of his cabinet and nearly 200 members of the White House staff to listen to feedback from the delegates and to defend his policies. The distance between administration Democrats and party Democrats caused some uneasiness among the delegates. In contrast, Senator Edward M. Kennedy's fervent appeal for support of the party's social programs evoked a warm emotional response more familiar at such gatherings of the faithful.

CONSTITUENCY TENDENCIES, 1948–1976

The prolific political research of the previous quarter century, that is, the period from Truman to Carter, permits well-quantified descriptions of the group characteristics of the

Democratic party-in-the-electorate during most of this time. The tendencies may be summarized as follows:

— Men and women tended to have comparable party and candidate preferences. Women, however, liked Harry Truman and Hubert Humphrey particularly well in 1948 and 1968, respectively. (Could it have been Truman's respect for "the Boss," that is, Bess, and Humphrey's for Muriel?) Conversely, women were cool toward Stevenson in 1952 and 1956. (Could it have been Stevenson's recent divorce?)

— After 1948, nonwhites, particularly blacks, were increasingly supportive of the Democratic nominees. This reached a 94 percent peak in 1964, but declined slowly thereafter. But the significant trend among blacks was their growing numbers, increasing turnout, and therefore their rising numerical contribution to the Democratic coalition. A similar up-and-down tendency was observed among Spanish-speaking groups.

— The less formal the education the voter had, more likely that he or she would vote Democratic. This correlated with the tendency of the poor, blacks, and manual laborers to be Democrats.

— Only about one-in-three voters in the professions and business were Democrats, but these groups were attracted in unusual numbers to Kennedy, Johnson, and Carter.

— Labor has always voted more Democratic than the national average, but the relative size of this group in the total electorate was declining gradually, as was its contribution to the Democratic coalition. White-collar workers were tending to refer to themselves as Weak Democrats and were fluctuating widely in their support of the party. Although more strongly Democratic, blue-collar workers also swung between the parties, blue-collar voters were particularly supportive of Eisenhower in 1956, Wallace in 1968, and Nixon in 1972. Union membership made a difference in favor of the Democratic party, ranging from 80 percent for Johnson in 1964 to 62 percent for Carter in 1976, but only 46 percent for McGovern in 1972 when the AFL–CIO declined to make its usual endorsement.

— Farmers have been one of the most fickle of Democratic constituencies, supporting the party only when in trouble, as in 1932–1936 and 1948. They are also one of the most endangered species among constituencies, rapidly decreasing in numbers. Corporate agribusiness has displaced the moderate-sized and small farm.

— Catholics and Jews were overwhelmingly Democratic in the past, but this attachment has been weakening in recent years, mainly as a consequence of growing affluence. Jews have also tended to give great attention to candidates' positions regarding Israel's fortunes in the Middle East and have been uneasy about expressions of strong Christian faith by some political leaders.

— The youngest and the oldest voters have been among the least reliable Democrats. While many of the young tend to be liberal and many of the old tend to remain New Dealers, these inclinations are often weaker than some more immediate concern such as campus protest or social security problems. The young and the old have also been highly likely to stay home on election day.

— Low-income families and individuals have tended to be Democrats. In recent years, this group's numerical contribution to the Democratic coalition has decreased sharply due almost entirely to the dwindling size of the group. The poor are also the most likely non-voters.

— The great party loyalty of the Irish, Italians, and Hispanic groups has been melting away.

— The once Solid South has become more competitive. About one-fourth of all Democratic votes have come from the South, in part because of the increase in voting participation by southern blacks. This contribution was particularly large in Johnson's case in 1964 and Carter's in 1976, both Southerners.

In the late 1970s Democratic constituencies continued to have their old labels—labor, blacks, nationality minorities, etc.—but each constituency was taking on a different personality. Industrial and white-collar employees of an increasing number of companies were voting "no union" in collective bargaining elections. The proportion of unionized workers in the labor force was decreasing. Blue-collar workers, with homes, cars, and recreational possessions, were voting with the affluent rather than their union leaders. More prosperous blacks were making their way into the Republican party while the poorest blacks were locked into a cycle of unemployment, poor education, welfare, drugs, and political inaction. Nationality minorities—Irish, Italians, Poles, Hispanics, Jews—were, to one degree or another, following their filled pocketbooks out of the party of the Underprivileged. Southerners were as likely to be Republicans as Democrats. A Democratic politician found it hard to know whom to represent.

The demands of some constituencies were not hard to identify, even if impossible to satisfy. Consumers were upset about inflation. Taxpayers were tired of the complexity and inequities built into the tax system. Environmentalists had had it with pollution, waste of natural resources, and extravagance in the use of energy. Good-health devotees went after more and cheaper medical care and recreational facilities. Retirees were becoming interested in activity as well as security. Among the employed, a "leisure ethic" was challenging the ancestral work ethic, resulting in a preference for part-time work or "elective unemployment." Educational policies were not only directed at the young but were taking into account persons inclined to be life-long students. Consumers, taxpayers, environmentalists, good-health devotees, retirees, part-time workers, life-long students—these were functional roles, not constituencies in the traditional sense. The same individual could incorporate several of these roles and belong to organizations propounding conflicting policies. The definition of "constituency" seemed ripe for reexamination and revision.

CONFUSING AND DILUTING THE NEW DEAL COALITION

A man given to philosophy and religion, President Carter wanted to discuss some of their implications and dilemmas with his citizenry. His efforts, particularly an address dealing with the "national malaise," were tragically misinterpreted and politically suicidal. A biblical reference to "lust in his heart" became a macho joke. His self-description as a born-again Christian was viewed as an intrusion of religion into public office. His shock over the Soviet invasion of Afghanistan sounded like the confession of a naive politician rather than as a declaration of renewed distrust of a foreign adversary.

Carter had equally poor luck in the management of foreign affairs. In a dramatic and masterful exercise of diplomacy, he brought President Anwar Sadat of Egypt and Prime Minister Menachem Begin of Israel into negotiations at Camp David. The Camp David Agreements laid the groundwork for a long-term peace process in the Middle East that had evaded previous presidents. Yet, on election day in 1980, as many as 10 percent of the Jewish voters, for whom peace in the Middle East is a salient issue, abandoned him for third-party candidate John Anderson or Ronald Reagan.

In a sensitive exercise of caution and behind-the-scenes negotiation, Carter spent most of one year working to free sixty-three United States diplomats and other citizens held hostage in the American embassy in Teheran by militant student followers of Ayatollah Khomeini. The eve of the 1980 presidential election was also the eve of their release, but a disenchanted electorate preferred to punish rather than reward the achievement.

In an attempt to make its invasion of Afghanistan costly to the Soviet Union, Carter ordered an embargo of grain and high technology and a withdrawal of United States participation in the Olympic games scheduled to take place in Moscow. Grain farmers and sports enthusiasts did not like this at all.

Some of Carter's troubles in the foreign policy field were not accidental. They began with the infusion of a generation of ideological conservatives into the Republican party during the Goldwater years in the mid-1960s. A dedicated speaker for Goldwater on the campaign circuit, former actor Ronald Reagan became one of the stars of this faction.

Elected governor of California in 1966 and reelected in 1970, Reagan let it be known that he would be a candidate for president at the end of his term in 1974. The conservatives fully endorsed him, but plans had to be modified somewhat in the unexpected circumstance that incumbent President Ford might also be a candidate. Ford edged out Reagan for the 1976 nomination, but his defeat in the election gave Reagan four more years in which to campaign. It also gave his conservative colleagues in Congress and in a large network of conservative groups time to harass the Carter administration.

The harassment took place most visibly in connection with foreign policy events. Carter's nomination of Ted Sorenson, a Kennedy liberal, as director of the Arms Control and Disarmament Agency had to be withdrawn under conservative pressure. A long-negotiated treaty with Panama, returning the Canal Zone to that country's jurisdiction, was vociferously opposed and barely accepted by the Senate. After Carter signed a SALT II agreement with the Soviet Union, its approval by the Senate was so problematical that he withdrew it from consideration. The conservatives never let up on their criticism of Carter's handling of the Iranian hostage crisis.

The Carter-Reagan contest in 1980 was practically a tie, according to most opinion polls conducted during the September-October period of the campaign. A complicating factor was the third-party candidacy of Congressman John Anderson, a liberal Republican who sought to build the foundations for a centrist party. Anderson started the campaign season with 20 percent support in the electorate. This dwindled to 7 percent by election day. What Anderson did provide was a cross-over path for Democrats unhappy with Carter but not quite ready to become Republicans. A large number were Democratic-leaning Independents, and the Anderson vote in New York and Massachusetts was credited with giving those states to Reagan.

As it turned out on election day, large numbers of blue-collar workers, disgruntled with high unemployment, and Jews, uncertain of the Democrats' born-again Christian, went over to Reagan or Anderson. Overall, 40 percent of the voters who identified themselves as Weak Democrats and 55 percent of those who were Independent Democrats defected.

A closer examination of the Anderson vote revealed important shifts in the Democratic constituencies and anticipated developments in the 1984 contest between President Reagan and former Vice President Walter F. Mondale, the Democratic nominee. Anderson voters in 1980 were more like Carter's in favoring government activity on social issues, yet resembled Reagan's on economic policy. Many Anderson voters were somewhat more liberal than both Reagan and Carter supporters, but felt that the Democrats had done poorly and that the Republicans would do better.

Survey data showed that the Democratic party was receiving its strongest support from groups with the following attributes, in the proportions indicated below.

	Dem	Rep	Ind
Women . . .	46	25	29
Southern Whites . . .	43	28	29
Nonwhites . . .	80	7	13
Grade School . . .	55	22	23
South . . .	49	25	26
East . . .	44	24	32
50 and older . . .	47	31	22
$15,000 to $24,999 . . .	41	35	34
Under $15,000 income . . .	49	23	28
Jews . . .	54	12	34
Unskilled workers . . .	51	17	32
Nonlabor force . . .	48	29	23
Union families . . .	50	20	30

The Democratic constituencies in 1980 looked like a diluted New Deal coalition—half a century later. Democrats were still being supported by women, blacks, the South, the elderly, the low-income families, Jews, and labor—but to a lesser degree.

REAGAN: DISMANTLING THE NEW DEAL

Ronald Reagan departed from his New Deal beginnings during the Eisenhower years and became a principal spokesman for Republican conservatism during the Goldwater candidacy. After his election to the presidency, his policy objectives brought no surprises. He had been stating and restating those objectives in stock speeches for more than two decades. Reagan wanted nothing less than to rescind as much of the New Deal, Fair Deal, and Great Society as possible.

Reagan wished to cut back the functions and the size of the federal government, decentralize public programs to the states and local communities, reduce the growth of entitlement programs and social security, promote the growth of the economy (productivity, real income, employment) by encouraging savings and capital investment, reduce taxes, control inflation, modernize the armed forces, deregulate industries to promote competition, and contain the Soviet Union and the Communist movement. Setting aside his conservative rhetoric, the pillars of this policy structure were his faith in the marketplace, the work ethic, and a version of Jeffersonian democracy.

With the exception of defense policy, most of Reagan's program was tried out during his two terms as governor of California. In the White House, he went immediately about the task of implementing his policies. He had a favorable congressional situation. Although Democrats controlled the House of Representatives, 243 to 192, some seventy-two Democrats—Boll Weevils, as they were called—tended to be conservative and supportive of the administration's positions. Republicans held a 54–46 majority in the Senate. The scenario was consistent: tax reduction (25 percent over a three-year period for individual taxes and numerous changes favoring business); budget cuts for innumerable federal social and economic programs, but increases for the military; adjustments in the social security system (with the help of a 1982 report from a special presidential-congressional commission); deregulation of transportation and other industries.

The administration had hardly gotten under way when a deranged young man shot Reagan, his press secretary, and two security officers on March 30, 1981. The president survived to address a joint session of Congress the following month. Other world leaders were not always so fortunate. An assassination attempt seriously injured Pope John Paul II in St. Peter's Square on May 13. President Anwar Sadat of Egypt was gunned down on October 6. Three years later, on October 31, 1984, Prime Minister Indira Gandhi was assassinated.

Assassination, terrorism, hijacking, war, and other forms of violence seemed ever present. The American hostages, held by Iran for 444 days, were returned on January 20, 1981, Reagan's inauguration day. Death squads in El Salvador continued to kill hundreds in defiance of United States protests and the best efforts of the interim government of Christian Democrat José Napoleón Duarte. The Soviet military ordered the shooting down of an off-course civilian plane, Korean Air Lines Flight 007, killing all 269 passengers and crew. In Beirut, 241 Marines and fifty-eight French soldiers were killed in terrorist suicide bombings. When Marxist hard-liners in Grenada assassinated Prime Minister Maurice Bishop, a moderate Communist, the Organization of Eastern Caribbean States, anticipating a threat to the region's security, requested United States assistance. U.S. armed forces invaded the island on October 25, 1983, and helped reestablish a democratic regime before departing.

Few would deny that it was a dangerous world, and this was always the context for Reagan's escalating defense budgets and Cold War rhetoric. Defense spending put money in circulation and workers on the job. Cold War rhetoric and the invasion of Grenada boosted patriotic feelings. Reduced unemployment and elevated patriotism were essential if Reagan was to bid for a second term. In contrast, some Democrats hoped to ride the nuclear freeze movement into the presidency. The freeze called for an immediate halt to nuclear weapons production and testing. On June 12, 1982, over a half million persons demonstrated in New York's Central Park in support of the freeze. Eight states and the District of Columbia passed profreeze referenda. Several Democratic presidential aspirants endorsed the freeze and sought the movement's support, only to find that it was a dispersed and frail enterprise.

On July 1, 1981, the 1.2 million member United Auto Workers rejoined the AFL-CIO. The times did not seem auspicious for the labor movement. Reagan, in keeping with his attack on the New Deal coalition, had few good words for unions and their leaders. When air traffic controllers struck in August 1981, Reagan ordered their employer, the Federal Aviation Administration, to fire all who failed to show up at work. This broke the union. By November 1982, some 11 million workers were unemployed, that is, 10.8 percent of the labor force.

Contrary to the usual correlation, the impact of unemployment on the 1982 midterm elections was modest. In the twenty midterm elections between 1900 and 1980, the administration party lost an average of thirty seats in the House of Representatives. In those instances when unemployment was going up, forty-six seats were lost, on the average. If unemployment was going down, only twenty-three seats were lost. With unemployment on its way up in 1982. the Republicans lost only twenty-six seats. Evidently the Reagan administration was not being very severely punished, if at all, for the high level of unemployment. In contrast, unemployment in 1979–1980 was a major factor in Carter's losses among blue-collar workers. It almost seems that those who talk most about unemployment, that is, the Democrats, also risk being blamed for it.

The midterm elections bolstered the party's morale. Democrats raised their margin in the House (269-166), with about a dozen fewer Boll Weevils returning. The Senate remained Republican (54-46), but Democrats won in twenty of the thirty-three contests for seats. Democrats controlled thirty-four state legislatures (holding 4,678 seats) to the Republican's ten (with 2,741 seats), with the remainder split. Democrats held thirty-six governorships to fourteen by the Republicans.

The 1982 results suggested that the Democratic presidential nomination was well-worth seeking. Former Vice President Mondale, Alan Cranston, Gary Hart, and Reuben Askew were the first to announce their candidacies as early as February 1983. Ernest Hollings and John Glenn followed in April. At the beginning, Mondale was the odds-on front-runner, having received the endorsement of the AFL–CIO— an unprecedented prenomination commitment by labor—and the National Education Association. Reverend Jesse Jackson entered the race on November 3, 1983, as the first black leader to make a serious bid.

The long preconvention contest was debilitating and full of surprises. Hart upset the Mondale lead in New Hampshire. Jackson, campaigning as the leader of the "rainbow coalition" of blacks, Hispanics, women, and other minorities, demonstrated substantial strength and held the attention of the press. The other candidates withdrew one by one, leaving the field to Mondale, Hart, and Jackson by convention time in July in San Francisco.

President Reagan had a much easier time of it, announcing his uncontested candidacy in January and saving his campaign funds and energy for the general election. It was also clear that he would enjoy the advantages of a favorable rise in the nation's economic activity: real income up about 8 or 9 percent over the previous year and unemployment down to the 7.0 to 7.4 percent (8.5 million individuals) range.

The Democratic national convention was a one-ballot affair, nominating Mondale and resounding with impressive rhetoric. The historic development was the selection of Congresswomen Geraldine Ferraro as the first female vice-presidential nominee.

The campaign was an uphill battle for the Mondale-Ferraro ticket against a popular incumbent president. Party officials spoke of turning out 100 million voters to assure victory. Endorsement of Mondale by John Anderson, the 1980 third-party candidate, had little consequence. A flurry of public attention to Ferraro's family finances was a major distraction. Hart campaigned for the ticket mainly in the West, where most of his prenomination strength was but where Republicans prevailed in the general elections. Jackson focused on the possibility of running for the Senate in South Carolina. The summer monotony was broken by the Olympics in Los Angeles from July 28 to August 12. Two televised debates between Reagan and Mondale and one between Bush and Ferraro received more press analysis than any of the issues. Opinion polls reiterated forecasts of a Reagan landslide.

The polls were correct, although their percentages differed from each other to an unusual degree. Reagan carried the popular vote by 59 to 41 percent. Only Minnesota and the District of Columbia went for Mondale in the electoral college. The congressional returns favored the Democrats. Two more seats were gained in the Senate. Only fourteen seats were lost in the House, where Democrats retained a seventy-five-vote majority. Democrats lost, net, one governorship. Democrats also lost full control, that is, both houses, in six state legislatures, leaving twenty-seven Democratic, eleven Republican, eleven divided, and one nonpartisan.

THE DEMOCRATIC ELECTORATE OF 1984

Registration and turnout statistics demonstrated once again that Democratic constituencies are the most difficult to get to the polls on election day, requiring far more effort, organization, and money than needed for Republicans. Since the 1960 high of 62.8 percent, percentage turnout of the voting-age population (twenty-one or older then, eighteen or older after 1972) had declined steadily, reaching a low of 52.6 percent in 1980. The 1984 turnout was not much better: 53 percent. This trend may in part be a consequence of the extension of the suffrage to eighteen-year-olds, the young tending to be a low turnout group. The trend may also be correlated to the rise in the proportion of the eligible voters who classify themselves as Independents, unaffiliated with any party.

Both parties and about 200 other organizations spent unprecedented millions to register voters. Republican party agencies are estimated to have spent at least three times as much as the Democrats. About 125 million voters were registered in time for the elections, an increase of 10 million over 1980. This represented 72.8 percent of the voting age population, as compared to 70.4 percent in 1980. About half of the new registrations were the result of drives by the two major parties. A CBS News survey reported that registration in precincts that usually vote Democratic increased 9 percent over the preceding four years, while registration in Republican precincts grew by 12 percent. Democratic registration rose substantially in four states, Republican in ten. Democratic strategists hoped that at least 100 million would actually cast their ballots; only about 93 million did.

Groups that are more likely to be Democratic are also those that are less likely to get to the polls. Voters tend to be older and more affluent than nonvoters. (The younger and the poorer have been predominantly Democratic.) Men were more likely to vote in past elections, although this may have changed in 1984 when more women than men registered. (Women have in the past leaned Democratic.) Whites turn out in greater proportion than blacks. (Blacks tend to vote Democratic.) The recent addition of some 2 million blacks to the 10 million already registered indicates that a change is occurring in this group, too. The employed are more likely to vote than the unemployed, retired, or others not in the work force; yet Democratic candidates make strong appeals to the latter. Those with college education tend to vote; those with less education (and these lean toward the Democrats) tend to stay home. Lowest turnouts have been in the South, a former Democratic stronghold. The newly enfranchised or newly registered—in recent decades, these have been the very young, immigrants, southern blacks, Hispanics, Democratic women—also tend to come into the electoral process gradually and at lower rates, and these have usually been Democratic.

These data explain why the now defunct urban party machines were so important for the Democratic party. Strong local organizations saw to it that eligible citizens were registered and got them to the voting booth by escorting many of them.

How did the various constituencies vote, and what was left of the New Deal coalition? The exit polls conducted immediately after voters cast their ballots tell the following about the sources of support for the Mondale-Ferraro ticket.

Women: 46 percent, only about 2 points better than the female vote for Carter in 1980. Some exit polls reported that Ferraro cost (by about 5 percent among women) rather than gained women's votes; for example, Italian women voted disproportionately for Reagan.

Men: 38 percent, just about the same as for Carter in 1980. The male vote has been fluctuating dramatically; 37 percent for McGovern in 1972, but 53 for Carter in 1976. It is easy to suspect a combination of military and patriotic rather than gender attitudes as the explanation. In 1976 Carter's background as a naval officer and in 1984 Reagan's defense posture were important features of their public image. In contrast, McGovern and Mondale took strong peace positions, while Carter caught blame for the failure of the hostage problem in 1980.

Whites: 37 percent, again as in 1980. The prominence of Jesse Jackson, particularly during the nomination campaign and at the national convention, caused substantial defections among white Democrats. This was especially true in the South; for example, only 27 percent of the white vote in Texas went to Mondale. It must be recalled, too, that a typical supporter of George Wallace in 1968—his white "backlash" campaign—was southern, white, male, with high school education or less, young, and a blue-collar worker.

Blacks: 89 percent, many responding to Jackson's appeal. Black turnout was up a percentage point or two from 1980. As the most cohesive constituency in the Democratic party, blacks were beginning to ponder how long it would be before their growing participation and success in local and state politics would be matched by recognition—and a diminution of racism—at the national level.

Hispanics: 56 percent, down from the 70–80 percent support of Democrats during the 1960s and 1970s. Hispanics are no longer a homogeneous constituency, with large numbers having come from Mexico (overwhelmingly for Mondale), Cuba (overwhelmingly for Reagan), Central America (divided), and Puerto Rico (heavily for Mondale). This has been a low-turnout group, but growing in participation and mobilization as local Hispanic leaders increase in numbers and skill. Only about a third of the 9 million potential voters among Hispanics vote.

Asian Americans: Many of the 2.5 million potential votes in this constituency are still uncommitted and unregistered, not yet a significant group in the voting statistics. Most respond favorably to anti-Communist and conservative appeals.

Catholics: 44 percent, a substantial drop in a constituency that voted for Democratic candidates by margins of 60 and 70 percent in the 1950s and 1960s. Higher income, sex issues, and lifestyle issues may be the most significant correlates of this trend.

Jews: 69 percent. This constituency currently consists of slightly less than 5 million votes, with a turnout rate that is probably the highest in the nation. Nine out of ten Jewish voters supported Lyndon Johnson in 1964 (Goldwater's partial Jewish background notwithstanding), and three out of four Jews were consistent Democrats until recently. Approximately 14 percent defected to Anderson in 1980, another 6 percent to Reagan, perhaps permanently.

Union households: 54 percent. Unionists supported Humphrey in 1968 by 56 percent, with another 15 percent voting for Wallace. When the AFL-CIO failed to endorse McGovern in 1972, union support dropped to 46 percent, suggesting that a good many unionists *do* follow their leaders. Carter attracted 63 and 50 percent of the union vote in 1976 and 1980, respectively. Thus, in 1984, the union vote for Mondale was proportionately average, despite the popular tide for Reagan in other groups. What made a big difference was the shrinkage in the number of union families: a membership of about 20 million in 1982, down from 23 million eight years earlier. The estimated size of the labor force in the United States is 112 million, of which only about 19 percent is unionized.

Nonunion workers: 36 percent. Voters in this group are a large sample of the population, and it is not surprising that their support for Mondale comes within 5 percentage points of the 41 percent that Mondale received from the electorate at large. Perhaps the most important inference to be drawn by comparing this group with the union constituency is that it pays to organize.

Unemployed: 64 percent. Of the approximately 9 million unemployed in 1984, the evidence is not clear how many went to the polls. Usually, turnout of the unemployed is at least 3 percent less than those working. This constituency clearly heard the Mondale call for more jobs.

Farmers: The nation's 3 million farmers tend to be Republicans except when they are in trouble. They gave Carter only 29 percent of their vote in 1980. In Minnesota, Iowa, and Illinois, states with troubled farm economies, Mondale received a few percentage points more farm support than elsewhere. In numbers and support, farmers are no longer the Democrats they were during the New Deal and Fair Deal era.

Age groups: Between 39 and 44 percent, with very minor differences associated with age. In other words, Reagan captured votes in all age groups across the board. The difference from previous age-related voting is that the young (under thirty) and the old (over sixty) have been more Democratic in the past regardless of tendencies in other age groups. When examined in relation to the voting behavior of the baby-boomers and the Yuppies, noted earlier, several generational questions come to mind. Are the declining Democratic loyalties among the young and the baby-boomers indicative of a long-term generational trend? What effect will the tendency for first-voters to stay with the party of original choice have on the Democratic future? Is the reputed affluence and conservatism of the older citizens beginning to manifest itself more than previously in their voting behavior?

Nationalities: The Irish and the Poles have been long-standing Democratic stalwarts in the past. In 1984, the Irish gave only 40 percent of their vote to Mondale, and the Poles 49 percent. These percentages are, of course, related to the decline in the Democratic vote of Catholics generally.

What, then, remains of the New Deal coalition? Most of its components are fewer in numbers and weaker in enthusiasm. Only blacks, an emerging force, and Jews, original members of the coalition, continue to be thoroughly committed. Relatively new constituencies that are subject to contest are the young, the baby-boomers, the Hispanics, and Asian Americans. With mass media and mass appeals increasingly cross-cutting constituencies and groups, perhaps the most reliable Democratic constituencies will be those that are well-organized.

King Andrew the First

The Whig Party took its name to emphasize a comparison between Jackson and the autocratic kings against whom the English Whigs struggled.

BORN TO COMMAND.

OF VETO MEMORY.

HAD I BEEN CONSULTED.

KING ANDREW THE FIRST.

A Live Jackass Kicking a Dead Lion

Although he did not invent the Democratic donkey, cartoonist Thomas Nast used the donkey to represent Copperhead—or Peace—Democrats who were sympathic to the South during the Civil War.

Democrats Split— Northern Democrats nominated Douglas. Southern Democrats nominated Breckinridge. The split elected Lincoln, even though he received less than half the popular vote.

PROGRESSIVE DEMOCRACY—PROSPECT OF A SMASH UP.

The Political Death of the Bogus Caesar—A parody of Shakespeare's *Julius Caesar*, showing Radical Republicans exulting over their political assassination of President Andrew Johnson.

Bryan Favoring Vote for Women

Many of Bryan's proposals were a generation ahead of their time. He appealed to emergent constituencies, often too soon. The first women to vote tended to be affluent, better-educated Republicans, hence the Harding landslide in 1920.

One Form of Preparedness He Does Approve of

As Wilson's Secretary of State, Bryan favored strict neutrality toward the warring European nations in World War I. His position was interpreted as preparation for something he could not resist, a fourth nomination for president.

Wets and Drys in Discord

The Prohibition Era split Democrats irreconcilably down the middle. In this cartoon, Miss Democracy pretends not to hear either Wets or Drys.

A BERRYMAN CARTOON, REPRINTED FROM RONALD F. STINNETT, *DEMOCRATS, DINNERS, & DOLLARS* (Iowa State University Press, 1967), WITH PERMISSION OF IOWA STATE UNIVERSITY PRESS.

Roosevelt Defends His Brain Trust and Programs

FDR's alphabet agencies and New Deal programs have been credited with saving American capitalism, although his opponents viewed him as a wildeyed revolutionary.

Yes, You Remembered Me

Roosevelt wanted his programs to help "the forgotten man," that is, the unemployed, the poor, the downtrodden. The Forgotten Man responded by electing him to the presidency four times.

"Yes, You Remembered Me"

David and Goliath, New Deal Version

Vice President Garner and Democratic National Chairman Farley led a serious but futile effort to head off an unprecedented third-term nomination of FDR.

Give-em-hell, Harry

Truman's hard-hitting campaign style became a model for later Democratic nominees.

"Dewey Defeats Truman"

The *Chicago Tribune* jumped the gun on the official election returns. Truman, just elected, relished poking fun at this hostile newspaper.

"Let's get a lock for this thing"

Kennedy appealing to Soviet leader Khrushchev to help keep a lid on the escalating nuclear arms race.

"Let's Get A Lock For This Thing"

REPRINTED WITH PERMISSION OF HERBLOCK CARTOONS, FROM *STRAIGHT HERBLOCK* (Simon & Schuster, 1964).

Kennedy and His White House Staff

— Kennedy's staff meetings were noted for their intellectuality and his commanding style. It is an understatement to say that Kennedy also had difficulties with the CIA.

FROM FEIFFER: JULES FEIFFER'S AMERICA FROM EISENHOWER TO REAGAN, BY JULES FEIFFER, EDITED BY STEVEN HELLER. COPYRIGHT © 1982 BY JULES FEIFFER. REPRINTED BY PERMISSION OF ALFRED A. KNOPF, INC.

Unity

Lyndon Johnson, who brought unity to the nation following the trauma of Kennedy's assassination, had announced the day previous to this cartoon that he would not run for re-election, the end of his own political life.

Portrait of Nixon; Vote McGovern

Artist Andy Warhol's caricature of Nixon, the sight of whom was presumably enough to unite all Democrats behind McGovern.

"But I Don't Think I Know Him"

Carter seemed to come out of nowhere—"Jimmy who?"—to win the 1976 Democratic nomination.

REPRINTED WITH PERMISSION OF HERBLOCK CARTOONS FROM *HERBLOCK ON ALL FRONTS* (New American Library, 1980).

"I'll give it to you straight—
You're in trouble."

The last year of Carter's Administration was devastated
by inflation and unemployment.

"With these rosy glasses, I don't have to do all my campaigning from the [White House Rose] Garden."

Despite favorable scores in the popularity polls, by 1980 Carter's credibility as a leader was shaken by the economic and hostage crises.

"WITH THESE ROSY GLASSES, I DON'T HAVE TO DO ALL MY CAMPAIGNING FROM THE GARDEN"

CARTER CREDIBILITY CANYON

©1980 HERBLOCK

Reagan and Recession—Reagan gives short shrift to typical Democratic constituencies: the old, the poor, and the unemployed.

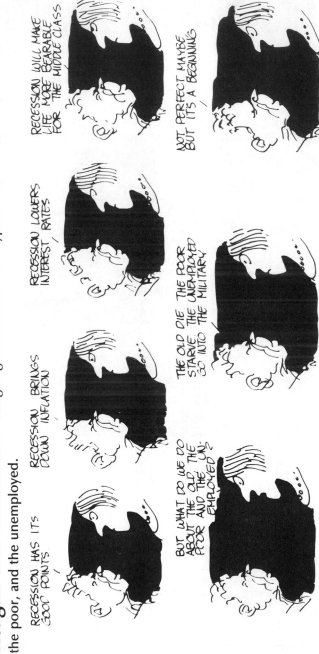

SEVEN

The Electronic Electorate: Organizing the Grassroots

For concerted action to occur, constituencies must be organized. This is an essential function of political parties. Without organization, a party, its leaders, and its programs are beholden to the vicissitudes of events, the whims of the moneyed, and the coincidences of popular attitudes. Organization identifies the constituencies to be represented, imparts a common purpose to them, provides them with an estimable leadership, mobilizes them to act in particular ways on particular occasions, and shares the fruits of success with them.

Different parties at different times organize the electorate in different ways. For example, some parties use money, others use people. Some use the mass media, others use precinct captains. Organizing styles employed in the past may tell much about a party's present and future problems and successes. Which leads to this historical review of the Democratic organizational experience.

POPULAR SOVEREIGNTY AND THE FOUNDING FATHERS

According to the doctrine of popular sovereignty, governments are organizations established by and operated according to the wishes and will of "the people" rather than any special group or elite. The doctrine was first argued in the eighteenth century. The Founding Fathers endorsed it cautiously.

Not quite sure how "the people" would behave politically, they created an electoral college which enabled the popular electorate to choose their president indirectly, a Senate whose members were chosen by popularly elected state legislatures, and a House of Representatives directly elected by popular vote but spread out among geographically dispersed districts. With popular constituencies broken up into so many pieces, the Founding Fathers believed that popular interests somehow would be represented at the center of government without much risk of some demagogue coming along to lead the masses in the overthrow of the government (as the French revolutionaries did in Paris shortly afterward).

The Founding Fathers did not prescribe how all these pieces would be put together for the purpose of operating a government effectively in some organized fashion. Most did not believe in political parties, having watched the machinations of parliamentary parties in England and having become annoyed by the way electioneering had developed in several of the colonies. This left unanswered the questions: Who are "the people?" How shall their collective "will" or choices be expressed and measured? The Founding Fathers were divided and hesitant about political parties and popular elections.

In his *Federalist* Number 10, James Madison recognized that "the people" are hardly a faceless mass. He saw them as a changing array of social groupings—farmers, laborers, merchants, bankers, coreligionists, veterans, etc.—with different social, economic, and political needs and objectives. He called these groups, particularly when organized, "factions" and noted that factional leaders were in constant search of allies to help them achieve their group objectives. Allies usually included leaders of other organized interests or politicians seeking election to public office. In a heterogeneous and changing society, the safety and advantage of all groups lay in how these groups conducted their conflicts and how well group leaders could carry on a politics of coalition. In modern terminology, this is the essence of pluralistic politics.

The Founding Fathers did appreciate, as no political leaders ever had previously, that elections are a principal means for measuring the popular "will" in a system of democratic representation. They also appreciated that the design of an election system would significantly influence how political groups would try to win control of government and government policies to further their own interests. A design that calls for majority rule, for example, compels disparate minority interests to negotiate with each other in order to pool their respective voting strengths. This combining process produces the requisite majority, and victory. Thus, majority rule procedures result in a politics of coalitions, compromises, and moderation. As a consequence, the vitality of a democracy would come to depend upon the skills of interest group leaders to identify political issues, speak for their constituencies, and build coalitions.

An effective political party in a pluralist democratic community has the capacity and the organization to allow political communication to flow influentially to and through its leadership. Communication is usually about group needs, demands, and resources (electoral strength, money, volunteers, etc.) in order to pursue the demands. If a political system requires majorities to elect persons to office, office-seekers will try to construct coalitions by reconciling the demands of their supporting groups in order to bring out the largest possible favorable vote. This is the way to get elected. This is the way, as Madison saw it, to moderate the extremes of political conflict. The process for the most part requires leaders who know how to be political brokers, groups that know how to compromise, institutional forums, such as legislatures or party conventions in which leaders and followers can communicate, in which an election system compels them to communicate, and parties must organize the competing constituencies to achieve the election outcomes required if they are to control the government.

During the colonial period there tended to be a basic clash between the mercantile-financial interests on the one hand and the independent farming interests on the other. These organized themselves into Court parties and Country parties respectively, in order to pursue their objectives in colonial assemblies and before royal administrators. In order for the Country party to capture as many seats as possible in the Massachusetts assembly and among local governments, for example, the Caucus Club of Boston was organized as one of the first urban political machines in America. The interests active in the club put together slates of candidates and statements of policy that they proposed to the tiny electorates of that day. They then electioneered in order to win the requisite majority.

The caucus model was copied elsewhere and in many places succeeded in capturing control of colonial legislatures. By the mid-1770s the committees of correspondence of these legislatures, if controlled by Country party majorities, formed an intercolonial network that was in effect the first "national" party on this continent. This network created the Revolution's First Continental Congress. Here were all of the components of a primitive party system: elections, electorates, representative assemblies, political groups, caucuses, nominated slates of candidates, and platforms.

A period of economic prosperity ended with independence. Deflation brought depression and a severe crisis for agrarian debtors. The currency of the Continental Congress became worthless. Banking, commercial, shipping, and fishing interests joined together under Federalist leadership to promote programs for stabilizing the economy and the credit structure of the new nation. Mortgaged to the hilt, farm families—and these constituted about 95 percent of the population—turned to the Jeffersonians for a voice in the national government. Alexander Hamilton's financial program, enacted by the First Congress of the United States, benefited the financial and creditor interests at the expense of the farmers. A coalition of farmers, debtors, and frontiersmen became the "normal" constituencies of Jefferson's Democratic-Republican party, and, later, the Democratic party. The Madisonian model of pluralist democracy was in operation.

THE EMERGENCE OF POLITICAL PARTIES

In the new federal system party leaders had to develop several levels of organization: at the local grassroots level, in the state legislatures, in each house of Congress, and for the quadrennial presidential selection in the electoral college. In the new and free political community, the press was unabashedly partisan and provided the principal mode of continentwide political communication. For example, one study of 512 newspapers published during the period 1790–1800 found that 139 were strongly Federalist, 121 moderately so, seventy-two were strongly Democratic-Republican, and fifty-seven moderately so. The remaining 123 were of doubtful leanings. Party organization and party communication were functioning from Day One of the new Republic.

In the period from 1789 to 1792 local party organization was uneven across the nation. In some places, notably New York and Pennsylvania, committees of correspondence remaining from the Revolutionary period continued to nominate and campaign for slates of candidates. In other places, the absence of electioneering organizations led to multiple candidacies and plurality rather than majority voting outcomes. In Boston, for example, there were twenty-seven candidates for the five presidential elector positions in 1792. Between 1793 and 1800 numerous patriotic societies were established in urban centers to debate the issues that divided the nation. These eventually opposed Federalist policies and stimulated local Democratic-Republican grassroots organization elsewhere.

The first patriotic society was organized by German-Americans in Philadelphia on April 13, 1793. Its announcement, in the quaint phrases of the day, makes all the fundamental connections between popular sovereignty, liberty, civic duty, and the functions of political parties.

> In a Republican government it is the duty incumbent on every citizen to afford his assistance, either by taking part in its immediate administration, or by his advice and watchfulness, that its principles may remain uncorrupt; for the spirit of liberty, like every virtue of the mind, is to be kept alive only by constant action. It unfortunately happens that the objects of general concern seldom meet with the individual attention which they merit and that individual exertion seldom produces a general effect; it is, therefore, of essential moment that political societies should be established in a free government, that a joint operation may be produced, which shall give that attention and exertion so necessary for the preservation of civil liberty.

A second society appeared in Norfolk, Virginia. A third was organized in Philadelphia, then the seat of the national government. The latter had important national leaders among its members. The Philadelphia patriotic society aggressively encouraged the formation of similar clubs throughout the nation: forty-one over the next few years, with from one to five in each of the thirteen states.

The patriotic society of Philadelphia was the first to proclaim the legitimacy and legality of political party alignments. Most of the patriotic societies directed their attention primarily to local and congressional issues and elections. Most were city or county associations holding monthly meetings in local courthouses. All had committees of correspondence that kept them in touch with each other. In time, they replaced mass meetings as nominating bodies.

A more fraternal type of local organization—the Society of St. Tammany (after Tamanend, a chief of the Delaware Indians who was known for his love of liberty)—was first established as an association of enlisted veterans of the Continental army. Branches appeared in New York, Virginia, Pennsylvania, Rhode Island, North Carolina, and one or two other states. By 1794, the Tammany Society of New York began to debate current public issues and engage in electioneering. Members were almost always in tune with the Jeffersonian leadership. Thus began the most famous of urban political machines, Tammany Hall.

In 1793, the patriotic societies helped return the first Democratic-Republican majority to the House of Representatives. In his message to the Third Congress on November 19, 1794, President Washington denounced the activities of "certain self-created societies." This caused the patriotic societies some loss of membership, but not enough to affect seriously Democratic-Republican activities. Washington's remarks removed all pretense of his nonpartisanship.

Federalist party organization was quite different structurally from the Democratic-Republicans'. Federalists condemned political parties as such and denied that they themselves were a party. Their coalition was based upon organized groups similar to modern pressure groups: chambers of commerce, professional associations, church-affiliated groups, associations of bankers or manufacturers, and the Society of Cincinnati, an organization of officer veterans of the Continental army.

Democratic-Republican organization in many localities took on a modern appearance. For example, Aaron Burr, a

Tammany leader, introduced the card index of voters' names, a device that came to symbolize party organizational proficiency in later years. The Tammany leadership understood that each vote counted. In 1796, for example, a shift of one-hundred votes in Pennsylvania would have lost the vice-presidency for Jefferson. In 1800, a shift of 214 votes in New York City would have given the presidency to the Federalists instead of the Democratic-Republicans.

A letter from the politically appointed collector of the Port of Middletown, Connecticut, Alexander Wolcott, to fellow-Jeffersonian William Plumer illustrates party organization procedure. Wolcott told Plumer to have each county leader appoint a manager for each town in his county. Each town manager should appoint district managers who would list the names of all male freemen, taking pains to divide this list into "decided Republicans" (short for Democratic-Republicans), "decided Federalists," and "doubtfuls." District managers should also get all eligible freemen to take the necessary oath at registration time and to furnish these freemen—particularly the friendly ones—with "votes," that is, the prepared paper ballots used at that time. Each town manager was to be assigned dates for forwarding their estimates of voter preferences to county managers who, in turn, were to consolidate and forward them to the state manager. In addition, every manager was to be active in the circulation of campaign literature. On election day each manager was to report his own estimates of local election returns. This letter was written in 1805 but could just as readily have been written by James A. Farley in 1936 when Farley's forecasts of voting in the states, based on party precinct reports, were so accurate and the *Literary Digest*'s forecast of Landon's election so wrong.

Extension of the suffrage during the 1820s and 1830s, that is, the beginning of the Jacksonian Era, lay heavier responsibilities on local party organizations. Migration to Ohio, Michigan, Tennessee, and Mississippi drained the older eastern cities and counties of loyal party voters. Eastern political managers had to look for replacements. Western managers had to track and enroll the newcomers, with a special appreciation that all rifle-bearing men (not only the propertied) were equals before the hardships of the frontier. Hence, the new western states, as rapidly as they became organized, extended the vote to all white men of legal age, that is, twenty-one years, in the Anglo-Saxon tradition. For party managers this meant mobilizing a large number of new voters, most of whom tended to share Jeffersonian and Jacksonian political views.

This egalitarian suffrage standard filtered eastward, particularly among workingmen's groups and fraternal associations among the foreign-born. Both groups were preponderantly Democratic-Republican. Both pressed for removal of property ownership and tax payment as suffrage requirements. By 1830 universal white manhood suffrage was radically altering the election environment in the older states.

The introduction of the penny newspaper provided a channel of communication to the new, less-prosperous voters. Local Democratic-Republicans enjoyed a revival after long dormancy during the one-party Era of Good Feeling (1816–1824). No one better organized these new voters than General Jackson's colleagues in Tennessee, unless it was Martin Van Buren and the Albany Regency in New York. By 1832, the year of the establishment of the national Democratic party, the Jacksonian political machine was in full operation locally and nationally.

LOCAL MACHINES: THE TAMMANY MODEL

For the next half century, the evolution of city "machines" and rural county "rings" continued. Variations in degrees of organization and amounts of electoral success depended upon types of party leaders, quantities of available patronage, movements of population, and similar circumstances. The most prominent and most strategically situated of the city organizations was Tammany Hall. The most significant rural machines were those that developed in the South and the Middle West after the Reconstruction Era at the end of the century.

Tammany Hall grew rapidly and rancorously from the 1840s on. As wave after wave of immigrants arrived from Europe, Tammany workers were at the docks of New York City to welcome and Americanize them. Tammany helped them find their relatives, places to live, jobs, recreation, and the big prize, American citizenship. In return, Tammany sachems asked only for unwavering loyalty to Tammany candidates at the ballot box.

Tammany leaders learned how to broker job and contract patronage in exchange for campaign contributions and public offices. Some leaders also broke the law. Thus, in 1868, Boss William Marcy Tweed, of Tweed Ring infamy, ordered a company, of which he was president, to print some 100,000 applications for citizenship and 69,000 certificates of naturalization. Then, at the rate of several thousand a day, Tammany-appointed judges certified new citizens, who remained obligated to Tweed for expediting their Americanization.

Technically, Tammany Hall was the New York (Manhattan) County Democratic party organization. So long as Manhattan remained the most populous and the richest of New York City's five boroughs, Tammany was the kingpin of the citywide Democratic party. During the 1920s and 1930s, as population surged into other boroughs (Brooklyn, the Bronx, Queens), other county organizations challenged Tammany's hegemony.

In the 1840s and 1850s, Tammany factionalism was embittered by the nationwide divisions over slavery and North-South hostilities. Tammany also established itself as the key party organization in the nation's key state in presidential politics. Tammany leaders were not reluctant to use this swing position in bargaining with national party leaders.

By the end of the 1860s, many Tammany leaders—John Kelley, Richard Croker, the Scannell brothers—and many wealthy New York Democrats—Samuel J. Tilden, Abram Hewitt, and others—were able to rid the city of the corrupt Tweed Ring and convert Tammany into a powerful and relatively honest political operation. By the close of the nineteenth century Tammany consisted of some 90,000 party workers and more than 220,000 reliable Democratic voters in a city of one million. There was a captain for each city block, another captain for each voting precinct, a leader for each of thirty-five assembly districts, a five-member finance committee selected by the leaders, and, at the top, the boss, usually the chairman of the finance committee. There was a million-dollar edifice, Tammany Hall, on Fourteenth Street. The thirty-five assembly district clubhouses, worth about $100,000 each, were scattered around the borough. A typical end-of-the-century Tammany campaign cost $300,000 (in 1890 dollars).

Tammany was a year-round enterprise. Unemployed laborers by the score could be found applying for work every morning at the doorstep of their Tammany captain. Builders, contractors, and other business enterprises could have their bids for contracts facilitated by Tammany's excellent access to city administrative departments. Police protection could be arranged when needed. Persons facing penalties for minor crimes frequently received bail or money for fines from the Tammany representative monitoring the particular city police court. Tammany leaders from the precinct up were constantly aware of the complaints of the disorganized, the under-privileged, the unemployed, and the newcomers. From the point of view of wealthy taxpayers, Tammany was often perceived as a useful agency for the prevention of vandalism, riots, unemployment, and misdirected public relief to the needy.

Such a model was imitated, with interesting variations, elsewhere during the nineteenth and early twentieth centuries. In Boston, the principal bosses were ward leaders rather than single city-wide leaders. Until the late 1920s the two most powerful organizations were the Hendricks Club of the Eighth Ward, dominated for forty years by Martin Lomasney, and the Tammany Club (modeled after Tammany Hall), run by James Michael Curley. Sometimes as allies, more often as competitors, and always in shifting coalitions with lesser ward organizations, these two wards gave Boston and Massachusetts Democrats whatever cohesion and effectiveness they had until the 1940s.

In Memphis, Tennessee, Edward Crump rose to the top of the city's politics as part of a reform movement in 1903 and remained there for more than half a century. The pillars of the Crump coalition were the city's long-resident blacks and a smaller community of affluent immigrants and their heirs. Mayor for four terms, Crump was allied with a tough, gun-slinging rural machine—the Sheriff Birch Biggs organization. The alliance enabled Crump to dominate state politics until the end of World War II. After the war, politically active veterans, as competent with guns as the Biggs machine, joined young New Deal-Fair Deal liberals to cut back Crump's influence. The rise of Senator Estes Kefauver as a presidential candidate indicated the extent of their success. Retreating to home base in Memphis by the mid-1950s, Crump hung on until his death.

Frank Hague won his first election as constable of Jersey City in 1897. The city was rife with political gangs. Hague was elected major in 1918 and put his first hand-picked governor into office in 1919. By 1925 he controlled a 100,000-vote block in Hudson County that assured his dominance of the Democratic party in the state for years. In the late 1940s Hague's influence was diminished by the growing effectiveness of the New Jersey Congress of Industrial Organizations (CIO), one of labor's most successful vote-getting organizations. The unions and a coalition of hostile county leaders finally isolated and overthrew the Hague machine by the end of the 1950s.

One of the most colorful and enduring party machines was in Chicago. During the decades between 1890 and 1920 Roger C. Sullivan built up a Cook County Democratic organization that was unbeatable when united. However, rivalry within the party was relentless in the period after 1910, and Republicans, with a strong machine of their own, were able to win numerous local elections. During the 1920s, two Democrats—Edward J. Kelly, chief engineer of the Chicago Sanitary District, and Patrick A. Nash, head of a sewer contracting firm—pulled together a winning coalition: the Kelly-Nash machine. Later in the decade, a reform movement supported by many of the city's nationality groups united under the leadership of Anton J. Cermak, a Czech-American party leader. Cermak's untimely death in an assassination attempt on President-elect Franklin D. Roosevelt returned control of the Chicago party to Kelly and Nash.

An aging Mayor Kelly advanced Jacob Arvey to the county chairmanship in the early 1940s. Arvey worked hard to revitalize the organization. He was instrumental in electing a businessman, Martin Kennelley, to the mayor's office, Adlai E. Stevenson as governor, and Paul H. Douglas as senator. Governor Stevenson appointed the former minority leader of the Illinois Senate, Richard J. Daley, as head of the state's Department of Finance, and Daley succeeded Arvey as Democratic county chairman in 1953. Daley beat Kennelley in the primary and in the general election to become mayor in 1955.

As mayor, Daley gave the city a unique combination of old-style machine management and new-style reform. A decade's immigration of southern blacks put a strain on the city's housing, educational, and employment resources, yet the party's assiduous attention to the population shifts and needs kept racial tensions to a minimum. Daley was elected in 1975 to his sixth and final term as mayor. It was Daley's organization that delivered the several thousand votes that carried Illinois and the presidency for John F. Kennedy. When he died in 1976, while on rounds of party and civic functions, it was recognized that an American political genre also died with "Boss" Daley.

SHIFTING POPULATIONS AND CHANGING FUNCTIONS

The Republic began with a population that was 95 percent rural. In 1790, there were only twenty-four communities with populations of more than 2,500 persons. By 1970, the last census to classify communities of 2,500 as urban, there were 6,435 urban sites, containing 70 percent of the nation's population. In 1980, there were thirty-nine U.S. cities with a million or more in population. In that same year, a mere 3 percent of the labor force was employed in farming. These changes have been accompanied by the changes between Jefferson's Democratic-Republicans and the Democratic party today.

The Jeffersonians and the Jacksonians were ardent representatives of rural agrarian interests. The succeeding Greenback, Populist, and Progressive parties that so greatly influenced the Democrats were in turn essentially rural organizations. Not until 1920 did the nation cross the line from its rural beginnings to its predominantly urban character of today. The South and the Midwest continued as rural regions until the 1960s when industrialization and agribusiness began to transform them.

From the point of view of party organization, a rural "neighborhood" is, of course, very different from an urban one. City precincts and wards exist on a block-by-block basis and are readily organized and served by an attentive party captain. A rural precinct may spread over many square miles, its voters are more difficult to reach, and its parties tend to be organized on a county rather than a precinct or ward basis.

Rural party machines have been unflatteringly referred to as "county courthouse gangs" because county governmental centers are where most local political action takes place. For much of the nineteenth century, rural communities were overrepresented in state legislatures and Congress. Hence, coalitions of county organizations with such names as Albany Regency, Richmond Junto, and Nashville Junto were able to control state legislative bodies. During the heyday of the Solid South, these county coalitions became the personal machines of individual leaders, for example, Huey Long of Louisiana and Harry Byrd of Virginia.

Beginning in the 1950s, a new type of population center emerged: the suburb. Large numbers of families were moving from central cities to outlying areas, much of the movement being racially motivated. The populations of the cities and the suburbs became self-segregating. Central cities were losing whites to the suburbs and gaining blacks, mainly from the rural South. President Johnson's National Advisory Commission on Civil Disorders (the Kerner Commission) reported in 1968 that, whereas 91 percent of American blacks lived in the Old South in 1910, by 1966 one-third lived in the nation's twelve largest cities. With urban party machines gone, very few of these cities had the organizational capacity to assimilate these new neighbors.

Internal migration of all types has become one of the major causes of the debilitation of local party organization. About 20 percent of the American people moved annually in the early 1960s. This decreased to about 17 percent by 1980, that is, about 39 million persons, of whom some 28 million were potential voters (eighteen and older). These are, to say the least, a great many voters for relatively nonexistent local party organizations to track. Local party leaders despair of keeping up with arrivals and departures of resident voters, of registering those who meet local residence requirements (an anachronism in a mobile and computerized society), of learning new residents' predispositions regarding candidates and issues, and of providing the traditional personal attention to get them to the polls on election day.

Another source of local party pathology has been the nationalization of party services and functions. By and large, local parties have from their earliest days provided political, social, and economic services of substantial benefit to their constituents. Local party facilities have served as fraternal and recreational centers, offering off hours places for neighborly comraderie. Local party organizations have been educational agencies for civic education, political discussion, and training for naturalization. Precinct and ward leaders, as personal acquaintances of most voters and their families within their districts, have provided social services that ranged from personal counseling to steady employment. Local machines were charitable institutions, providing food, shelter, clothing, and holiday gifts to the poor and the lonely. They gave legal aid, in the form of counsel or money, to petty criminals, and occasionally drove the not-so-petty criminals out of the community. Local organizations promoted community development projects, albeit largely in the interest of contractors they favored.

All this changed radically during the New Deal and subsequent administrations. The national government assumed or financed most of the functions previously performed by the local party machines. Jobs were provided through such New Deal agencies as the Works Progress Administration, the Public Works Administration, the Civilian Conservation Corps, and so on. Charity came to be dispensed through an elaborate federal system of social security, unemployment benefits, and food stamps. The United States Employment Service, CETA (Comprehensive Training and Employment Act) programs, and other national agencies have taken over the function of job placement. An entire federal agency—Housing and Urban Development—is concerned with community growth and development. Legal aid is provided to the poor through national legal assistance programs such as the Legal Services Corporation. Political discussion and civic education are conducted for the citizenry by panelists on national television networks.

With the federal government providing all these services and functions, who needs local party organizations? One answer was suggested by President Johnson's National Commission on Civil Disorders, which also mentioned another source of debilitation of local party organization: nonpartisan local elections and city-manager government, both among the list of reforms of the progressive movement earlier in this century:

> [T]he needs of ghetto residents for social welfare and other public services have swelled dramatically at a time when increased affluence has diminished the need for such services by the rest of the urban population. By reducing disproportionately the economic disability of other portions of the population, particularly other ethnic urban minorities, this affluence has left the urban Negro few potential local allies with whom to make common cause for shared objectives. The development of political alliances, essential to effective participation of minority groups in the political process, has been further impaired by the polarization of the races, which on both sides has transformed economic considerations into racial issues.
>
> Finally, these developments have coincided with the demise of the historic urban political machines and the growth of the

"city manager" concept of government. While this tendency has produced major benefits in terms of honest and efficient administration, it has eliminated an important political link between city government and low-income residents.

Another answer: Most citizens need human contact in order to experience a sense of community and party affiliation. The bureaucratization—i.e, depersonalization—of nearly all of the services of local parties has probably been the single most influential factor in the dramatic increase of voters who identify themselves as Independents rather than party members. The disappearance of a sympathetic neighbor, that is, the precinct or ward captain, the personification of one's political party, has destroyed the voter's personal sense of party and transformed party into a remote and relatively meaningless organization—something "out there somewhere."

PARTY IDENTITY AND INDEPENDENCE

There are several ways of finding out the extent of a voter's sense of party. One is to ask the voter for a self-description: "Do you consider yourself a Strong Democrat or a Strong Republican, a Weak Democrat or a Weak Republican, or an Independent?" Another is to ask the voter for his or her actual voting record: "For which party did you vote in the last congressional election?" A third is to determine how he or she recorded party affiliation at the time of registration to vote. A fourth is to ask for the voter's attitudes on typical partisan issues: "Do you favor government involvement or government abstention in providing employment for those seeking but unable to find work?" Of these methods, the most commonly employed is the first, self-description.

The proportion of the electorate identifying itself as Independent has risen dramatically in the past thirty years, from 22 percent in 1952 to as high as 35 percent in 1980.

Roughly, one-third of these Independents lean toward the Democratic party, one-third toward the Republican, and the final third toward neither party. About 40 of the remaining 65 percent consider themselves Democrats and 25 to 30 percent Republicans, with the latter gradually increasing. This would appear to give the Democrats a 2-to-1 voter advantage nationwide.

The problem for the party is that Weak Democrats and Democratic-leaning Independents are the voters most likely to defect from their party's candidates, sometimes at the rate of more than half their number. It is also true that Weak Democrats and Democratic-leaning Independents are very much more likely to stay at home on election day than other voters.

Why do they defect? Why so large a number of Independents? One much-overlooked explanation has been suggested earlier, namely, the lack of a sense of party because of the absence of the formerly ubiquitous local party official. There is also the transfer of social and economic functions from familiar local leaders to impersonal bureaucracies. Why bother identifying with or voting for a party that offers nothing tangible and immediate in return? After all, in other affiliations in their lives, most individuals *belong* to groups which they experience personally and from which they receive concrete gratifications. This latter point can be illustrated by the party role assumed by unions and the Democratic club movement at just about the time that city machines and other local party organizations were disappearing.

UNIONS, CLUBS, AND LITTLE CITY HALLS

Always interested in rewarding political friends and punishing enemies, American labor maintained a nonpartisan posture during the years it was led by the Knights of Labor and the American Federation of Labor. The New Deal gave unprecedented encouragement to union organization, and labor responded by becoming a charter member of the New Deal coalition.

When the Congress of Industrial Organizations departed from the AFL in 1936, several of its ten founding unions involved themselves directly and heavily in party politics. The Amalgamated Clothing Workers and the International Ladies Garment Workers Union joined hands to organize the American Labor Party, which later played a significant role in New York politics. The United Mine Workers gave substantial contributions and campaign energy to Democratic candidates. By 1944, national, state, and local CIO unions were major participants in Democratic party politics, the AFL much less so.

Unions approached the party and election processes in a variety of ways. In some instances, they helped the campaigns of friendly candidates, with money, publicity, and volunteers. Where they had the balance-of-power in primaries or elections, unions threw their resources to the candidate or party that offered the most. A union slate might challenge unfriendly party regulars in a primary. Unions would also develop alliances with other groups in order to influence party decisions. Sometimes a union would take over a party organization's activities year-round. Where there was a complete absence of precinct or ward organization, union locals became the organized representatives of the Democratic party interest.

A new high in trade union electoral effectiveness was achieved in support of Franklin D. Roosevelt in 1944 and Harry Truman in 1948. In 1955 the AFL and the CIO merged to form a united labor movement of some 15 million members. Soon after, the new organization created a Committee on Political Education (COPE) as its political arm. COPE was financed by a political levy on union members and became a major supplier of voter lists, election statistics, opinion survey data, campaign management skills, and field workers. Labor's role continued to grow during the 1950s and into the Kennedy-Johnson years in the 1960s.

By the mid-1960s it was becoming more difficult for union leaders to deliver the labor vote. In 1968, despite Hubert Humphrey's solid labor record, significant numbers of workers followed George Wallace into a third party. In 1972, the AFL–CIO refrained from endorsing George McGovern and participated in the formation of the Coalition for a Democratic Majority (CDM), an organization of Democratic centrists. Standing behind McGovern was a Coalition of American Public Employees (CAPE), including the rapidly expanding American Federation of State, County, and Municipal Employees (AFSCME).

As the 1980s began, a new generation of labor leaders and new approaches to the political parties began to take hold. COPE acquired computers and other campaign technologies indicative of new approaches. Realizing that a third or more of the membership was voting for candidates other than those endorsed by the AFL–CIO, COPE became more sophisticated and selective about the labor vote it sought to register and turn out on election day.

In 1984, under the leadership of Lane Kirkland, George Meany's successor, the AFL–CIO gave its first endorsement of a candidate during the presidential primaries to Walter F. Mondale. When Mondale lost or did poorly in some of the early primaries, AFL–CIO state and local unions contributed the funds, publicity, and door-bell ringers that turned the nominating process in Mondale's favor. With their political prestige on the line, the unions went all out for Mondale in the general election campaign against President Reagan: registering eligible voters; cajoling dissident members to vote Democratic, getting the reluctant and the forgetful to the polls, in short, performing the duties of a Democratic precinct organization. As noted earlier, the union vote remained firm but insufficient against the Reagan landslide.

Another grassroots development was the Democratic club movement. In the 1950s the club movement had many of the impulses of turn-of-the-century reform and progressive movements. Citizens of somewhat better education and income, who were antimachine, and who tended to focus on ideology and issues joined these movements. An important difference between the earlier movements and the clubs was the willingness of the latter to work within the parties.

Clubs were a natural development in California, where there was a strong progressive tradition, where parties were weak, and ideology strong. California Democrats, enthusiastic over the Stevenson candidacy and frustrated by the lack of local organizations to campaign for him, created clubs that avoided the geographical requirements of the old precinct or ward organizations. Instead, clubs tended to be gatherings of friends, persons with common ideological interests, groups from particular occupations, or individuals sharing a lifestyle.

By 1954, local clubs throughout the state joined to form the California Democratic Council (CDC), which thereafter endorsed state candidates, took stands on issues, and campaigned actively. While the clubs have felt free to endorse any candidate they wish for party nomination, they have generally remained committed to work for whichever Democratic nominee is chosen. Democratic clubs were subsequently organized in Illinois, New York (where they defeated Tammany Hall on occasion), Michigan, Kansas, Pennsylvania, and Colorado.

In some respects, the Democratic club movement has been a grassroots attempt to develop new modes of participation for new kinds of participants: the educated, the affluent, the ideological, the issue-oriented; in effect, an endeavor to incorporate reformism directly into the party structure. The club movement has perhaps also reflected the decline in material rewards (job patronage, contracts, etc.) for party work and an increase in symbolic and psychological rewards (ideological postures, charismatic leaders, club sociability, etc.) for the more educated, more ideological, and more issue-involved of the party's rank-and-file.

By the end of the 1970s, local party organization was in disarray throughout the nation. Interest groups, unions, personal political machines, minority ethnic and nationality organizations, and even public social service agencies were treading where precinct and ward captains had walked before. The reformers and progressives of the first half of the twentieth century succeeded in making local elections technically nonpartisan, and in installing city managers as the chief executives of "clean" municipal administrations. Primary election systems further weakened party management by allowing the wealthy to win party nominations by media blitzes rather than peer review, and by allowing unsubstantial interests to impose costly primary contests upon party regulars.

As noted earlier, the weakened local party organization has debilitated community life in general. The informal neighborly social network provided by earlier precinct and ward organizations has withered. Civic duty, patriotism, and civic education are no longer the tutorial responsibilities of a nearby precinct captain. Equally serious is the inability of local party groups to identify, recruit, and give civic responsibilities to natural leaders, a shortcoming that is often cited as a cause of many urban political maladies such as crime, riots, and street gangs.

The Kennedys and Lyndon Johnson were disturbed by these local developments as early as 1960. Johnson's War on Poverty, particularly the Community Action Program (CAP), was intended to put federal money into slum projects, bring the poor into the political process, and provide opportunities for ghetto leadership to emerge. But without the constraints of party loyalty or accountability, CAP was often exploited by street gangs such as the Blackstone Nation in Chicago, radicals interested in disrupting normal political processes, and program administrators who were untrained or corrupt. In many communities, CAP spawned "para-governments," in the phrase of D. Patrick Moynihan, that were a direct challenge to responsible local party leaders.

Another attempt to fill the gap left by disappearing local party organizations was the "Little City Hall." Initially, but unsuccessfully, attempted in New York City, Little City Halls have since been established in more than a hundred municipalities across the nation, the largest of which has been Boston. A Little City Hall is, in effect, a miniature replica of the mayor's office. It is usually located in a trailer, office, or storefront in a residential community. Boston, for example, has had seventeen Little City Halls spread among its twenty-two wards. Each is staffed by five to ten city employees providing such services as consumer protection and rent control information, voter and selective service registration, property and auto excise tax collection, notarization and copying of official documents, translating and interpreting services, visitations to nearby nursing homes, and local emergency help of various types. In many respects, the Little City Hall has been a public and ostensibly nonpartisan replacement of the old party clubhouse and precinct captain.

There is also renewed interest in returning to partisan local elections. As the antimachine movements of the past are forgotten and as the illusion of local nonpartisanship wears thin, the advantage of party slates on the local ballot will undoubtedly reappear. There is evidence that nonpartisan elections tend to favor candidates who are Republicans in other guise, but it is generally a debatable fact best judged on a city-to-city basis.

REBUILDING THE PRECINCTS: SPECIFICATIONS

To repeat, different political parties have different organizational needs and different approaches to meeting those needs. What are likely to be the Democratic party's organizational needs during the next decades, and how should the party approach their solution? If these were questions addressed to engineers—and there are *social* engineers—their first response would be to specify objectives. Product designs would then be developed within the limits set by these specifications. Why not adopt a similar approach to the future of the Democratic party's grassroots organization?

1. *Contact.* A party of the people needs to be in direct and close contact with its people. Historically, Democrats have achieved this contact through their local machines and by the personal campaigning of their nominees and party officials. The wisdom of this has recently been confirmed by behavioral

research indicating that person-to-person communication is one of the most effective forms of influence. Yet, the party's current local organizations are, for the most part, nonexistent, frail, or in shambles.

2. *Funds.* Money is admittedly the mother's milk of politics, particularly when free and given in generous amounts. Beyond mother, there is no free lunch. It is one of the misfortunes of politics that politicians must trade in unfamiliar currencies (votes, access, policies, recognition, favors, etc.) and are under suspicion when handling money. Unlike the fiscal operations of the supermarkets, local party organizations have yet to install a check-out register.

The current need for local party funds is substantial, particularly if all the activities familiar to the old urban machines are taken seriously. Party workers need to be compensated for the time they spend on organizational matters, a function that patronage jobs used to provide in times past. Clubhouses, party literature, services to voters, and similar expenses need to be covered; kickbacks from job-holders and favored contractors, contributions from the wealthy, and less-savory raids on the public treasury used to take care of this part of the budget. These types of fundraising are, to put it mildly, inappropriate today and in any foreseeable future. But the activities and the financial needs are essential elements of any local organization at any time.

3. *Information.* Sam Adams, Aaron Burr, Alexander Wolcott, and James A. Farley were among the astute party managers who understood that political knowledge is power and they knew how to get it. Know thy constituent! Today's professional campaign managers, pollsters, computerized data banks and mailing lists, and other high-tech approaches are testimony that the proposition is equally appreciated by contemporary party leaders.

Great volumes of data about registered voters and unregistered citizens have already been gathered. Since most of the information is from public sources, it is inevitable that controversial questions will eventually arise regarding privacy and the use of the data by unauthorized, incompetent, or malicious individuals. For Democrats, information-gathering needs to be conducted so as best to serve the local organization. Further, the information should be in sufficiently standardized form to facilitate national compilations and analyses.

4. *Service.* What can the local party official do for his constituents, locally, in exchange for the voters' loyalty and support at the ballot box? A difficulty here is that most economic benefits and social services are now provided by remote state or national agencies and are discussed during campaigns in broad, national terms. The personal services of the friendly precinct captain need somehow to be recovered.

5. *People.* The Democratic party usually has more people than money. The local use of volunteer help can be a major resource or a big headache, as most party managers will agree. The recruitment, assessment, training, and effective employment of volunteers year-round and during campaigns require management skills that would humble most old-style army top-sergeants. Underemployed or poorly treated volunteers can be costly not only as a wasted resource but also as party voters.

6. *Hierarchy.* No large-scale human organization can function without complete and clear channels of communication among its executives. Hierarchy is more a problem of communication than of prerogative, although the opposite interpretation is more often made. Party hierarchy in a federal system is almost never the neat pyramid of the organizational charts. The challenge of this specification will be to separate communication-of-information from power-to-decide at the different levels of organization—precinct, ward, county, congressional district, state, and national.

Given the many layers of government and politics in the American federal system, the more direct the relationship between local and national party units, the swifter the flow of information to meet party needs. Ways of sharing information or being in communication with intermediate levels of organization will, of course, need to be built around the local-national framework.

The six specifications are fundamental and particularly relevant to the organizational history of the Democratic party. There are, of course, other specifications worthy of consideration; and those given here can probably be better formulated. The purpose of *any* listing is to facilitate systematic thinking about approaches to its application to the problem at hand, in this case, rebuilding the grassroots organization of the Democratic party.

Contact

Who will provide the contact between party and Democratic voter? There are over 100,000 election precincts, an uncounted number of wards, and some 3,300 counties in the United States. These have been the typical local units of party organization, each type with particular advantages and disadvantages for party operations. Ideally, 100,000 personable and well-trained Democratic precinct captains, with sound organizational backup, would provide the kind of personal contact desired. This assumes that each captain will get to know intimately the several hundred voters in his or her precinct.

The difficulties leap out at the reader. Where will the 100,000 Democratic captains be found? How will they be compensated for what would be a full-time job? How will they keep track of the migrants: current constituents moving away and new constituents arriving? What will be their functions between and during campaign periods? What happens to their responsibilities when precinct boundaries are changed, as they regularly are? Given the committee structure of American parties, to which party committee should the precinct captain be accountable?

The same general questions would pertain whether the captains' districts were wards, counties, state legislative districts, or congressional districts. Only counties present a slightly different aspect; counties have permanent boundaries and can be geographically stable units of a party organization.

Perhaps sustained, informed, and politically meaningful personal contact with all constituents is, after all, no longer possible to achieve satisfactorily. But, for the party, the difficulties do not remove the need: contact remains essential for Democratic constituencies. Clearly, the difficulties require more thought, more questions, more data, more analysis, and more proposed solutions from which to choose. An example follows, in full recognition that the close contact between local party official and voter achieved in earlier eras is no longer attainable, if it ever was. It offers a less than ideal solution.

The number of local party officials must be fewer than the 100,000 precincts or the 3,300 counties, yet numerous enough to make citizen contact everywhere in the nation at least theoretically feasible. The 435 congressional districts come to mind.

The local party official should function within a geographical unit that is closely related to a dynamic and significant political office. The congressional district meets this requirement.

The territory covered by these district captains and the size of the electorate they serve should be larger than precincts and wards but not so large as to make travel, information management, and direct communication with voters too costly or impractical. Again the congressional district comes to mind. The areas of most congressional districts are of reasonable and comparable size. The extremes should be noted: the 580,000 square mile district of an Alaskan congressman and the densely populated city blocks of a New York City district. As a consequence of the one-person, one-vote rulings of the Supreme Court, district populations—between 200,000 and 700,000 inhabitants (not to be confused with registered or active voters)—are also comparable. Again, extremes should be noted; congressional district voter turnout as a measure of political participation may vary from several thousand to several tens of thousands.

Admittedly, the congressional district can be an excessively large geographical and population unit for local party purposes. Yet, it demonstrably comes within the range of practicality. Ask most congressmen. The experience of the home district staffs of most members of the House of Representatives could provide relevant data.

An important difficulty of the congressional district is its changing boundaries. The census results and decennial redistricting alter the population size and shape of many districts. The proposed party captain would have to drop former constituents and track down new ones every ten years. Previous voting data and analyses would have to be substantially revised. However, the articulation of the problem may be more serious than its reality. In former days, alert party managers simply reshuffled or prepared new index cards. Today, with computerized data banks containing the addresses and other data about individual citizens, it may be but a few hours work to retrieve and transfer information from one district captain to another, and take just a few days to reanalyze voting and other political patterns of the new district.

During the next several decades, the American voter will undoubtedly become the most observed and most analyzed political creature in the world. For Democrats, perhaps the most significant application of this knowledge will be to facilitate direct and effective contact with the party's constituents.

Money

How would the party pay for the above or any other form of local organization? The question seems so awesome that most party managers simply throw up their hands in frustration or hold out their hands for contributions from some unusually interested source. No chain of supermarkets operates this way. (The comparison is financial, not facetious.)

Whatever the structure of the local party organization, it is practical rather than visionary to speculate about possible optimal and minimal budgets. Will the local party unit be a one-person operation or have a staff, as in the case of congressional home district offices? Will an office space be necessary or will it be an out-of-home operation? What equipment—computers, telephones, files, etc.—will be necessary? How will the size of the electorate (for workload) and geographical area (for travel) of the district be taken into account? To what extent will the system of administrative accountability add to the operating costs? Will funding come from the party, from the public treasury, or a matching combination of both? An agenda of questions of this type gives reality—and, of course, some sense of futility—to the problem of grassroots organization.

Both to illustrate and suggest, assume that the congressional district is indeed designated as the local unit of the party organization. Assume also that both major parties in Congress agree that grassroots political party vitality and services are in the interest of the party system and will strengthen our democratic institutions, hence worthy of some degree of public funding. This reasoning would follow the logic that led to public funding of primary and general elections. Furthermore, in other nations, it is not uncommon to provide public funding for party functions in parliamentary districts.

Given these assumptions, the budget for grassroots organizations now becomes a matter of designing an appropriation formula. A successful formula would put in operation principles of allocation and allow initial funding to be modest but capable of growing with experience.

A formula would presumably establish fixed expenditures: for example, standard salaries for a district captain and one assistant, standard allowances for office rent and expendable supplies, basic startup funds for furniture and equipment, and a minimum telephone and postage allowance. The formula would then apply explicit criteria for the variable expenses: for example, travel (area of district in square miles), size of electorate (number of registered voters), and incumbent or opposition status of the parties in the district. Each party might have to meet a matching requirement in order to receive public funds. Each party would be free to add whatever additional funds it may raise.

The above observations serve as both an illustration and a recommendation. There are a number of other ways to raise money that should be mentioned briefly. Some of these will be nothing less than small businesses. For example, a modern version of the old Democratic clubhouse might require party-club membership dues, rent office space, contain a health spa or workout center, operate a restaurant or amusement center, or engage in other nonprofit enterprises. Extensive use of competent volunteer workers could keep expenses down and help make these small-business pursuits a source of steady income.

There are also the traditional political contributions, which today have the added incentive of tax deductibility. Organized direct personal solicitation, feasible at the local level, is likely to produce more contributions than the direct-mail approach, although both should be employed. Contributions could also be dealt with in the form of party membership dues or as a subscription to a party newsletter or other publication, giving the Democratic contributor something immediately tangible for his or her money.

Contributions from local organized groups and political action committees (PACs) should be welcomed but handled with special care. One of the dilemmas of modern democratic politics is giving contributors of funds as fair a representation as is given to contributors of votes.

The question of party finances fills countless volumes. Democratic party fundraising is characterized by small amounts and large deficits. However, if we lend some detail to an otherwise broad and ambiguous subject such as finances, it soon appears that money may be an attainable goal after all if approached in an explicit and business-like manner.

Information

The future of political intelligence work is already here. For Democrats, the issue is how, when, and with what resources can the party implement the known and available informational activities. Republicans, flush with funds and organizational talent, are already well along in this field.

The mere listing of present informational functions only begins to touch all that is possible with the new electronic technologies:

— Computerized name lists drawn from local voter registration rolls, local directories, public lists of driver's and other licenses, telephone directories, and similar public sources, to cross-index and produce voter profiles.

— Computerized address lists to check residency requirements and mail campaign appeals, fundraising requests, registration reminders, questionnaires, and other political correspondence. Special lists may be produced to enlist volunteers and locate party members interested in particular projects.

— Attitudinal data gathered by various methods of polling the electorate, along with individual information regarding race, sex, age, occupation, income and other socioeconomic attributes, and policy preferences.

— Election return statistics to identify and analyze local voting patterns and trends.

— Decennial census tract data, perhaps resurveyed every two or three years for current local changes.

— Textual materials from local press, television, radio, and other media, for purposes of content analysis regarding political orientation, positions on public issues, and other communication messages.

— Data about the opposition's personal and political record and statements.

The possibilities seem unlimited. Once established, the costs of maintaining and employing these data sources are surprisingly modest. Cooperation among local, state, and national party managers would undoubtedly keep costs down and broaden the coverage, for example, joint data and mailing lists, data analyses covering nearby and mutually influential districts, and data analyses for joint election campaigns.

The critical phrase is "once established." Without vast quantities of money and large staffs, data banks of the magnitude suggested may require years to put together. Republicans have been able to embark on this enterprise from the top, at the level of the national party agencies. In the absence of money and personnel, Democrats may make a manageable beginning at the local level, taking a few districts at a time and debugging programs as the coverage expands.

Service

The models for local party service are again the urban machines and their modern counterpart, the Little City Halls. The services rendered will be many: assistance in the preparation of legal and other forms and applications; information and guidance for job-seekers; education and training counseling; help in identifying legal, health, and other service professionals in the community; year-round voter registration; community orientation programs for new residents; preliminary, nonprofessional counseling in family, landlord-tenant, and other disputes. These are but a few of the pertinent activities.

Party services should be informal and informational, designed to assist with minor procedures or to direct citizens to available professional or commercial services. The services would provide an excellent opportunity to employ trained volunteers from among the community's retiree or teenage population. The activities of the latter could possibly become a precareer work experience and even earn school credit. It would be no coincidence if these same volunteers turned out to be loyal partisans frequently found working at the local Democratic headquarters.

Unlike the publicly funded Little City Halls, the party's service centers should be financed strictly by the party and its more affluent local contributors. The management personnel and volunteers should be openly party members. The object is, of course, to earn citizen good will and voting loyalty for the party. "Thank you for visiting this Democratic party service center" should be the message relayed at the end of every session with a client. After all, the Democrat who renders the service may be the one who gets the client to the polls on election day.

An innovative form of public service would be the use of the party's grassroots organizations as informal but authoritative planning agencies. Some experts in the field of public planning are skeptical of centralized, top-down systems, as exemplified in various socialist and mixed-economy nations. They prefer decentralized, community-based systems whose needs and proposals are eventually coordinated and reconciled by central agencies. There are those who point out that this is exactly what political parties do. Parties are planning agencies in disguise. If we accept this characterization, it should not be difficult to devise procedures by which Democratic grassroots organizations could produce local planning documents as data and demands to be incorporated in quadrennial Democratic National Plans. These plans could perhaps be the agenda of the Democratic midterm conventions.

People

In an era of huge television budgets, mass media political messages, massive mail solicitations and campaigns, and the perception of voters as computerized profiles, it is almost sacrilegious to suggest that most of the costly advertising is worthless. Yet, there is much to be learned from the merchant or professional who has a zero advertising budget and a large word-of-mouth network of customers or clients. Word-of-mouth tends to attract and keep loyal followings. As mentioned earlier, behavioral research findings clearly support the observation that direct person-to-person communication is far more influential than other forms. This is increasingly true as one goes down the scale of socioeconomic status—the less-educated and poorer the person, the more influential the person-to-person communication.

Again, the problem is how to find and employ the appropriate Democratic persons. We have already mentioned the local district party captain. There would also be the inevitable district party committee. Members of party committees are chosen by registered Democrats in primary elections. Ideally, candidates for district committee membership should have certain qualifications in addition to the ability to garner votes for themselves: for example, instructional talents for training party volunteers, analytical skills for getting the most out of district data sources, business skills for supervising the party's small-business enterprises, counseling competencies for management of the party's service centers, an ability to raise funds, and so on.

Such an array of elected talent on a local district committee would make for a powerful organization. In a more realistic world, an elected committee and a district captain would be achieving a great deal if they could bring together as many of these talents as possible in the form of a district advisory committee. For the more educated and activist among the local party faithful, responsibilities such as these would surely be more challenging than stuffing envelopes or writing a campaign contribution check.

In addition to a full-time district captain, elected district committee, and talented advisory committee, the other significant members of the local organization would include party volunteers and regular party voters. Each group requires distinct modes of treatment and involvement.

Volunteers are special persons requiring special attention. They are usually motivated by nonmonetary rewards: sociability, that is, an opportunity to meet others with similar interests; convenience, that is, great flexibility of time and place of participation; recognition, often in the form of simple and sincere flattery or expressions of appreciation; and curiosity, or the opportunity to become informed. The supervisor of volunteers who fails to respond to these motivations subverts an important component of the party enterprise.

Democratic training programs should give particular attention to instruction in the recruitment and management of volunteers. There is a wealth of behavioral research that is relevant to this training objective. Supervisors of volunteers need to know how to design interesting, specific, short-term tasks for their charges. Supervisors need to be counseled regarding specific responses to reinforce the usual motivations of volunteers. Skill in handling disruptive or other problem volunteers is essential. In short, elections are won by well-directed and enthusiastic volunteer troops. No political party can afford to neglect this resource.

Democratic "Regulars" are those voters whose participation rarely goes beyond turning out to vote the party ticket. They are registered as Democrats. When questioned by an opinion-polling organization, they identify themselves as Strong Democrats. What these Democrats need is attention, information, and reminders.

Attention may be as simple as a telephone call or house visit once or twice a year by a local party captain, committee member, or volunteer. Attention should be given after as well as before elections.

Information relevant to party affairs should be communicated as conversationally, briefly, and clearly as possible. Whatever the form of communication, it should convey information about party nominees and officers, party and election procedures, public policies endorsed or being considered by the party, and events of likely interest to party members. The purposes of these informational activities are straightforward: give the Regular a sense of connection to the party, disseminate information of potential practical use to the Regular, and occasionally attract the Regular into more intense participation in party activities.

There are many channels through which to communicate party information. In the early days of the Republic, certain newspapers were explicitly partisan and served as the principal channel. Today, there is such a great variety of channels that party communicators are limited only by their energy, funds, and enterprise. Telephone calls, house visits, and newsletters are considered the simplest and least expensive means. Club or other public meetings are another standard approach.

Whether they really are nonpartisan or not, local newspapers, television stations, and radio stations must respect the concept of equal time for partisan views. These media—particularly local cable television—have not yet been fully exploited for regular, noncampaign programming of party news, commentary, training, or entertainment. Finding ways to use these media would be a challenge to innovative Democrats.

There are many situations in which a party reminder may produce important results: registration to vote; voting; the location of the polls; the names and backgrounds of party nominees; the party's statements about issues; how to handle political items on income tax forms. The function of reminding often is the sole purpose of much campaign literature. For the politically disinterested, uninformed, or distracted, a very great many of whom consider themselves Democrats, reminders have particular importance and seem best communicated by local party workers.

Hierarchy

The place of local organizations in the state and national hierarchy of the Democratic party is inevitably a subject of great controversy. These disagreements are a consequence of several complicating truths. In the first place, there are not many local organizations worthy of the name. Then, there are several ways to stack up the hierarchies:

—precinct captain, ward leader, county committee, state central committee, and national committee, or

—state assembly or senatorial district, state legislative party, and state commitee, or

—congressional district and party leadership in one or both houses of Congress, or

—some combination of the above, or

—personal organizations of important party leaders.

It will take more than two centuries to arrange these party units in anything approaching pyramidal symmetry. Thus far, Democrats have been dedicated states righters and decentralizers. Whatever nationalization of the Democratic organization has occurred since the New Deal has taken place mainly in connection with the national convention and the presidential-nominating process. If there is to be a rebuilding of the party's grassroots organizations, there must be a direct link between new kinds of national and local units. The means (telecommunications, computers, etc.) are available. What is needed is an organizational design that puts the local and the national in direct communication, at the same time keeping the intermediate layers of organization (county and state) fully informed.

Here again the congressional district offers certain advantages. It is the basic unit of a significant public office; political forces mobilize meaningfully within its boundaries. Organizationally, it is directly related to a major national party leadership in the House of Representatives. The congressional districts within a state may be coordinated structurally with membership in the United States Senate where another major national party leadership is found. The presidency may become part of this organizational structure through the selection of delegates to the national nominating conventions principally in the congressional districts. With some modifications, the national committee could become the national coordinating agency of the party's leaders in all three branches of government.

Of course, the rebuilding of the party's grassroots organization and the restructuring of its national organization will require massive adjustments: new attitudes, new conceptions of the party's role in American and world politics, new functions, new relationships between party units and offices, major redistributions of resources and prerogatives; and time—lots of time, perhaps reaching beyond the party's bicentennial.

Above all, the process must begin with an appreciation of the fact that no political party can successfully mobilize its constituencies without touching each constituent in some meaningful way. This is a particular requirement for the Democratic party.

EIGHT

Organizing the Leadership: State, Congressional, and Presidential

Political parties are pointless without leaders. By definition, a political party must have leaders who wish to hold office in government in order to implement the public policies they and their constituents favor. Where there is true popular sovereignty, the leaders and the constituents maintain a binding two-way relationship through political parties and the processes of nominations, campaigns and elections.

The leaders of a political party must be able to communicate with each other, particularly if there are as many as in the Democratic party. The federal structure of the government and the parties of the United States add to the party's communication problems. The division of powers among the branches of the national and state governments makes matters even more complicated. Trouble becomes certain when communications, prerogatives, and competing ambitions get into the picture. Political parties are in crisis if their basic functions are assumed, intruded upon, or stolen by other institutions: public relations firms, the press, television, organized interest groups and their political action committees (PACs), the military-industrial complex, or the personal political organizations of candidates for office under the party emblem. Party leaders who fail to deal with the problems of communication and coordination among themselves, let alone with their constituents, will some day discover that they no longer have either a political party or a leadership.

THE PARTY AT THE STATE LEVEL

In addition to its experience with grassroots organizations, the Democratic party has also had a history of state and national organizational development.

State party affairs usually involve a complex set of relationships among a governor, two United States senators, a congressional delegation, party members in each of the two houses of the state legislature, and the members of the party's state central committee. Then add the fringe groups—the state capital press, lobbyists, citizen groups, and administrative bureaucracy. Besides the horizontal relationships there are those that dip down to local party leaders and rise to regional and national party leaders.

Under the Constitution, states were assigned powers and responsibilities that are of critical importance to party functions. These include the power to regulate elections and establish the qualifications of voters. The states prescribe the manner in which presidential electors are chosen. These selections were a state legislative activity for several decades. Selection of United States senators was also a power of the state legislatures until the Seventeenth Amendment in 1913 transferred that power to the electorate. To be eligible to vote for members of Congress a citizen must also be eligible to vote for members of the lower house of the state legislature. Thus, state laws and practices have for generations shaped the development of the state and national parties. But the direction of influence was reversed after the Democratic loyalty-oath requirements were established in the 1950s. Since then, the requirements of the national party have influenced the formulation of state legislation.

Two of the earliest state-level party machines have been previously noted, namely, the Richmond Junto in Virginia and the Albany Regency in New York.

The Richmond Junto had its base in the Virginia Assembly, with Antifederalist patriot Patrick Henry very much in charge. Henry was powerful enough to prevent the selection of James Madison to the Senate in the First Congress of the United States. Virginia, at the time, was not only the state with the most votes in the electoral college but also the home of the Virginia Dynasty, that is, Presidents Jefferson, Madison, and Monroe. It was the Richmond Junto and its allies that later sustained the presidential candidacy of William H. Crawford in the 1820s, elevated John Tyler to the vice-presidency in 1840, and denied a renomination to Martin Van Buren in 1844. The Junto, managed by politicians residing in Virginia's state capital, was well-connected with party leaders throughout the South.

The Albany Regency was a later arrival, constructed from the Democratic-Republican membership of the New York state legislature by Martin Van Buren beginning in 1816. Two years later the Regency was able to elect the speaker of the New

York Assembly and control the principal sources of state patronage. Van Buren's election to the United States Senate by the legislature in 1821 firmly established the Regency.

The Regency did little to organize at the local or county levels in New York but, instead, nurtured allies in nearby state legislatures. The object was to broaden the influence of these states in the national affairs of the party. The Regency also welded together an enduring alliance with Tammany in New York City. Thurlow Weed, who created the Whig-Republican equivalent of the Regency, spoke of the Regency's leaders as "men of great ability, great industry, indomitable courage and strict personal integrity."

Over a century later, in the 1950s to 1970s, the Democratic party continued to have a strong presence in the politics of the states. Democrats controlled state senates, state assemblies, and governorships over 60 percent of the time. As might be expected, much of this strength lay in the states of the South. The predominantly Democratic state governments in recent times have been in South Carolina, Georgia, Louisiana, Mississippi, Texas, Alabama, Arkansas, Florida, Virginia, North Carolina, Tennessee, Oklahoma, Kentucky, Arizona, West Virginia, Maryland, and New Mexico.

The first state governors to be nominated for president were Samuel J. Tilden of New York and Rutherford B. Hayes of Ohio in 1876. Governorships have since become a prime source of candidates for president, about one hundred having been in contention since Hayes-Tilden. With the establishment of popular elections of United States senators in 1913, senators have competed equally with governors for the affections of state voters and the party rank-and-file. Senators have enjoyed two advantages: their presence in the nation's news center, Washington, where opportunities for publicity are greater, and their ability to take credit for dispensing federal munificence while the governors struggle with state deficits.

For generations, state party organizations operated out of the pockets of their leaders. These leaders were usually United States senators, governors, assembly speakers, or state party chairmen. The address of a state party's headquarters was generally the residence or business office of one of these individuals. Expenses were paid personally or from funds collected from a small coterie of political friends. There were no rented headquarters, party staff, or organizational funding.

Since the 1960s, the situation has changed. Most state parties now have headquarters offices and staff. In off-years, the staffs number five persons on the average, doubling during elections. Annual costs for each state party range from $25,000 to $1.5 million, with a median figure of about $360,000. Costs go up appreciably during election campaigns.

The need for permanent state headquarters arose when new campaign finance laws and new national convention requirements imposed record-keeping and rule-making responsibilities on the state parties. Furthermore, as state elections became more competitive, parties were moved to employ media, polling, computerized information, and other technology in a more systematic and centralized way.

Strengthening the state party organization has tended to strengthen the national parties. The more proficient these state party agencies, particularly as they coordinate competing centers of power within the state parties, the more stable and coherent the relations between national and state organizations. Leaders in the state parties are identified more readily by national leaders, factional issues are dealt with more openly, national and state administrative functions are more easily arranged and monitored, and political information is more accurately and cheaply gathered and analyzed. Such advances inevitably strengthen party operations in the electoral wars.

SECTIONALISM: THEN AND NOW

Sectionalism in American history has not quite led to regional party organization, although perhaps something close to it. The Richmond Junto and the Albany Regency, for example, branched out beyond their state bases to become the political hubs of regional party collaborations. In time, the nation's continental size and diversity compelled politicians to think and organize themselves by regions.

At first, the sections were simply North and South. National tickets responded to the need for balance: Washington from Virginia and Adams from Massachusetts; Adams from Massachusetts and Jefferson from Virginia; Jefferson from Virginia and Burr from New York, and so on. The Old West, that is, today's Midwest, became part of regional ticket-balancing with the arrival of Henry Clay of Kentucky and Andrew Jackson of Tennessee. In the twenty-five national tickets put together by Democratic national conventions, from 1832 to 1928 inclusive, only four failed to choose a pair of nominees from different sections of the country, the Midwest and West having been added to the two original sections.

The role of sectionalism in American politics was handled in classic exposition by the eminent historian Frederick Jackson Turner. Throughout the nineteenth century, according to Turner, rival societies, free and slave, existed in the North and the South. Emigrants from each of these societies marched side by side into the unoccupied lands of the frontier West, each attempting to dominate the back country. With the disappearance of the frontier, a more stable pattern of sectionalism developed, each territorial unit with its own political characteristics and interests.

The deliberations of Congress and national party conventions led to decisions which could be characterized as "treaties between sections," in the manner of treaties between nations. The national political parties were, in Turner's opinion, the most effective single political institution for the prevention of sectional disunion. Party ran across all sections and evoked intersectional or nonsectional loyalties. A dissenting minority within one section had an organic connection with party associates in other sections at the same time that the majority interests of a section received their proper political recognition. Thus, the voter could act continentally and the politicians were compelled to act on policies that transcended their particular sections. When this criss-crossing of sections within the parties broke down in the period 1850–1860, civil war and the near destruction of the Union followed.

From the 1880s to the 1930s, a major factor in sectional politics was the noncompetitive one-party character of politics in nearly two-thirds of the states: twelve one-party Democratic states in the South and nineteen one-party Republican states, mainly in New England and the Midwest. By the 1960s, the trend was toward party competition in nearly all the states. Regional political traditions persisted but were further weakened at each succeeding election.

Regionalism took an administrative form from the 1960s on. Regional associations of members of the national committee and state chairpersons, such as the Western States Democratic Conference, began to share political intelligence and draft policy statements on regional issues. During national elections, artificial administrative regions were created to coordinate multistate presidential campaign operations. These campaign regions usually followed Bureau of the Census regional lines or the voting patterns of the area. In another half century, all that remains of sectionalism may be the accents of regional speech.

THE CAUCUS OF THE PARTY-IN-CONGRESS

It all began with legislative parties. The first parties were organized among like-minded colleagues in the English Parliament during the seventeenth century. Legislatures, as the most numerous set of governmental officers, continue to be one of the most significant arenas for party activity in democracies. In a bicameral legislature such as the Congress of the United States, it is more accurate to refer to the Party-in-the-House and the Party-in-the-Senate. Each has had a distinctive history.

The first United States Senates were almost completely Federalist in membership. The first serious partisan divisions appeared in the House of Representatives as "Hamiltonians" and "Madisonians." Madison's Democratic-Republicans, contending with a Federalist administration, formalized a consultation procedure among fellow-partisans, namely, the caucus.

The first such formal caucus was held on April 2, 1796. The purpose was to mobilize the party's vote on a controversial issue, the Jay Treaty. In the Senate, the treaty was adopted by precisely the two-thirds required, 20–10. In the House, a related appropriation was passed by a one-vote margin. Those Democratic-Republicans who dared defect were verbally drawn-and-quartered in their home districts by loyal Jeffersonians.

The caucus gained great power and notoriety from 1800 to 1820 for its presidential and vice-presidential nominations. Both Democratic-Republicans and Federalists held secret caucuses in 1800 to decide which candidates to sponsor. Disenchanted with the procedure, the Federalists never again used it. But the Jeffersonians continued, in effect choosing the president of the United States after the Federalist opposition disappeared. The electoral college, then chosen mainly by Democratic-Republican state legislatures, simply confirmed the congressional caucus choice.

The caucus was at its most disciplined when demanding party loyalty under conditions of close competition, as in 1796. In the one-party, noncompetitive circumstances between 1816 and 1824 (the Era of Good Feeling), however, the caucus was rent by factionalism, divided in its decisions, and under public suspicion for its secrecy.

In 1824, when Jackson was denied the presidency by Speaker Clay's withdrawal in favor of John Quincy Adams, the Democratic-Republican caucus was not technically involved in the maneuver. However, the action took place in the House of Representatives, where secret caucuses had been conducted. This was enough to cause Jackson to depart from the capital condemning "King Caucus." And it ended the use of the caucus in the presidential selection process.

The influence of the Democratic caucus waxed and waned

over the decades. Its most persistent function has been as the vehicle for selecting the party's leadership in the House: the speaker or minority floor leader, the party whip, the chairman of the Ways and Means Committee, and the principal appointed staff. When a speaker was powerful, he tended to give the caucus little or nothing to decide in the making of public policy.

A strong president could, as Harry Truman declared, occasionally ask the caucus to decide an issue as a "party matter." The House caucus became a potent machine under Woodrow Wilson's guidance and again in the New Deal era. Franklin Roosevelt's capacity to pull in Democratic congressmen on his "coattail" at election time and the reduced number of southern Democrats in Congress after 1934 enabled this activist president to revitalize the policymaking functions of the caucus.

The LaFollette-Monroney Legislative Reorganization Bill of 1946, among other proposals, unsuccessfully proposed creation of a policy committee for each major party in each house to enable the party leaders to coordinate their respective legislative agendas and policy postures. Seen as a threat to the authority of the speaker and the agenda-making Rules Committee, both Democratic, the policy-committee concept was deleted from the bill. The following year policy committees were established in the Senate, where minority Republicans, under the leadership of Robert A. Taft, built theirs into a strong arm of the leadership. Democrats preferred to leave Senate leadership in the hands of the majority leader, who also served as chairman of the Democratic Policy Committee, used primarily to schedule Senate legislation. The majority leader was also chairman of the Democratic Steering Committee (which assigned party members to standing committees) and the Democratic Conference (which formally confirmed the party's choice of its Senate leadership).

Under Speaker Sam Rayburn and Senate Majority Leaders Alben Barkley and Lyndon Johnson, the party's House caucus and Senate conference were rarely convened. With conservative southern Democrats so strongly entrenched in the leadership positions, eighty liberal congressmen, later calling themselves the Democratic Study Group, inaugurated cooperative consultations in 1957. After the DSG formalized itself two years later, members contributed staff on a regular basis. The liberal caucus grew to over one hundred members, almost as potent a voting bloc as the Southerners.

After long years of power concentrated in the party leadership positions in Congress, the dispersion of power to the caucus membership was stepped up in the 1970s. In 1970, the Democratic caucus changed its rules so that the election of each standing committee's chairman could be voted on by secret ballot separately rather than en bloc. This later enabled caucus liberals to remove the more objectionable of the senior conservative committee chairmen.

In 1972–1973, Democrats in the House created a Steering and Policy Committee to recommend legislative priorities and policy positions to the caucus. The members of this new twenty-four-member committee were to come from a wide range of interests: the black caucus, congresswomen, freshmen, and different regions. One major committee and subcommittee assignment for every Democratic member regardless of seniority was guaranteed.

In the post-Watergate election of 1974, seventy-five of the 291 House Democrats elected were freshmen of moderate-to-liberal orientation. A liberal, Phillip Burton, was elected chairman of the newly composed Democratic caucus. Responsibility for committee assignments was shifted from the conservative Ways and Means Committee to the more liberal Steering and Policy Committee. The caucus also assumed the prerogative of electing chairmen of the powerful subcommittees of the House Appropriations Committee.

Changes, perhaps less dramatic, were taking place in the Senate. The Democratic conference, mirroring the House caucus, arranged to vote by secret ballot on each standing committee chairman, requiring a four-fifths majority for election on a first ballot. Without the four-fifths, other candidates could contest the position.

Outside the conference, under Democratic pressure, the

Senate modified its cloture rule. To end debate, the rule required a vote of two-thirds of those present and voting. If the entire membership of one hundred was present and voting, cloture would thus require sixty-six votes. The new rule allowed three-fifths (sixty members) of the constitutional members to cut off debate. This applied only to substantive issues, *not* those dealing with procedure.

CONGRESSIONAL CAMPAIGN COMMITTEES

Another party agency in the Congress is the campaign committee. There is one in each house. The Democratic-Republicans' campaign committee was the first. At the conclusion of their tumultuous nominating caucus of June 1812, the Madisonian managers felt a need for a national campaign coordinating organization, in part to keep the more reluctant Madison supporters in line. A Committee of Correspondence was appointed, one representative from twenty-five of the twenty-seven state delegations in Congress.

Similar campaign committees were created from time to time over the next three decades. Usually headquartered in Washington, their principal responsibility was the presidential campaign. In 1842, Democrats created a more exclusively congressional committee. Democrats from most state delegations in both houses, with the encouragement of titular leader and former president Martin Van Buren, agreed to publish a joint platform and mount a unified attack on the Whig administration of President Harrison.

In 1860, the new Republican party created a joint presidential-congressional campaign committee, calling it the Republican Executive Congressional Committee. In 1864 it was the Union Congressional Committee. Both committees issued scores of campaign pamphlets and undoubtedly prompted the formation of the pro-Johnson National Union

Campaign Committee of 1866, the first of the modern congressional campaign committees.

This Johnson committee chose a nine-member Resident Committee to coordinate campaign efforts from Washington. Working with the resident group, President Johnson embarked upon an unprecedented personal "swing around the circle," a campaign tour of the country between August 28 and September 15 in support of pro-Johnson congressional candidates. On the other side, the Radical Republicans organized their own congressional campaign committee which helped them win a majority in both houses.

In 1868, congressional campaign committees became settled in their principal modern functions, namely, gathering information about the electoral situation in the districts, fundraising (particularly on behalf of candidates in closely contested districts), and the distribution of party literature in local races.

Early Democratic committees often involved themselves in both presidential and congressional campaigns. During the closing quarter of the nineteenth century, the committees were made up of members from both houses. During the 1880s, the committees did less and less in presidential races and attended almost entirely to the election of members of the House of Representatives. With the direct popular election of senators after 1913, Democratic senators established their own senatorial campaign committees.

From the turn of the century to the New Deal period, congressional campaign committees were temporary agencies whose membership changed with each session of Congress. Their main tasks continued to be electing fellow-partisans to Congress, fundraising, and disseminating propaganda through party literature and speakers. For tactical reasons, the committees divided districts into, to use M. Ostrogorski's phrase, "the good, the hopeless, and the doubtful," determined by continuing analyses of district voting patterns and conversations with party factional leaders. Committee efforts focused on the doubtful districts to the almost total neglect of the good and the hopeless. The congressional campaign committees were most actively concerned with midterm elections, subordinating themselves to the national committees during the presidential years.

THE FUTURE OF THE PARTY-IN-CONGRESS

Congress, particularly the House of Representatives, has been preponderately Democratic since the New Deal. As a consequence, many changes in congressional organization and procedure have been motivated by Democratic party needs. These have occurred from the Legislative Reorganization Act of 1946 to the recent strengthening of the Democratic caucus. Congressional party organization also continues to evolve. Most recently the trend has been toward decentralizing power from the leadership to subcommittees and individual legislators.

The House Democratic caucus and the Senate Democratic conference will probably continue to develop methods of decentralizing leadership in ways that keep the factional balance current and moderate. Such changes are most likely to take place in steering, policy, and other management committees. Seniority, the leadership standard of the past, will continue to give way to party, expertise, regional concerns, and other criteria of leadership selection.

There is no long-term Democratic institutional strategy for strengthening party organization in Congress. Further change will depend upon the composition, experience, and ideological orientation of the Democratic members in any given session. This, in turn, may vary with the extent to which congressional districts become more generally competitive, how much the turnover in office increases as a result of competitiveness, and with the extent to which congressional candidates become beholden to such national party agencies as the congressional campaign committee or the national committee for their recruitment, nomination, and campaign resources. For the next decade or two, districts will certainly become more competitive, but turnover will increase only slightly, and, among Democrats, few will become beholden to the national party agencies.

The electoral competitiveness of congressional districts, while spreading to more districts in the next half century, continues to be problematical. Long-standing one-party districts persist and incumbency is a potent factor in any contest. Fully two-thirds of House members tend to be reelected by 60 or more percent of the popular vote. The battles are closer in the Senate, where only about one-third of the incumbent members manage to achieve the 60-plus victories. Turnover also continues to be modest. About a third of House members manage to stay on for six or more terms, a proportion that was closer to one-half of the membership in the 1960s. Turnover after a first or second term has risen by a mere 5 percent of the members.

The thrust for more competition and more turnover will probably come from the national party agencies. Republicans have already moved in this direction, aided by the availability of substantial funds. Republican congressional and senatorial campaign committees have increasingly subordinated themselves to their party's national committee, principal holder of the organizational purse. Republican recruiters have aggressively sought out and funded attractive local political talent, even in predominantly Democratic districts. Considering their disastrous losses in the post-Watergate midterm elections of 1974, Republicans have since done well in holding their losses and gains to long-term averages in both midterm and presidential years. They also make no secret of their efforts to integrate the work of their national agencies.

Whether Democrats will be able to integrate their national organizations for similar party objectives will depend less on the availability of funds than on modifying the states–rights and decentralizing propensities that characterize the leaders in the party. For many Democrats, national intervention into local, including congressional, races is anathema, loyalty oaths and recent party nationalizing rules notwithstanding. For these

Democrats, "national" is a euphemism for constraint and uniformity, unpopular in a party which is proud of its diversity and its obstreperous minority and local factions. It will probably require a series of costly defeats and a party "backlash" against the public relations and other intruders upon traditional party functions to motivate Democratic leaders to gather up the reins of their organization in new ways in order to create a team more capable of winning.

A more fundamental question is whether the Party-in-the-House and the Party-in-the-Senate can ever unite as a Party-in-Congress and as the principal center of direction of the national agencies of the party. In certain respects, this development would reflect the manner of parliamentary parties elsewhere. Could the Party-in-Congress some day, for example, coordinate its components in both houses sufficiently to be the decisive influence at the national nominating conventions? Could the national committee and its chairmanship be composed in such a way as to be brought regularly into line with the policies and strategies of the Party-in-Congress? Can a system be devised that would place a "loyal opposition" spokesperson at the head of the Party-in-Congress in the wake of a lost presidential contest? Coming from another direction, can the presidential wing and the national convention reform themselves sufficiently to exercise a more comprehensive and constitutionally responsible influence over the Democratic Party-in-Congress? Such questions will undoubtedly be more frequently asked in the near future.

Answers to some of these questions may be implicit in recently proposed reforms. The McGovern-Fraser and the O'Hara commissions explicitly advocated a more centralized party structure, with the congressional districts serving as the base of the national organizational hierarchy. This change could conceivably be a first step in the coordination of congressional, senatorial, and presidential units of representation within the party suggested in the previous chapter. It would also provide the party's nominees with campaign-ready organizations in the districts.

A serious effort to organize at the congressional district

level would lend new significance to the perennial proposal to extend the term of representatives to four years, to be elected in the presidential years. This modest constitutional amendment would have important consequences for party organization. The most obvious would be the reduction by half in the campaign funds required for House races. As suggested earlier, the congressional district, despite its possible decennial change in size and shape, would become the basic grassroots unit of party organization. Integration of campaign effort at the district level would promote joint campaign activity and close coordination between the congressional and national committees, bringing economies of effort and funds. Voter response to party conduct in Congress and in the presidency would have greater political connection, a consequence that may disturb those dedicated to the principle of the separation of powers. But this closer congressional-presidential connection in the voters' perception would undoubtedly make for greater congressional participation in the platform and the nominating work of the national conventions.

Another perennial proposal with potentially profound consequences for the Party-in-Congress and the national party organization generally is the plan to terminate the electoral college and have a direct popular election of the president and vice president. If every citizen's vote were to count equally with every other, national parties would have to direct their campaign appeals to each and every voter. Under the present electoral college system, nominees may conserve their campaign resources by choosing to campaign primarily in those states where they have important constituencies. Under a system of direct popular elections, however, the presidential campaign would need to create grassroots organizations capable of reaching all 100,000 precincts. Either that or forego party organization entirely in favor of campaigning through the mass media. These two unsatisfactory extremes could be avoided if joint congressional-presidential organizations were in place at the local level, enabling the two campaigns to complement each other.

Other schemes appear to move toward a national-congressional organizational bonding. For example, the 1974 Democratic Charter expanded the membership of the national committee to 350. If another eighty-five members were added and a new method for selecting the 435 were developed, representation on the new national committee could be somehow related to organization in the 435 congressional districts. This assumes that each district would have a year-round party staff, serve as the basic unit for selecting delegates to the national conventions, and more actively submit statements of policy concern for use in party platforms, campaigns, and congressional legislation.

Such changes are also bound to bring the work of the congressional campaign committee and the Democratic caucus into much closer harmony, making for party programs that are better coordinated and more politically sensitive to constituency needs and preferences.

THE PRESIDENTIAL PARTY

The 538 members of the electoral college are the official presidential constituency. Each state's voters choose as many electors as there are members in the state's delegation to the two houses of Congress. For example, if a state has a delegation of twenty congressmen and two senators, it will have twenty-two electoral votes. A plurality of the popular vote in a state elects a party's entire slate of electors. An absolute majority in the electoral college elects a party's nominees for president and vice president. Thus, an American presidential nominee has a distinct constituency, requiring a "presidential party" organized to campaign in a presidential party-in-the-electorate. This presidential party does what it can to bring together the activities of the national nominating convention and all the national, state, and local units of the party that are scattered about by the federal system and the separation of powers.

Organizationally, the national convention is presumed to be the supreme unit of the national party, yet it has no directive power over the Party-in-Congress and, prior to the 1950s, even less influence over state party organizations. The national convention meets quadrennially to select the presidential slate, adopt a platform, review the organization and procedures of the party, and select a national committee to function as the party's permanent agency between conventions.

Until recently, the state delegations to the national convention selected their representatives—one man and one woman—to the national committee. The 1974 charter added the state party chairperson and the highest ranking state officer of the opposite sex. The charter allocated additional members apportioned according to the same rules applying to the apportionment of national convention delegates. To this were added representatives of other party groups, such as the Democratic Governors' Conference, party leaders from the Senate and the House, and others. The 350-member national committee is more a convention than a committee.

The national committee elects a national chairman, who is usually someone associated with the presidential nominee. The chairman's task is to maintain the operation of a permanent national headquarters in Washington. If the nominee for president loses the election, his national chairman may be replaced by someone supported by a new coalition of factions.

In the time between the national convention and election day, a presidential campaign organization is created that is usually an expanded version of the nominee's preconvention campaign organization. The nominee's campaign team is often a group apart from the formal party structure. The campaign is usually run by the nominee's most trusted political colleague (who, in earlier times, was also the nominee's national party chairman). In recent years, public relations and technical staffs have had larger campaign roles than party regulars.

A major task of this short-lived campaign organization is to bring together the nominee's defeated opponents for the nomination, the party regulars who may be less than enthusiastic about the ticket, and his own loyal followers—all soon enough to allow time for convincing the electorate to support the ticket on election day. The content and style of the campaign, the media through which the nominee's message will be communicated, the constituencies to which appeals for support will be directed, the overall strategy and the daily tactics, and the responses to the opposition must be planned and implemented. In the end, each nominee will have in effect fashioned his own presidential party, including the coalition of national convention delegates who nominated him, the national committee and its chairman who presumably will support his campaign and his administration (if elected), and the campaign organization that works to reunite all Democrats and get them to the polls.

Perhaps the weakest link in a presidential party is the titular status of the presidential nominee, particularly if he is defeated in the election. A defeated presidential nominee has no legal or traditional basis for continuing to serve as the leader of a loyal opposition, a familiar and official position in many parliamentary systems. In their efforts to keep the Democratic party together while it was the out-party, leaders like Martin Van Buren, August Belmont, Samuel J. Tilden, William Jennings Bryan, and Adlai Stevenson did their best to serve as the party spokesman and to increase popular awareness of the need for an opposition leader. Their difficulties—lack of legitimacy and funds, disregard by adversary factions within the party, lack of a coherent out-party program of public policies, etc.—in many respects supports the argument for such a position. A major argument favoring the present system is that the absence of a formal opposition leader enables the out-party to find new leaders and new constituencies more readily.

The elimination of the century-old two-thirds nominating rule in 1936 and the election of Truman in 1948 opened the way for major changes in the party's national convention. By reducing the probability that majority coalitions would be frustrated by a one-third minority, new and more fluid coalitions were made possible. Battles shaped up over which of the constituencies should be recognized as the party's most significant. Disagreement arose over whether recognition and representation should remain with the party's established constituencies or be given to emergent constituencies that hold promise of future support for the party. The issue was whether to stick with the reliable customers or solicit the new.

At the conventions of 1948 and 1952, this issue became entangled with President Truman's civil rights program. Should the party give recognition to the reliable, all-white Solid South and its discriminatory system of electoral politics or to the emergent political aspirations of black citizens arriving in pivotal northern cities? President Truman, Mayor of Minneapolis Hubert Humphrey, Americans for Democratic Action, and northern liberals generally preferred the new constituency.

The southern leadership, determined to retain a major role in the party, tried, unsuccessfully, to reinstitute the two-thirds rule, to modify the 1948 civil rights plank, and, finally, to prevent Truman's election. To achieve the latter, they bolted the party's nominees in favor of a States-Rights Dixiecrat ticket. In Alabama they were able to keep the Truman-Barkley ticket off the ballot entirely. This led four years later to the adoption of a loyalty pledge by the national convention requiring each delegate to give assurance that he or she would exert "every honorable means" to make certain that the nominees of the convention would appear on his or her state's election ballot under the name and emblem of the Democratic party.

The 1952 loyalty pledge fight inaugurated three decades of change in national party rules and procedures. In its report to the 1956 national convention, the national committee's Special Advisory Committee on Rules proposed twelve new rules that laid on state parties full responsibility for getting the national ticket onto the ballot, sending only "bona fide Democrats" to the national convention, and appointing representatives to the national committee who would publicly support the national ticket. Other rule changes sought to speed up preparatory work for the convention, to provide ways to fill vacancies on the ticket, and to deal with other technical issues.

At the 1964 convention, the seating of the regular delegation from Mississippi was challenged by a predominantly black delegation on grounds that racial discrimination prevented black citizens from participating in party affairs. A compromise, rejected by both delegations, included provision for a Special Equal Rights Committee of the national committee to help states give voters the opportunity to participate in party affairs "regardless of race, color, creed or national origin."

The 1968 national convention took place amidst urban riots, campus protests, antiwar demonstrations, and the assassinations of Martin Luther King, Jr., and Robert F. Kennedy. In pursuing his candidacy, Senator Eugene McCarthy challenged as unrepresentative those delegations selected in some states as long as two years before the national convention rather than in the more current year of the convention. This was another version of the choice between previous and future constituencies. The national convention responded by urging state parties to send delegates to the 1972 convention who were chosen in 1972, by abolishing the antiminority unit rule (long out of practice in most states), and by establishing the McGovern-Fraser Commission on Party Structure and Delegate Selection and the O'Hara Commission on [Convention] Rules.

The McGovern-Fraser Commission recommended eighteen guidelines for national convention delegate selection. Among the guidelines: publication by state parties of written rules for delegate selection; prohibition of the unit rule at all stages of delegate selection; adequate notification of all public meetings; prohibition of proxy voting; a quorum of 40 percent required of all party committees participating in the delegate selection process; a limit of 10 percent in the number of delegation members chosen by state party committees; no ex officio seats on the delegation for public or party officials; and, in states using the convention system for delegate selection, the choice of at least 75 percent of the delegation from congressional district or smaller constituencies. Most importantly, state parties and presidential candidates were called upon to take "affirmative action" to assure minority representation on their delegations "in reasonable relationship to the groups' presence in the population of the state." Minority representation was *not* to be accomplished by mandatory quotas.

The ambiguous terminology of the affirmative action requirement touched off a decade-long controversy. The dilemmas of the requirement were vividly demonstrated in the course of the McGovern candidacy in 1972. Older, perhaps more conservative, delegates who had long served the party (for example, Mayor Daley and his delegation from Chicago) were shunted aside by newer, less-experienced minority delegates (in this case, the Jesse Jackson delegation), with all the bitterness that such actions engender. The McGovern candidacy, using the affirmative action and other commission guidelines, carried on seating controversies in twenty-one delegations. In the ensuing general election, it was evident that many offended Democrats stayed home or voted for Richard Nixon.

The O'Hara Commission brought in a host of recommendations dealing with convention management: apportionment of representation among the states, designation of hotel facilities by lot, regional public hearings by the platform committee, the elimination of favorite-son nominations, and other rules intended to speed the convention's work and compel clear decisions on the issues before it. The O'Hara recommendations urged a tightening of the party's loose organizational structure: enactment of a party charter; formal memberships; a national organizational structure *with congressional district committees at the base*; regular midterm national policy conferences; a national party executive committee to include the national committee chairman, Senate and House leaders, regional chairpersons, state and local representatives, and an elected general party chairman. Members of the House Democratic caucus and representatives of organized labor were uneasy about the latter recommendation, and the 1972 convention put it off for later consideration. The shelving of the O'Hara Commission organizational recommendations may, in a perverse way, be a compliment to their merit. They will surely be resurrected when the party leadership again confronts the party's structural handicaps.

The 1972 national convention came at the end of a generation of effort to improve the representativeness of the Democratic party and strengthen its capacity for disciplined and responsible decision-making. Dislocations were inescapable during so much change, particularly when exploited by the McGovern candidacy. On the one hand, the party and the McGovern candidacy reached out to incorporate hitherto low participation constituencies: blacks, Hispanics, youth, and women. On the other hand, the older and most loyal constituencies—labor, city machines, party regulars—were dealt with harshly. On the issues of the day (welfare, busing, crime, etc.), the 1972 delegates also placed themselves a substantial distance to the left of the party's electorate. Somehow, the search for representativeness seemed to be leading the party up a dark alley.

Yet another commission was created by the 1972 convention: a new Commission on Delegate Selection and Party Structure, chaired by City Councilwoman Barbara Mikulski of Baltimore. The convention also created a Charter Commission, headed by former Governor Terry Sanford of North Carolina, to write a draft charter for the party and to convene a midterm conference in 1974 to consider the draft. Both the charter and the midtern conference were first-time innovations. Another significant step in 1972 was the adoption of a resolution asserting the national party's claim to primacy over state party organizations and state laws. The nationalization of the party was making progress.

On December 6, 1974, the Midterm Conference on Democratic Party Organization and Policy met in Kansas City. The proposed charter brought together in a single document most of the organizational and procedural changes instituted during the preceding two decades. Rules for national convention delegate selection were much as the McGovern-Fraser Commission had prescribed. The controversial affirmative action provisions were broadened and refined. For example, representation of minorities was to be based not on their "presence in the Democratic electorate" but on the general population of the state. The composition of the Democratic national committee was enlarged, as noted earlier. The executive committee of the national committee was given the responsibility for coordinating the congressional and presidential wings of the party. Regional caucuses were encouraged.

Special functions were assigned to three national councils: one on education and training, another on finance, and a third for adjudicating delegate-selection disputes. For some, the charter was the end of a long journey; for others, only a beginning.

By 1976, it was time for review. After the election, the national committee put together a Commission on Presidential Nomination and Party Structure. Its chairman was a former chairman of the state party in Michigan, Morley Winograd. The object was to determine the effects of the recent party reforms and to do so on the basis of the best evidence available.

The Winograd Commission discovered, for example, a radical decrease in the number of senators and representatives—perhaps the most knowledgeable and concerned of the party's leaders—who participated officially in the presidential nominating conventions. The commission tried to determine how closely the Democratic electorate was being represented in the national conventions. It therefore examined the socioeconomic attributes of voters in the Democratic primaries, assuming that this was where the "Democratic electorate" was to be found. The facts revealed that proportionally far fewer voters from minority groups showed up in Democratic primaries than supported the Democratic party in the general elections. Clearly, the party rules and the electoral realities were mismatched.

The Winograd Commission recommended increasing the size of delegations to include state party and elected officials, shortening the number of months during which delegate selection takes place, banning cross-over primaries, requiring primary states to set candidate filing deadlines for 30–90 days before the primary election, and other reforms.

Rule-making continued after the 1980 convention under the aegis of a commission headed by Governor James B. Hunt of North Carolina. The Hunt Commission favored limiting the primary season to three months, providing delegation seats for leading but uncommitted party and elected officials, diluting the provisions for binding delegates to constituency instructions, allowing candidates to approve which delegates would appear on their local slates, and other already established or slightly modified rules. Close observers of the rule-making trends could see a gradual return to stronger representation of party professionals and elected officials, that is, to the proven old rather than the sought-after new partisans.

FUTURE DILEMMAS OF NATIONAL PARTY ORGANIZATION

"Reorganization" is a common way of labeling the hiring-firing process. As ordinarily used in the context of party politics, the term refers to kicking out the losers in the last election and putting a new team in charge. When applied to structural changes, reorganization often means adding a position or a committee here and there. Rarely does party reorganization deal with fundamental bottom-to-top redesign of the executive structure and the functions and relations between them. Political parties rarely do what the Founding Fathers did at the Constitutional Convention in Philadelphia. In writing its current charter, the Democratic party engaged in this rare type of reorganization, most of which has yet to be implemented. The following discussion speaks of redesign dilemmas that are fundamental and comprehensive: how to coordinate the leaderships at the national level; how to cope with national factionalism; how to achieve representativeness; how to fund the growing costs; and how to communicate with the Democratic constituencies.

Coordinating the National Leaderships (Plural!)

Political party leaders, as the managers of government, cannot avoid having their party mirror the structure of the government. In the United States, however, the major parties have been more federal than the nation and more divided among their national units than the national branches of government. Yet, parties have the special obligation to serve as connectors between the separated branches and the different levels of governments. If political parties do not coordinate political and governmental leaders, who will? If political parties do not compile the agenda of current community problems and citizen concerns, who will? If political parties do not mobilize the leader-selection processes, who will? Intensified party competition, expanding party organization, and increasingly complex public problems have directed attention to these questions over the past forty years and will probably continue to do so over the next forty.

How can the Democratic party coordinate its national level organs? A widely acceptable institutional design is not readily available. Party leaders in the House of Representatives and the Senate are likely to protect their constitutional prerogatives and resources with the energy of a lioness defending her young. Titular leaders of the presidential party come in two extremes. In the presidency, the titular leader has both the opportunity and the resources to build a potent national party machine *if inclined to do so*. But why should a president bother? Why build a powerful organization that the president may not be able to control or that may be more petitioner than provider of political resources? At the other extreme is the titular leader who has just lost a presidential election. He has little opportunity, no resources, and few supportive party leaders with whom to mount a major opposition role in national politics.

The separated turfs of party leaders is not the only obstacle to national-level coordination. Dispersion of party influence has given leaders the political elbowroom needed for pulling together new coalitions in response to changing circumstances. The large number of routes to party or public office has afforded new leaders many opportunities for winning promotion in the system. Competition among leaders is also considered laudable; the greater the number who *must* listen to their constituencies, the better.

Some coordinating schemes have been tried. Most tend to be informal and extracurricular. In recent decades, for example, Congress, particularly the Senate, has been a major source of presidential timber, which has built-in coordinative consequences. When congressmen show up as delegates to the national conventions, they often play an integrative role by mediating antagonistic factions and providing policy input for the party's platform. Presidents and presidential aspirants are increasingly available to campaign for fellow-partisans in midterm congressional elections, a process that requires cooperation.

In the Stevenson years, the Democratic Advisory Council was created in the hope of bringing into consultation the titular leader, party leaders in Congress, and leaders at several levels of the federal system. The council concept had modest success despite the refusal of the Speaker of the House and the Senate Majority Leader to participate. A similar attempt was the national committee's Advisory Council of Elected Officials created in 1973. This council organized eight policy panels for the Kansas City midterm conference. To pick up the problem, the national committee's new executive committee, as prescribed in the 1974 Charter, currently has the responsibility for inventing an acceptable national coordinating mechanism.

Presidential-congressional coordination is further complicated by the Democratic preference for strong titular leaders. Woodrow Wilson and Franklin Roosevelt are the unforgettable models for presidential activism, although Truman, Kennedy, Johnson, and Carter were far from sedentary. The oft-told story has it that Dwight Eisenhower was elected in 1952 because the voters had been exhausted by years of Democratic activism; they chose repose. Even defeated titular leaders—Bryan, Smith, Stevenson, and Humphrey—created whirlpools of political activity as they simulated the role of Leader of the Loyal Opposition. To make matters more difficult, there are several combinations of party control that must be accommodated: the party in the presidency, but without party control of either house of Congress; president plus one house of Congress; president plus both houses of Congress; one house of Congress, but no president; two houses, without president.

Reconciling National Factions

Another problem facing presidential-congressional party coordination is factional politics, that is, the development of relatively enduring factions within the party. Factional politics are a subuniverse of party politics. Much of this book is the story of factional struggle within the party. Factions are often short-lived collaborations, organized around a single candidacy, a single election, or a single issue. Others are more enduring.

The early factions in the Democratic party tended to be regional and enduring: North, South, Old West. Prior to the Civil War, disaffected factions were more likely to bolt the party than to remain. Policy factions began to acquire some durability during and after the Civil War, often as overlays on regional considerations; the War (East) versus Peace (Midwest); tariff protectionists versus reductionists; Gold versus Silver, etc. Leadership factions are perhaps best illustrated by the divisions surrounding Van Buren, Andrew Johnson, Tilden, Cleveland, Bryan, and Wilson.

Since the revolt against Speaker Cannon in 1910, and particularly during the New Deal, enduring factions have tended to gather along liberal-conservative ideological lines. The elimination of the two-thirds rule and the decline of the southern wing speeded this trend. Liberals appeared as Americans for Democratic Action and the congressional Democratic Study Group. Moderates established a Coalition for a Democratic Majority. Democratic voters during the 1970s classified themselves in a three-way split on the ideological spectrum: slightly more than a third conservative, slightly less than a third liberal, and the rest middle-of-the-road.

Factions will assuredly continue to operate within the Democratic party and probably become more institutionalized. As factions acquire long-term organizations, regular memberships, and cohesive issue orientations, they will carry on sustained contests on nominations, programs, procedures, and whatever issues the political occasion demands.

One of the most disruptive strategies of factional politics is the decision of a minority faction to bolt and form a third party or simply to stay at home on election day. To avoid this, factional reconciliation has been handled in a number of ways: a place on a balanced ticket, recognition in the campaign or in an administration, or a share in the distribution of patronage. Factional disenchantment has occurred frequently enough in recent decades to suggest that the more decisive and threatening the victory of the majority faction, the more likely the losing faction is to bolt (the Dixiecrats in 1948) or stay at home (Democratic regulars and moderates in 1972). In the future, if factions become more organized—acquire names, maintain headquarters, adopt programs, and develop procedures—new methods of reconciling factions will need to be developed.

The future development of factions within the Democratic party is likely to be influenced more by circumstances outside the party than within. The direct popular election of the president, unless qualified by special majority-rule requirements, would probably lead to plurality victories and a multiplication of factional defections. Regional primaries or the general extension of the system of primary elections could promote the development of regional as well as national factions. If the two major parties become closely competitive in all states, as seems to be the long-term trend, factional competition within the parties is likely to intensify. If the party takes on transnational party attachments, as described in a later chapter, factions may attach themselves to different transnationals. Enduring party factions will of course bring a host of consensus problems.

Competition between the major parties is most visible and influential in presidential politics. However, interparty competition is likely to spread to constituencies at all levels: congressional, state, and local. Intensified competition will require more campaigning and increased organization. As party operations become year-round, as growing numbers of competitive districts have to be coordinated, and as financial and other resources have to be regularized, it will become

increasingly important to maintain permanent party headquarters, full-time professional staffs, and reliable lines of
communication and political intelligence at all levels of the
party. This will require more skill, money, and people.

Achieving Institutional Representativeness

One organizational concern will remain the same, perhaps with new twists. As changes occur, as new political
circumstances appear, and as the Democratic party becomes
more institutionalized, party leaders will ponder the dilemmas inherent in the representation of its constituencies.
Representativeness has almost always been a fundamental
concern of party leaders, periodically reaching crisis proportions, as in the 1970s.

Should a criterion of apportionment of units of representation, hence decision-making power, within the party be
electoral performance (bonus votes for success in previous
elections) or some form of outreach into new voting populations (minimum number of seats for all districts or for particular groups)? Stated somewhat differently, should
apportionment favor reliable traditional constituencies (labor,
certain religious groups, etc.) or entice emergent ones (youth,
Hispanics, women, blacks, etc.)?

How should the significant differences between Democrats who vote in party primaries and those who vote in the
general elections be accounted for in the system of
representation?

In a highly mobile electorate, how should the interests
of the residentially migrant Democrats be reconciled with those
of more settled residents? This issue may be complicated by
new technologies in election administration. It requires no
great futuristic imagination to anticipate a time when voters
will be registered nationally (as credit-card holders now are),
present registration cards at the polls that match their sig-
natures and other identification information with that in the

national data bank, and possibly cast their ballots by interactive computers or telephone devices. Would facilitation of voting administration bring more Democrats—those inveterate stay-at-homes—to the polls? While it may become easier to monitor voter changes-of-address, how will the movers be represented in party affairs? And at what cost to the party if they are not adequately represented?

How should new factions coming up behind new leaders and issues be accommodated without casting aside the older factions? Behind this question lie age-old issues of generational differences in experience, perception, assessment, and ambition. No human organization can endure and thrive without the renewal that must come through the recruitment of new leaders. Nor can an organization preserve its traditional values and goals without the knowledge acquired from the struggles and experience of previous leaders. For a political party that prides itself in its adaptability, this dilemma may become extreme in the twenty-first century for several reasons: the need to find leaders who can keep political pace with rapid technological and social change; the diminishing size of the pool of young leaders and the increasing longevity of the older ones; the disappearance of the wise generalists in party politics and the growing tendency toward specialization, expertise, and compartmentalization; and, perhaps most threatning of all, the rise of new centers of political leadership in competing institutions (the media, interest groups, political action committees).

Funding the Financial Costs

When the National Conservative Political Action Committee (NCPAC) sent $1,873,000 in support of Ronald Reagan in 1980 and over $3.5 million to unseat Democratic liberals in the 1982 midterm races, the role of PACs in electoral politics became a worrisome public issue. Party leaders were worried long before this. Financial contributions that had previously gone into party coffers were beginning to go to the PACs. The amounts are awesome: a total of $190 million to Republican PACs and $29 million to Democratic PACs in 1982. The conservative NCPAC alone raised over $10 million, with a half dozen similarly conservative PACs doing almost as well. The most a liberal PAC could raise was the $2.4 million of the National Committee for an Effective Congress.

Channeling campaign contributions through the PACs debilitates the political parties. Individual candidates receiving PAC money can ignore party needs. Party operations lose much-needed operating money that could serve the interest of the entire party slate. PACs need not account to any political constituency other than their donors. While money—along with volunteer effort and votes—may be a legitimate political resource in a democracy, publicly undisclosed or unaccountable money is not. Party leaders, even those timid about offending the PACs that support them, must eventually confront the questions of disclosure and public accountability of PAC money. How, for example, can a party harness these funds for the general good of the party?

In many respects, PAC funding of party nominees is a form of trademark theft. The Democratic party name, emblem, and nomination, for example, carry goodwill, group endorsements, assured votes, and other forms of support that are invaluable. If the parties were private corporations, there would be a specific dollar value placed on their trademarks and the public goodwill earned by their name and reputation. Also, if the parties were private corporations, they would sue any perpetrators of encroachments on their trademarks. Party leaders do not usually think in terms of trademarks or law suits, but this is an aspect of fundraising that must eventually gain their attention. If a party's leaders do not fulfill their responsibility to defend valuable party property, in this instance, the trademark, who will?

What political parties do that PACs cannot do is to nominate candidates for public office. As in the case of the party emblem as trademark, what is a party nomination financially worth? A valuable party nomination that is subverted by campaign resources contributed from nonparty sources is—as is the party emblem—a diminished or stolen property. Leaders who fail to protect their party's nominations are wasting a resource and may be considered negligent in their organizational duties.

The Democratic loyalty pledge battles of the 1950s show how difficult it is to design ways of protecting what belongs to the party: its name and emblem, its right to a place on the ballot, its nomination, and its expectation of loyal support from its own officials. Protective impulses along these lines require a strong sense of the individual and collective benefit that can be derived from the successes of the party as a whole. Getting the competing interests within the party to give something up for this collective good may be as difficult as trying to overcome the competitive escalation of an arms race; self-defense usually seems much more important than collective defense. In both situations—political self-interest and military self-defense—it may require some kind of crisis and certainly a special kind of leadership to demonstrate that the collective interest should be given primacy.

Whether funded by private PACs and similar sources or by grants from the public treasury, the Democratic party will increasingly need to consider by what formula it should "represent" money in its system of representation. Today and well into the future, passing out cold cash in the lobbies is hardly likely to be an acceptable method of influence. Nor will informal "understandings" about the purpose of giving contributions pass muster. Studies of the impact of financial contributions on party behavior indicate that access—the opportunity to communicate with an elected public officer—is perhaps the main consequence. Of course, communication is itself a not-too-subtle form of influence. Communication associated with financial contributions should perhaps become a more explicit and systematic process, a goal that is only partially achieved by the current rules for public disclosure of campaign contributions.

One possible solution may be to combine the issues of

funding and representativeness is some explicit way. To illustrate (rather than to suggest), assume that a pool of, say, 350 national nominating convention votes (in a total of 3,500) is set aside for award to groups or persons in proportion to their contributions to the party over the preceding quadrennium. Assume that one major PAC has contributed 10 percent of the total given to the party over this specific period. This PAC would receive 35 votes in the convention; if not in the nominating convention, then perhaps in a midterm or other convention dealing exclusively with the party platform. This example is not presently realistic, but it does illustrate an approach.

Extension of public funding of the parties is highly likely over the next decades. The circumstances are compelling. The costs of campaigning are mounting rapidly. The notion that only the rich can participate in electoral politics is unacceptable. The advantages of incumbency—and it would be incumbents who vote for public funding—are too precious to lose. The rationale is more than sufficient. The parties are, after all, public services in a broad sense.

Several principles should prevail in any system of public funding for the parties. The goal should be to provide a minimum of party service for all parts of the electorate:

—Funding of year-round party activities should be separated out from funding for election campaigns. The components of year-round support should be clearly identified, for example, salaries for specific official positions, rent, newsletter publication costs, etc.

—While there should be no ceiling on private contributions to either the year-round organization or to particular contributions to either the year-round organization or to particular campaigns, a standard minimum in public funds should be granted to all year-round party organizations meeting specific requirements.

—No funds should be awarded to individual candidates for public office. Money should go only to certified party committees, with a requirement for public audits of these accounts.

It is asking a great deal to strive for the legitimization of public funding of party functions. In the United States, politicians and political money are suspect almost by definition. It is also a favorite posture of candidates to charge their opponents with unsavory financial connections. This is not the place to argue the merits of this way of campaigning or monitoring party finance. What is certain is that the charges and countercharges reinforce the public's suspicions and skepticism. It may well be that a sound system of public funding of the parties could dissipate the suspicions and help place the matter of party funding in a more positive light.

Communicating with the Constituencies

The traditional pillars of a democratic society are an informed citizenry and free discussion; hence, the strong commitment of democracies to public education and a free press. Since their inception some three-hundred years ago, modern political parties have been among of the most important vehicles for conducting civic education and discussion about public issues. In addition, the parties have been the principal recruiters and presenters of public leaders. If these were the only functions of parties, it would suffice to confirm that parties are vital institutions of public communication, deserving of ample public support to maintain this function.

What does this mean in a practical sense? The ramifications of the question are many and profound. If the citizenry were to review the services rendered it by the communicative activities of the parties, the public's obligation to the parties would be irrefutable. Admitting the biases and distortions inherent in competitive party campaigning, the parties do inform the citizenry of the salient problems before the community and the available options for resolving them. In their use of patriotic and ideological language and symbols, the parties reinforce basic community values and keep alive the sense of community itself. By closely monitoring and reporting the public and private conduct of their opponents, the parties in a democracy, as compared to most communities in the world, are able to keep corruption to a minimum and compel governmental responses to public problems.

If the parties were to review their responsibilities for sustained communication with the citizenry, it would become clear that more and better communication is essential. One question pertains to the relations between party and press. How can the parties regain their capacity to communicate directly with the citizenry, without going through the too-often distorting filter of the press? Should the parties return to the semi-official party newspapers of the early years of the Republic? In addition to newspapers, should the parties take on the ownership of cable television stations? Should the new communication technologies—from computer modems to videoconferencing—be incorporated into the party's network of media? How can any or all of this become self-financing?

The organizational needs and dilemmas of the Democratic party are many and challenging. These dilemmas require data, analysis, and careful deliberation. Panaceas and from-the-hip solutions are costly forms of trial-and-error. The knowledge and talent for developing a successful strategy of reorganization are available. The Democratic party needs to find the leadership, collective self-interest, and courage to employ them.

NINE

Reconstructing the Constituencies: Traditional and Contemporary

In a constitutional democracy such as the United States, political parties are representative institutions made up of competing coalitions of constituencies. Achieving representativeness, putting together winning coalitions, and organizing constituencies is not easy work. But it *is* the highest civic calling in any political system, particularly in democracies. In the United States, as in most democracies, the job of political management requires of leaders consummate skill and patience, despite the press' frequent caricature of party politics as a soap-selling business. Party leadership also depends fundamentally upon self-conscious, organized constituencies.

If a party is a coalition of constituencies, then its leaders must be interested in the strengths and weaknesses of their constituencies. American party leaders have an important stake in how well-led and well-organized a supporting constituency is and they often help their constituencies in this respect, for it is essential for a powerful coalition and party success. For example, unions had relatively modest influence in national politics before the party's leaders stepped in; that is, before the Wagner Act and other New Deal legislation gave them rights and opportunities that enabled organized labor to become a major constituency in the Democratic party and a major power in the country. Franklin D. Roosevelt understood the strategy of constructing and reconstructing constituencies, and he carried it forward successfully.

Examining, diagnosing, and helping to cure the organizational and programmatic difficulties of party constituencies is an important aspect of the party leader's job. In the case of Democratic party leaders, the 1980s are the beginning of a time when a fifty-year-old coalition seems to be falling apart and traditional constituencies are diminishing in size and power. The Democratic trends sometimes leave one wondering if the party is going to make it to its bicentennial. What is happening to the traditional Democratic constituencies? With what probable consequences? And what can the party leaders do about it?

Some constituencies have been Democratic in varying degrees most of the time. These may be called the traditional constituencies, mainly labor, farmers, and immigrants (the latter usually referred to by election analysts as ethnic and nationality minorities). Other Democratic constituencies—substantial blocs of voters—are relatively new to the fold: blacks, women, youth, and seniors. Finally, there are some constituencies that have yet to bloom and be gathered; these are constituencies of the future. What will be the relationship of each of these to the Democratic party over the next two or three generations?

REPAIRING THE TRADITIONAL CONSTITUENCIES

Labor, farmers, and immigrants just "ain't what they used to be" as basic elements of the Democratic coalition. They are fewer and less loyal.

Labor

Labor has never been a homogeneous group in American politics. After all, whoever is employed—whether ditch-digger or doctor—is presumably a worker. The unemployed are also workers, but without income-producing work. The range of political behavior among workers is equally varied.

In the first days of the Republic, most working people were engaged in agriculture. More will be said about them shortly. But in that era, those who spoke of "workers" had in mind the craftsmen, shipbuilders, dock hands, merchants' helpers, and others who were mainly employed in eastern seaboard towns and cities such as New York, Norfolk, and Boston. Many workers in the early nineteenth century were also recent immigrants, not particularly welcomed by native workingmen (themselves descendants of recent immigrants).

What little organization these early workers had usually took the form of fraternal associations such as the Society of St. Tammany. Social comaraderie led to political awareness and to participation in patriotic societies, but not always in elections. In most states, unpropertied workers did not acquire the vote until the 1820s, when leaders such as Martin Van Buren and the Nashville politicians who promoted the candidacy of Andrew Jackson promptly solicited the electoral support of the new constituency. Van Buren drew the Albany Regency and Tammany Hall, by now predominantly an Irish working-class organization, more closely together. In 1828 and 1832 the great coalition of eastern labor and southwestern frontiersmen surged to the polls to elect Jackson as the Democratic party's first "people's" president.

Within a single generation, Van Buren and the Democratic party became confused and divided over the issue of free labor versus slave labor. The Democratic party began splitting on the slavery issue. Black freemen and escaped slaves were finding their way into the northern labor market, competing with older, native workers and the new immigrant labor. After straddling the issue of slavery during his presidency, Van Buren left the party and came down on the side of free soil, that is, an end to slavery. Northeastern workers worried whether this meant that ex-slaves would remain in the South or come north in greater numbers. By the later 1840s, black workers in the Northeast were listening to a new champion, the Whig editor of the *New York Tribune*, Horace Greeley. Ex-slaves in cities like New York were beginning to vote against Democrats as the party of racist immigrant laborers, the southern aristocracy, and opponents of abolition.

By the late 1850s, the Democratic party was losing its labor constituents, both black and white, to the new and radical Republican party. The offspring of northern Whig, Free Soil, and other abolitionist parties, the Republican party was clear about its hostility to slavery and, faintly echoing the new Marxist theories imported from revolutionary Europe, angry about capitalist exploitation of northern workingmen. During this decade, with the expansion of railroad-building, manufacturing, mining, and various trades, and with a sharp increase in immigration, the ranks of labor were swelling and the number of farmers had begun its long-term relative decline. Tiny craft unions, numerous fraternal organizations, and incipient Marxist parties could be seen here and there. The Democratic party's labor constituents could most often be found following the local guidance of urban political machines, loyal to the local candidates but uncertain as a source of support for the party's national ticket (then as now).

Civil War and Reconstruction brought industrialization, contract labor (hiring and importing foreign workers at extremely low wages), severe depressions, high unemployment, the founding of the secretive Knights of Labor, the establishment of the American Federation of Labor, strikes, strike-breaking state militia, northern and southern Democrats reunited as a national party, and a rising sense that the federal government should have a significant role in the nation's economic affairs. It took another seventy years to implement the latter view in the Full Employment Act of 1946.

It should have been a Democratic era. But a Democratic president (Cleveland) turned out to be a strike-breaker, a friend of Wall Street, and the incumbent during a catastrophic depression. When William Jennings Bryan repudiated strike-breaking, gold, and Wall Street in 1896, it was too late. Workingmen joined farmers and capitalists behind the Republican banner, skillfully wooed by Republican National Chairman Mark Hanna and, later, by Theodore Roosevelt during his terms in the presidency.

Unionists and other wage-earners came back to the Democratic party as beneficiaries of Wilsonian policies. The new immigrants, once naturalized, began to vote for the party, particularly in support of Al Smith's candidacies and in response to nativistic tendencies in the South and elsewhere. Democratic city machines, at the height of their influence, continued to be essentially working-class service organizations and mobilizers.

By building significant pro-union legislation into his New Deal, Franklin D. Roosevelt assured that the Democratic party would have a powerful and enduring labor component in its coalition. Electorally, organized labor was at first a supplement to the city machines; later, an alternative. As one of the most important constituencies in the Democratic coalition, labor was impressively successful in helping elect Truman in 1948, punitive in 1972 when the AFL-CIO failed to endorse McGovern, and just held its own behind the candidacy of Walter Mondale in 1984.

This thumbnail review of the relationship between labor and the Democratic party suggests that when both are well-organized and mutually loyal, they are favored by political success, witness the Jacksonian and New Deal eras. Fundamental divisions between them or within either lead to political deserts: the Republican victory and Civil War in 1860; the floundering Bryan era between 1896 and 1912; the devastating internecine battles within the party during the 1920s. Is an era of decline in the influence of organized labor currently in the making? And what of the consequences for the Democratic party?

The most recent parting of the ways between unionists and the Democratic party began, ironically, in the late 1960s, with the defeat of one of organized labor's truest friends, Hubert Humphrey. Prior to 1968, approximately six or seven out of every ten union families regularly voted Democratic. The first important unionist defection was part of a "white backlash" against black demands; large numbers of blue-collar workers followed George Wallace into a third party. Unionists and their leaders, perhaps unwittingly, reinforced the process of defection by staying away from McGovern in 1972. They returned to support Carter in 1976 but left him in 1980. But vigorous union campaign drives in 1980 and 1984 did succeed in holding a 6-in-10 unionist vote for the Democrats, despite the pro-Reagan tide. The percentages, however, were misleading. The absolute number of unionists in the nation was decreasing, and votes are counted in absolute numbers, not in percentages.

The workers who knew where their interests would be best represented were the unemployed. Six-in-10 voted for Carter in 1980, 7-in-10 for Mondale four years later. The 8-to-9 million unemployed, however, are one of the lowest turnout constituencies in the electorate, hence one of the least attended-to constituencies.

What are some of the problems confronting organized labor and its relationship with the Democratic party in the decades ahead? Several have been indicated earlier. Others deserve mention here. The general trends present substantial challenges to both labor and Democratic leaders.

On the question of union membership, workers have been voting "no union" increasingly in collective bargaining elections. Between 1976 and 1981, unions lost 72 percent of the collective bargaining elections in large companies (those with more than five hundred employees) and 48 percent in smaller companies. The trend toward diminishing membership has been reflected in the decline in the absolute number and the proportion of organized workers in the labor force over the past decade. Adding insult to injury, antiunion management consultants have prospered to the point of becoming a specialized profession. Perhaps the situation requires new concepts of union membership as well as the more traditional organizing campaigns.

The politically "acceptable" level of unemployment has reached 7-8 percent, and is going up. Eight to 12 million unemployed, as currently counted in the official statistics, will undoubtedly be a permanent fixture of the economy over the next decades, particularly as the labor market becomes less national and more global in structure. The figures for the unemployed, it should be added, do not include discouraged workers who are no longer seeking employment, the underemployed, and those healthy and active retirees who are for all intents and purposes unemployed. The all-inclusive numbers become staggering and the social and economic consequences immeasurable. Unionizing these varieties of unemployed will require new assumptions about the nature of unions. Bringing these various parts of the labor constituency to the polls in support of Democrats will require a fresh look at the achievements of the city machines of old.

Blue-collar unionists, formerly the staunchest of Democrats, are becoming relatively fewer in the labor force and are approaching a 50-50 split in their party loyalties. Those who are regularly employed have acquired property, upper middle-class attitudes, skepticism about their union leaders, and a propensity to vote for Republicans now and then. It is not quite clear how similar their economic views are to those of Yuppies, but the comparison may provide significant data for the future political strategies of union and party leaders.

White-collar workers, increasingly better educated, include those who hold technical as well as clerical occupations. They are increasing in number and in their Republican leaning. They are destined to be the backbone of a computerized Information Society. Although many have attitudes usually associated with social consciousness, workers of this type are not natural recruits for a class-struggle, antiboss unionism. Party leaders and union leaders are likely to disagree for a long time about the best appeals to the white-collar occupations, particularly those in the public sector. The "hated" public official, or "boss," may well be an honest and faithful Democrat.

The reduction of the work week to twenty-five hours is a trend well on its way. Related practices—job-sharing and flexible hours—are already popular. The implications of so short a work week for the recreational and educational industries, now multibillion dollar enterprises, have yet to be thoroughly assessed from the perspectives of employment, unionization, and party affiliation. As we shall speculate below, entire new psychocultural constituencies may emerge from the realms of recreation and education, yet another challenge to the representativeness of the Democratic party.

New forms of worker-sharing of company income and management are developing. This trend is redefining, if not circumventing, the role of unions in labor-management relations. There are now at least five hundred companies in which employees are a majority of the stockholders, many more if holdings of 25–50 percent are included. The concept of adding union and public representatives to those of stockholders on corporate boards of directors is no longer novel and will grow in complexity as different patterns of worker-representation are adopted. The Japanese theory that employment in a company is a lifetime relationship, that is, the company as permanent employer, may well be a version of the American practice of seniority and tenure, the differences being in the modes of worker participation and responsibility. Adapting union practice and Democratic policies to these changes is likely to be a long and difficult process, particularly in the light of the American preference to do things on a case-by-case basis rather than in accordance with a comprehensive and integrated plan.

The growing corporate practice of establishing manufacturing plants overseas, where labor is unorganized and cheaper, may simply be a form of post-Civil War contract labor, this time taking the company to the cheap labor in its foreign location rather than bringing the cheap foreign workers to the United States. What will be the form of transnational union structure that can deal with the challenges of a world labor market, global unemployment, and collective bargaining with multinational corporations, sovereign foreign governments, and supranational political regimes?

President Reagan's personal image, political philosophy, and administration policies are no help to either the labor movement or the Democratic party. His personal identification with sports (as a former radio announcer and in his acting roles), heroic cowboys (in his movies), and good-guy roles generally have given him a lopsided majority among male voters that may have less personal and more long-term cultural implications for party politics than is ordinarily perceived. In earlier generations, military heroes and crusty frontiersmen were the models of American manhood. Athletes and entertainers may be taking their place, representative of a new kind of masculine constituency, particularly among the "working stiffs" belonging to unions. How should a union interested in politics or a political party with a labor constituency deal with this in their recruitment of leaders?

The Reagan philosophy is unabashedly for free enterprise, decentralization, antibureaucratic, and chauvinistically patriotic. This seems consistent with and reinforcing of the personal attributes just mentioned. As a former union president, he is unusually aware of the foibles as well as the strengths of union organization and leadership. His treatment of the Airline Pilots Association, which led to the demise of that union, set the context within which unions will be operating during the decade of the 1980s. His willingness to keep hands off business failures and unemployment among unprofitable enterprises has put unions on the defensive—more concerned about job security than wage increases, more eager to commit themselves to political friends than to pick-and-choose or remain aloof from the party process. The early prenomination AFL-CIO endorsement of Walter Mondale in 1984 was an experiment in labor-party relations that will continue to be assessed and reassessed, as it should be. Meanwhile, it may be some time before the labor movement recovers from the Reagan era.

All this is happening within the context of other major long-term social, economic, and political transitions to a postindustrial society in the United States. A postindustrial society is one in which technology has multiplied worker productivity well beyond the basic needs of the population. Such a society is expected to have automated factories, a highly skilled work force, and comprehensive industrial planning, which, combined, make the manufacture of goods a simple and relatively secondary concern. Productivity in many fields is limited only by the availability of natural resources and the tastes of the consuming public. Those who are in professional, technical, service, artistic, and information-processing occupations increase in numbers and general importance. Their products seem less tangible than those of the smokestack industries, yet no civilization could become postindustrial without them.

In the postindustrial society, work time takes fewer hours per week than leisure time. Entire industries develop around leisure. New demands are placed on education. Serial careers over a single lifetime become more common. The pace of technological change steps up. The drain on natural resources compels systematic conservation and motivates the search for synthetic and other alternatives, both becoming important new industries. These are but a few of the projected characteristics of a postindustrial society. The pace of change inevitably leads to a severe testing of ponderous social institutions and major social organizations such as unions and political parties.

The United States has been described as the first of the world's postindustrial societies. Its labor force is one of the most skilled in the world. Its high technologies are without peer. Its per capita productivity has been on a long-term rise for decades, with recent indications of a leveling off that, given the pace of American invention, may simply represent a pause before another rise. The tastes and consumption demands of Americans seem unlimited and are disseminating rapidly throughout the world.

In what ways will the trade unions adjust to postindustrial America? In what ways can the Democratic party help this traditional member of its coalition? The unions may well have to assume new functions, pay less attention to traditional functions, develop new modes of organizing themselves and of relating to business, politics, and the world. The Democratic party may well have to design legislation and allocate public resources so as to facilitate the union metamorphosis. Some of these changes are illustrated below.

Traditionally, American unions organize workers, represent them in collective bargaining with management on issues of wages and working conditions, and provide counsel in grievance proceedings. Unions are basically protective associations of workers. There is, of course, much more, but these are the predominant functions. The union posture toward management is fundamentally adversarial. With the looming employee ownership and participation in management, a cooperative posture will become more appropriate. Given traditional worker hostility to bosses and the organizational dynamics within most unions, the transition from contestant to partner will not be an easy one. Nor will it be easy for Democratic defenders of unionism to make a similar about-face other than in close tandem with the unions themselves.

The change in posture, however, may be facilitated by the manner in which unions respond to certain trends. As the high tech, leisure, educational, and service industries and occupations increase, unions will probably need to modify their approaches to craft and industrial unionism and assume many of the functions and styles of professional associations.

Examples of the problems arising from this shift may be found in union experience in organizing health professionals and university faculties. In the case of universities, faculties usually have significant management responsibilities, confounding the adversarial posture. The strike is relatively ineffectual and inappropriate. Individual faculty have great professional autonomy, making it difficult to achieve militancy and unity. In effect, at unionized universities, collective bargaining tends to blend into management decision-making, the latter requiring new styles of labor-management communication and cooperation.

Another factor favoring cooperative postures will be the high rate of job obsolescence and the high turnover in job-holding. Technological change brings change in occupations and job skills. Scores of occupations become obsolete each year or require skills and numbers of workers significantly different from previous requirements. For example, between 1900 and 1975, workers in agricultural occupations dropped from 38 to 4 percent of the labor force, blue-collars went from 36 to 34 percent, white-collars rose from 18 to 48 percent, and professionals increased from 4 to 15 percent. The rates of obsolescence and turnover can only increase in the future as the nation's pool of skills and careers stays abreast of the post-industrial Information Society. The trend will increasingly shake up union organizations based on stable categories of occupations.

If unions are to respond to the growing need in the working population for occupational training, job retraining, general education, and even preparation for the New Leisure, organized labor may have to take on large educational functions, in effect becoming an educational institution. To meet workers needs, unions may have to provide informational and training services directly. These services are too important to leave to others (schools, corporations, etc.), unless, of course, unions are willing to watch over their own obsolescence. The point is underscored by a 1984 Louis Harris poll that found that 49 percent of nonunion wage and salaried employees would be willing to pay $50 a year in dues to get a number of associational benefits: information on job openings and job training, group medical and dental insurance at reduced rates, discounts on consumer products, and legislative lobbying—a distinct departure from the traditional concept of unionism.

The basic fact is that the "working class" of the United States is not at all a homogeneous ideological class. American workers are union *members* who, like all rational consumers, want goods and services in return for their union dues. They are as disgruntled if they are burdened by a do-nothing dues-collecting union as they are by a miserly low-wage company. As economic enterprise in the United States moves from mass production industries into an age of diversity in the production of goods and services, the categories of labor organization also change, multiply, and develop distinctive needs and goals. Can unions keep up with the pace of change? Can the American labor movement continue to be a movement? Can the Democratic party ride out the turbulence in one of its principal constituencies, or will the party have to mobilize its labor vote by its own means? The answers to these questions will be slow in coming.

Farmers

The Federalists, under Hamilton's leadership, were dedicated to preserving the resources of creditors, establishing the new nation's currency, and facilitating the productivity and trade of several eastern seaboard crafts and industries such as shipbuilding. With nine-tenths of the populace living on family farms and plantations, had the Jeffersonians not taken up the cause of the nation's principal debtors (the farmers) others would have.

As it happened, Jefferson's concepts of limited government and personal freedom were highly compatible with the needs of the American farmers of his day. He helped elevate the family farm to its longstanding eminence as a major American ideal. If Jefferson were alive today, however, he would find it extremely difficult to believe that less than 3 percent of the American people now live on farms. He probably would understand the role of agribusiness; he was, after all, a plantation owner. He knew about farm workers, living, as he did, in a slave economy. As a scientist, he would relish the technological ingenuity that characterizes American agriculture.

Jefferson was also a successful politician. He would immediately recognize that the modern farm vote is no longer an electoral pillar for his party. *His* Democratic-Republican party did so well among farmers everywhere that it was overwhelmingly the majority party for more than two decades. Jackson added urban workers to the Democratic farm constituency and this coalition also prevailed. But Jacksonian experiments with the banking and credit system inadvertently brought on an agricultural depression that turned many farmers away from the party. Southern agrarians also began to leave the party during the 1850s, and particularly in 1860, over the issue of slavery. Thus not until the end of Reconstruction and the creation of the Solid South did the farm constituency again become a major component of the Democratic coalition.

From the 1880s through the New Deal, the Democratic party—or a major faction within it—was dedicated to cheap money and easy credit, the staples of the family farm. The land-grant college system and its accompanying farm bureaus flourished as the nation's great investment in agricultural technology. Democratic (and Republican) failure to accommodate this constituency drove farmers at different times into the Greenback, Populist, Free Silver, and Progressive parties.

Rural districts with little population were, and in many cases still are, overrepresented in Congress and state legislatures. Despite this, congressmen and state legislators rarely enacted farm policy that anticipated and prevented the economic crises of this highly competitive, high-risk sector of the nation's economy. Most presidents were equally remiss. In contrast, Woodrow Wilson responded to farmer distress by pushing through Congress such agrarian legislation as the Federal Farm Loan Act, the Rural Credits Act, and the Cotton Futures Acts. These were also important steps in his efforts to build an agrarian-labor-business coalition. During the 1920s, however, divided Democrats, minority Progressives, and disinterested Republicans did almost nothing about the decade's worsening farm economy. This farm crisis eventually became a major cause of the Great Depression of 1929–1933.

The New Deal solutions included limited production, easy farm credit, and price supports. New agencies were created with abandon: the Agricultural Adjustment Administration, the Farm Credit Administration, the Farm Mortgage Corporation, the great regional development program of the Tennessee Valley Authority, and so on. Small and medium-size farms were still numerous enough to be a significant constituency. Farmers responded appreciatively with Democratic votes and became a part of the New Deal coalition.

But by the 1960s the high cost of the farm price support programs, the rapid increase in the size and number of agri-businesses, and the drastic decline in the number of smaller family farms created a profound political dilemma for politicians generally and Democrats particularly: how to take away the benefits of a powerful constituency. Though this constituency was no longer numerous in voting strength or strategically located (the decline in farm families in overrepresented districts), it was very powerful through its lobbying organizations and campaign contributions (agribusinesses and their lobbies). It was difficult for Democrats to look for, let alone find, an answer. The deed was to be undertaken by a Republican—Ronald Reagan—devoted to free market economics.

United States agriculture accounts for more than a fifth of the nation's gross national product. American farms are one of the production wonders of the world, with continuing technological advances. Yet farmers operate under conditions of constant crisis that have still to be dealt with adequately: overproduction due to many producers in a highly competitive market; heavy borrowing amidst wide swings in interest rates; big risk-taking with respect to weather and soil conditions; vulnerability to fluctuations in exports caused by shifts in currency exchange rates and foreign agricultural conditions; and sudden changes due to consumer dietary preferences. Government purchase of surpluses, crop reduction, price support programs, preferential loan arrangements, and similar policies have ameliorated symptoms but have apparently failed to heal causes.

Motivated by budgetary rather than production considerations, the Reagan approach has been gradually to reduce farm support, to bring it down from its current $14 billion level to something closer to $5 billion. The Reagan administration would also lower the upper limit on crop loans. If this approach is implemented, distressed farmers—what few remain—may once again turn to the Democratic party for help. How much help would this be to the party, and vice versa?

This is another constituency that needs to reconstitute itself if it is to fit into a modern Democratic coalition. And it is also a case where the party needs to provide an innovative program that will facilitate such a constituency change. Much easier said than done. If current trends continue, as they are likely to, almost nothing may be left of this traditional constituency by the time Democrats come to its aid. Agribusinesses will continue to grow in number, size, technology, and financial capacity to absorb the risks. Small and medium-size farms—where Democratic votes are most likely to be found—will continue to go under as interest rates remain high, weather hazardous, land prices low, overproduction rampant, and price support programs reduced. Aquaculture and newly "designed" grains, fruits, vegetables, and livestock may require capital, equipment, and plant facilities of such magnitude as to sound the death knell of small farms in the United States. Who is going to prevent this, and should they? The family farm may become nothing more than a suburban avocation for those dedicated to fresh produce and meat.

Who will take the place of the disappearing Democratic-leaning small farmer? The answer is likely to be a new breed of farm worker. Until technology, particularly robotics, catches up, agribusiness and aquaculture will undoubtedly require substantial numbers of semiskilled and unskilled workers. These will probably be organized on an industrial union basis and tend to vote Democratic. In time, however, automated farm factories, aquaculture farms, and space farming will require substantial numbers of skilled and fewer semiskilled technicians, a trend that will not be favorable for Democrats. This changing farm constituency will surely be a continuing problem for the party, often placing Democrats in the position of apparently opposing or deterring technological advances in their efforts to represent and protect whatever farm constituency there is.

The specifications for a Democratic farm program over the next several decades will not be easy to design. How can a competitive farm economy be maintained within the framework of some system of national coordination and planning? Former systems of acreage quotas will have to be modernized to take into account new technologies and the tendency toward large-scale and oligopolistic agribusinesses. What new methods of crop insurance will better protect farmers from the ravages of weather, blight, environmental pollution, and energy shortages? Can a new specialized national banking system be created to cope with the special needs, interest rates, and risks associated with crop loans and farm mortgages? Perhaps a new concept of parity is needed which would correlate agrarian interest rates (rather than prices) with another economic index such as the wholesale price index. Perhaps agribusinesses will develop new ways of acquiring capital funds through the stock markets. Rather than purchasing whatever happens to be a surplus crop, the federal government may become a more regular purchaser of farm products for its Food-for-Peace and other foreign policy programs. Could similar governmental purchases channel agricultural products on a regular basis into the welfare system, e.g., benefits made up partly of food (in lieu of some proportion of food stamps) and partly of cash? In what new ways should American farm production be related to the global market? These questions merely hint at the complexity of United States farm issues. The challenge for Democrats as well as for the farm constituency is the preparation of a farm program directed toward the long-term development, stability, and prosperity of United States agriculture.

A closely related set of questions pertains to the probable emergence of a "politics of diet." This will arise from Americans' antipathy to the existence of hunger in the United States or abroad, increasing popular attention to healthful diet and the purity and quality of foods, and the widespread consumer interest in experimental cuisine. Agricultural producers and processors will undoubtedly have to respond not only to the data of the supermarket check-out registers but also to the growing volume of legislative and legal actions by consumer groups. In a politics of diet, the Democratic party will have opportunities to serve as honest broker among domestic interests. It will also be called upon to adjust the points of friction between United States agricultural interests and the overseas needs of a world still burdened by famine. There is manifestly much creative work ahead for the party on behalf of its farm and food constituencies.

Immigrants

The Democratic party has played a special role in the Americanization of immigrants ever since the founding of the Republic. In great part, this has entailed the points of entry into the United States, the early establishment of the party's urban machines, and the match between an immigrant's country of origin and that of former immigrants already in the United States. For example, New York City has been from the outset a—if not *the*—major point of immigrant entry into the United States. The Statue of Liberty and Ellis Island, great symbols of refuge and freedom, are, after all, located in New York harbor. Tammany Hall early became that city's principal

Democratic organization, dominated by Americans of Irish origin. The waves of Irish immigrants who came to the New World throughout the nineteenth and early twentieth centuries usually arrived in New York, were welcomed by their Irish relatives, were Americanized and naturalized with the help of the Tammany machine, and voted overwhelmingly Democratic until many of them became "lace curtain," that is, affluent and Republican. A similar pattern has prevailed among other immigrant groups: Italians, East European Jews, Poles, Hispanics, and others.

Population of and Immigration to the
United States

Period	Total Population at End of Period	Immigration for the Period
1776–1820	9,638,453	250,000 est
1821–1830	12,866,020	143,439
1831–1840	17,069,453	599,125
1841–1850	23,191,876	1,713,251
1851–1860	31,443,321	2,598,214
1861–1870	39,818,449	2,314,824
1871–1880	50,189,209	2,812,191
1881–1890	62,979,766	5,246,613
1891–1900	84,371,985	3,687,564
1901–1910	102,370,018	8,795,386
1911–1920	118,017,150	5,735,811
1921–1930	138,439,069	4,107,209
1931–1940	150,621,231	528,431
1941–1950	154,233,234	1,035,039
1951–1960	179,323,175	2,515,479
1961–1970	204,765,770	3,321,477
1971–1980	226,545,805	4,020,300

In the 1971–1980 period, 690,200 immigrants came from European countries, 1,452,400 from Asia, and 1,766,800 from the Americas.

Given its great land mass, wealth in natural resources, empathy for the oppressed of other lands, and Melting Pot heritage, the United States has over its two centuries as a nation (not counting the initial period of colonization during the seventeenth and eighteenth centuries) received and naturalized a major share of the world's migrants. The figures in the table above are impressive. Since 1820, when immigration data was first included in the census, 49,174,353 recorded immigrants have been admitted to the United States. The current rate of about a half million legally admitted immigrants and another half to one million "undocumenteds" clearly indicates that the nation continues to be a human magnet. What is different is the absence of local Democratic party organizations to serve as principal civic educators and electoral mobilizers of the newcomers.

At the time of the adoption of the Constitution most residents of the United States were of northern and western European descent. About 22 percent of the population were enslaved blacks from Africa. Of the estimated 10 million native Indians on the North American continent north of the Rio Grande River at the time of Columbus' discovery, an uncertain number were in the new republic at the close of the eighteenth century. Most of the Europeans were of English, German, Scotch, and Irish backgrounds. Most belonged to Protestant faiths. The extension of the suffrage during the 1820s brought large numbers of unpropertied Scotch-Irish into the Democratic-Republican party and in enthusiastic numbers to the polls to support their fellow-countryman, Andrew Jackson.

During and after the 1840s, millions began to arrive on American shores, most escaping the potato famine in Ireland or fleeing poverty and revolution in Germany. The majority were of the Catholic faith, and religious considerations began to take on new importance in domestic politics. Most of the Irish crowded into the cities of the East Coast, with Democratic city machines working overtime to shape them into

American citizens. The Germans continued on westward, subsequently inclined to follow Henry Clay out of the Democratic-Republican party into the Whig and, later, the Republican parties.

Another upsurge of immigration came between 1880 and 1920, mainly from southern and eastern Europe: Italy, the former Austro-Hungarian Empire, and Russia. These immigrants were for the most part Catholics and Jews, and were eventually brought into the Democratic party by the city machines, the presidential candidacy of Alfred E. Smith, and the New Deal.

On the West Coast during the nineteenth century, the importation of Chinese laborers and the immigration of Japanese marked the beginnings of an Asian influx. The Chinese were brought in from 1840 to 1882, when the Chinese Exclusion Act was passed; their numbers declined over the next four decades. Japanese began to arrive in the 1890s, but in particularly large numbers about 1910. Racism reared its head and led to the further enactment of exclusion laws, immigration quotas, and even ordinances prohibiting Japanese children from attending public schools.

Since the 1950s, many Chinese and Vietnamese wishing to escape the civil wars in their home countries have managed to enter the United States under one or another immigration category. The proportion of Asian immigrants from the total influx into the United States has risen annually from about 10 percent in 1960 to over 40 percent in twenty years. With the arrival of the Pacific Century during the next decades, immigration from Asia is likely to increase appreciably and, in the light of recent civil rights developments in the United States, is likely to be more welcome than a hundred years ago. Many Pacific Islanders will be part of this movement.

In the past, Asian-Americans have tended to be a low turnout category of voters—one could say, natural candidates for membership in the Democratic party. This is changing, probably as a consequence of ethnic pride, ambitious young community leaders, and improving family economic circumstances. However, a substantial number of better educated, more affluent Asians—for example, those South Vietnamese who escaped during the last days of the Vietnam War—are likely to prefer what they perceive to be the "upper class" party, that is, the Republican party, unless actively recruited by Democrats.

In the last quarter century the number of Mexicans and other Latin Americans who have entered the United States, legally and illegally, temporarily or permanently, may never be accurately known. Whereas 1 in 5 immigrants were from Latin America in 1960, the proportion rose to 2 in 5 by 1980. A peak of some 6 million Hispanics, according to some official estimates, seems to have been reached in 1976. These immigrants range from seasonal farm workers coming into California, Texas, and other southwestern states to permanent escapees from Castro's Cuba or civil war in Central America. The range of educational, occupational, income, and cultural differences among Hispanic-American immigrants is quite broad, making it difficult to predict which party will receive most of this constituency's support. The constituency seems up for grabs.

In the past two decades, the odds have favored Democrats, probably as a consequence of migration into Democratic cities and farm labor organizing by charismatic leaders such as César Chavez. But this is far from an assimilated group. The situation is illustrated by data from California and Texas. In the early 1980s, there were an estimated 4.5 million Spanish-surnamed residents in California, that is, about a fifth of the state's population. Of these, some 2.5 million were adults, but only about 1.7 million were U.S. citizens. Of those who were citizens, only around 1 million were registered to vote. Between 550,000 and 590,000 were turning out to vote, a proportion some nine or ten points higher than the average for Democrats at that time. In Texas, Mexican-American voter registration rose from 488,000 in 1976 to about 1 million in 1984. Turnout fluctuated between 32–38 percent in nonpresidential years to approximately the national average of 52 percent in presidential elections. Surveys conducted in San Antonio and Los Angeles in the late 1960s found that two-thirds of the Mexican-Americans considered their votes worth nothing. In 1982, respondents in the same areas believed that voting was important.

Many Hispanics tend to be conservative, religious, attached to family values, and upwardly mobile, suggesting that their loyalty to the Democratic party may be short-term and tenuous. It is also true that the number of Hispanics living in poverty rose 22 percent nationwide in the early 1980s. Hispanic political organizations are also growing in number, membership, and astute political leadership. While Democratic leaders have already given much attention to attracting Hispanic voters into the party, so too have Republicans. This constituency will require constant and close attention in the future.

Since strife in the Middle East is likely to take a long time to subside, Arabs, Persians, Israelis, and North Africans— usually students or temporary workers—will continue to seek refuge in the United States. Most will endeavor to acquire American citizenship. In time, this will become another volatile constituency. Despite the radical rhetoric of many, particularly among the students, the economic and religious importance of their homelands as well as their pursuit of education is likely to carry disproportionate numbers into significant business and civic roles in the United States. The sooner the party solicits their support, the better, even though Middle Easterners are hardly a full-blown constituency of any sort at this time.

In general, how should the Democratic party deal with future versions of its traditional immigrant constituencies? The historical patterns suggest some humorous observations. Have them enter the country at a Democratic place. Take the lead in their Americanization and naturalization. Make them feel at home, find them jobs, but keep them poor. Recruit them into the local Democratic organization. Develop party leaders from among them. Have them bring over as many relatives as possible from the old country. Watch out for that one second-generation child in five who will "defect" to the other party. Be reconciled to the fact that higher education and income will loosen the party ties of future generations.

More realistically, in America, you cannot keep immigrants uneducated, poor, and dependent on the local Democratic machine; less so when there are no local machines left.

More likely the same difficulties will pertain that have been associated with immigrant constituencies in generations past: the costs of community assistance to the arriving poor; the competition for jobs between native workers and cheaper immigrant labor; the political strains and violence that arise with the intensification of racism and nativism; the burdens placed on party, civic, and educational facilities by the process of Americanization; and the near-impossibility of controlling the flow of immigration into an open society consisting almost entirely of immigrants and the descendants of immigrants.

REINFORCING THE CONTEMPORARY CONSTITUENCIES

Several Democratic constituencies have taken shape only recently and, in some cases, have not yet fully developed. They are often referred to as "minorities," which is redundant in a society which consists entirely of minorities constantly forming coalitions in order to become majorities. Among these contemporary evolving constituencies are blacks, women, seniors, and youth.

Many black citizens are coming out to vote for the first time. Some women's organizations are still making the transition from consciousness-raising programs to party and electoral operations. Seniors are increasing in numbers more rapidly than they can be mobilized. Young first-voters are spread all across the political spectrum. The requirements for holding or winning greater portions of these contemporary constituencies for the Democratic party are perhaps more difficult to assess than the traditional types. The contemporary constituencies have too brief a history from which to extrapolate.

Blacks

By 2032, the proportion of blacks in the population of the United States will have risen to 16 percent from about 12 percent in the 1980s. This will be within a percentage point or two over or under the Hispanic portion of the population.

Many blacks will have followed the model of the Irish and other ethnic-nationality minorities by pursuing upward social mobility on the ladder of the Democratic party. Blacks will not only be a major force within the Democratic party organization but will also have helped elect a member of their race to the presidency.

Non-Caucasian races will continue to assert themselves everywhere, from South Africa to Mississippi, particularly on issues of equal participation in the democratic political process—a version of "no taxation without representation." Policies of racism in most contexts will increasingly become a political and economic liability in the United States. For example, the costs of motivating and training black youths—whose over 40 percent level of unemployment is a national blight—will be compared increasingly with the costs of maintaining these young people as unemployeds on welfare, as criminals in prisons, or as psychologically disturbed patients in mental institutions. As economic dependents, they augment the costs of running American society; as taxpaying employed workers, they would be contributing their share to those costs.

More importantly for the Democratic party, if these black youths remain economic and social outcasts, they will undoubtedly become an entire generation of political isolates and nonvoters, a constituency lost to the party for the next half century. Here is a case of constituency-party relations for which party understanding is not enough. The party will have to contribute ideas, programs, resources, and leadership actively and promptly to this disabled constituency if Democrats are to reap a political benefit at any time in the next several decades. In humanitarian terms, of course, the needs and their urgency should require no further justification.

Proponents of a "rainbow coalition" of blacks, Hispanics, Asians, and others (presumably Caucasian women and the poor) are writing themselves a prescription for frustration. These groups may be parts of someone's classification of "minorities." They may share the burdens of poverty and poor education. But, culturally and economically, the members of these constituencies are sufficiently competitive, different in background, and hostile to each other to make coalition-formation an extremely difficult but *not impossible* undertaking. Black, Hispanic, and Asian citizens will not come together because their leaders urge them to. They will not come together because the political logic of coalitions makes it clear that they should. They *may* form coalitions in the manner of the old Chicago machines, that is, because they choose national party leaders who can recognize their separateness and separate interests, yet serve as honest brokers among them.

In general, however, most black citizens as a group will continue their slow march up the educational, occupational, and income ladders. Intermarriages and residential mobility will tend to moderate public manifestations of racism. The irony of these evidences of black progress is that it will weaken black voters' loyalty to the Democratic party. The party's support in group after group has weakened as group members go up the income scale, and there is no apparent reason for the tendency to differ among black constituents. As it has in the past, the party will pay a price for the success of its constituents.

As has happened with other ethnic and nationality groups before them, the American black community will become a magnet for an increasing volume of immigration from Africa, particularly as the economic distress of many Third World nations worsens after the turn of the century. If it is to benefit from this immigration, the Democratic party will need to be prepared to function as a national version of Tammany Hall, welcoming and Americanizing the newcomers in exchange for their loyalty at the ballot box. In time, these black immigrants will have their equivalent of Al Smith and Jack Kennedy, and another social barrier to the American presidency will fall.

Women

This largest "minority" of them all (51 percent of the population of the United States) will continue its advance toward sex equality over the next half century. Women will also continue to perceive the Democratic party as better attuned to their interests. After all, the women's suffrage amendment was added to the Constitution during a Democratic administration, the Democratic party gave women equal representation in its conventions and committees during the 1970s, and Walter Mondale chose Geraldine Ferraro as his partner on the national ticket in 1984. All this notwithstanding, only *some* women tend to lean strongly in the Democratic direction: younger women, black women, unmarried women, and women at opposite ends of the educational scale (the less educated and the highly educated).

Just as the Pill liberated women from the dependencies associated with their biological function as childbearers, jobs will continue to liberate them from their economic and familial dependencies. The trends are already in place. Opinion surveys prior to World War II revealed that three out of four Americans disapproved of married women working for pay. More recent surveys show the disapproval rating down to one out of four. About 43 percent of the current labor force of 109 million are women, a number that represents more than 52 percent of the female working population, a proportion that will soar to 85–90 percent by 2032. While the male-female wage gap is still a serious problem, it too continues to diminish under the pressure of legislation, law suits, and changing employer attitudes. In the two decades following 1960, the number of women in professional, managerial, technical, and administrative jobs rose from 4 million to 11 million. More than 700,000 run their own businesses.

Women's entry into the work force will be accompanied by a rise in the numbers of single mothers, more substantial male participation in child-rearing and homemaking, and increased serial marriages as the career and lifestyle needs of spouses become less synchronized, and new concepts and publicly managed capacities to care for preschool tots and school children are organized.

With educational, occupational, and economic growth, women will also appreciate their growing stake in public policy developments and political party fortunes. Current female activism in the politics of the Democratic party and the electorate will be looked back upon as generally awkward and in some respects primitive. In contrast, female participation as the party's bicentennial approaches will be sophisticated and exert a preponderant influence in Democratic operations. A woman will have long since been elected vice president and president of the United States.

At present, however, there continues to be a need for ameliorating relations between the organized women's constituency and the party. The strains are those that plague relations between the unilinear thrust of most single-issue groups on the one hand and the coalitional requirements of political parties on the other hand. Further, women's groups are only recent arrivals on the scene of electoral mobilization, and their skills and resources have hardly reached that of, say, the unions. If invited, the party could probably make a substantial training contribution to the women's organizations along these lines. In general, however, the female side of the electorate—for reasons of sheer size and diversity—will remain an unwieldy constituency for any political party, and the Democrats in particular.

Seniors

One-fifth of the American people will be over sixty-five years of age in 2032: 61 million persons, a high proportion of whom will be well-educated, skilled, and in good health.

Long before 2032, some of the economic and social realities of this enormous sector of the populace will have become evident and controversial. The high and actuarily demanding cost of social security will have been debated time and again. Each debate will dilute by one iota the concept of retirement, as will the increasingly obvious fact that such numerous seniors, when retired from the work force, will result in a massive waste of the nation's most cherished resource, its human capital. Dealing with the problems and wishes of the seniors constituency will be a challenge to both parties, but particularly to the seniors themselves.

Unable to rescind retirement, legislators will tend to surround it with qualifications and conditions. Mandatory retirement ages will be delayed a year at a time. Certified disability will increasingly become a condition of certain retirement benefits. Many efforts will be made to bring retirement annuities in line with the actuarial facts of longevity. Public provision for the comfort, health, and safety of less self-sufficient seniors will be attended to more thoroughly and comprehensively, probably with an eye to achieving these objectives effectively at reasonable cost. These are not easy changes for politicians to make, and there will be much tip-toeing around obvious solutions. The more astute party leaders will try to arrange for the reforms to come from the seniors constituency itself.

By the twenty-first century the distribution of time among education, work, vacation, leisure, and retirement will probably be quite different from what it is today. More of an average American's lifetime will be spent on education, not necessarily in schools or other formal settings. In fact, as the practice of serial careers—two, three, and four career lives— grows, education and training are likely to continue throughout the individual's lifetime. One proposal would have mandatory savings for the costs of such educational endeavors made a part of the social security system, with modest regular contributions coming out of employees' wages and matched by employers' contributions. Thus, at age fifty-five or sixty a citizen may choose to reduce his or her work day to take a work sabbatical in order to train for another career with funds for tuition and related expenses from this lifespan educational insurance program. All this will be in addition to the continuing education of the most informal sort available to the individual through the mass media on a daily basis. It will truly be an Information Society.

Time at work will surely be reduced to a standard 25–30 hour week, raising the demand for the offerings of the recreational and educational industries. Vacations may well begin to expand to two and three months as is common in the teaching professions, allowing individuals to occupy the time in study, travel, play, or work at another occupation.

The redistribution of time commitments will inevitably affect seniors, particularly retirees. However, it will be a reverse process: the permanent "vacationer"—bored, eager to exercise his or her old or new skills, seeking the associations and friendships of the workplace—returning to work, full-time, part-time, or as a member of a new type of unpaid "activity group." The steady march of inflation will undoubtedly motivate many seniors to move in this direction, as it already has.

"Activities"—only a social science concept at this time—will probably be a cross between paid employment and strictly voluntary work. There are evidences of this type of work at hospitals and other social service facilities, that is, seniors working at relatively unskilled tasks such as serving food, folding linen, engaging in simple clerical duties, etc. The only "wage" may be free meals, cash for transportation to and from the workplace, or other minor perquisites. The social and psychological rewards are significant: the company of others, the self-esteem that comes with doing something socially useful, new knowledge and skills, and more. But as the practice grows, activity-work is likely to generate some difficult social and political management, such as the concerns of unions about the displacement of their members by free labor, the concerns of seniors' representatives about the exploitation of the elderly, the wasteful underemployment of persons with substantial skills, the forms of material compensation and its relationship to the underground economy, and other issues.

There is enough here to give politicians a migraine headache, and it will.

Perhaps the most emotionally laden and important political issues concerning the seniors constituency will be those relating to health, life, and death. The very definition of life itself is already an issue before the courts and on campaign trails, and is being pressed by right-to-life anti-abortion groups and right-to-die euthanesia groups. When is the fetus a living person? The failure of which organ determines whether a person is dead? Who will be the lucky recipients of scarce organ transplants or lifesupport equipment? Who should decide when to "pull the plug" to relieve a patient of the misery of a lingering death? Such questions are loaded with deeply felt religious, moral, and ethical problems among persons of any age, but have special poignancy among the elderly and their families. They already are grist for the Democratic party's platform mill, and will become more so. Their complexity and emotionality will demand close and thoughtful communication between the seniors constituency and the party's leadership.

Youth

The young are the fourth of the contemporary Democratic constituencies. Until a decade ago, the political young were citizens twenty-one years of age (the legal voting age) or in their twenties. Those who went to the ballot box (a lower percentage than the national average) tended to be enthusiastically Democratic. The same general tendencies—low turnout, Democratic leanings—persisted when the suffrage was extended to eighteen-year-olds. George McGovern, in 1972, was supposed to be the beneficiary of this suffrage expansion. Some of his advisers foolishly anticipated that all 25 million new voters between the ages of eighteen to twenty-five would flock to the Democratic nominee and sweep him into office.

The trends among young voters is quite different today. As we noted earlier, in the elections of 1980 and 1984 the young first voters, the Yuppies, and the baby-boomers lined up heavily on the Republican side. This is likely to be the worst of the long-term bad news for the Democratic party. While the party's leaders are constantly trying to revive the New Deal coalition, the New Deal generation of voters now makes up only about 15 percent of the electorate. An entirely different generation, the baby-boomers and the Yuppies, make up one-third of the electorate in the 1980s, with most still forming their long-term political predispositions.

The young between the ages of eighteen to twenty-five and the seniors sixty-five and over constituted half of the voting population in the 1984 election, with quite divergent interests. By 2032, these two age groups combined, with fewer young and more old, will make up two-thirds of the electorate. Some of the young are already complaining that they are unfairly taxed to support the social security benefits of the elderly. On the other hand, today's twenty-five-year-olds will be in their seventies in 2032, when, it is estimated, at least half of the federal budget will be devoted to programs for persons sixty-five and older. Here is an issue involving the distribution of the nation's wealth between two potent constituencies. Party leaders will need their best brokering talents to accommodate both constituencies.

There are several other significant tendencies in the youth constituency. Most forecasts anticipate lower birth rates over the next several decades. This trend will presumably mean fewer youth, emptier classrooms in elementary and secondary schools, a smaller college-age population, more entry level jobs for the fewer young, and less crime (since the young are more involved in crime than any other age group). Such forecasts, however, may overlook the probability that the new immigrants arriving during the next generation or two will tend to be younger on the average than native Americans and produce larger families. In other words, an important part of the future youth population will be among the next waves of immigrants—Hispanics, Africans, and Asians. This should be considered significant news for Democrats, as we have seen.

The young voters of the near future will be intensely interested in a number of special issues. The requirements of an Information Society will make them keenly aware of the quality of education for themselves and their children. The anomie and disorientation generated by a rapidly changing world will undoubtedly put additional strain on the mental health facilities of the nation. Looser family structures, higher divorce rates, serial marriages, and the many new attitudes and social adjustments necessary to cope with each of these trends are bound to be stressful enough to warrant a greatly expanded system of social and psychological services. Born into a shrinking and interdependent world under constant threat of nuclear holocaust, the young are likely to look askance at nationalistic chauvinisms and acquire a taste for internationalist approaches to domestic and world problems. More about the latter tendency will appear shortly.

If the Democratic party is interested in its future, it must be particularly interested in attracting the young—Yuppies, baby-boomers—into its ranks. The future leadership of the party and the nation is among the young. To neglect this constituency is to hazard the future of the party, the nation, and, indeed, the world.

Of the several contemporary constituencies discussed here, the elements for the emergence and development of several entirely new party constituencies are today faintly visible among the young.

TEN

Constructing New Constituencies: Prospective and Global

Cultural and social changes are occurring among today's youth that are likely to have long-term political consequences, particularly as they stimulate the emergence of new electoral constituencies. Lifestyle changes, particularly those related to sexual preferences, have already led to ambitious new constituency organizations. Recreational considerations have manifest themselves in sports, in the environmentalist and other movements. The family is being restructured in a number of ways that are only beginning to be grasped. The different mass media, notably television and radio, have attracted audiences with politically significant characteristics. All this change has given rise to issues, organizations, and constituencies that are new to the American political scene and, prospectively, to any new Democratic party coalitions.

PROSPECTIVE CONSTITUENCIES

Lifestyle

Major elements of the traditional American lifestyle have revolved around the workplace, marriage, the nuclear family, the home, and the church. Fairly standard patterns of expectations and attitudes used to be associated with each of these elements. For example, the typical male head of the household spent long working hours at the workplace in some smokestack industry, marriage was a heterosexual relationship entered into shortly after graduation from school on a till-death-do-us-part basis, the family was largely a child-bearing and child-rearing enterprise with important economic undertones, and so forth. For most Americans, these patterns are still in place, but the numbers who live life differently—in a wide variety of ways—grow continually. Freedom and affluence have made social experimentation readily available for novel experiences and excitement. Of course, when experiments become habits, they acquire the status of lifestyles. What begins as deviant becomes normal. Either way, there are usually political implications.

Perhaps one of the most bizarre manifestations of deviancy in recent decades was the drug subculture of the

1960s. The use of marijuana, heroin, LSD, and a candy counter of other hallucinogens was the principal symbol and weapon of youthful rebellion and was taken over by adult chic. The production and distribution of street drugs became a multi-billion dollar industry. Personal freedom was the great political banner under which users could seek their particular forms of "high" and psychic experiences. Street drugs, like alcohol, tea, and other gustatory devices, also became accompaniments, sometimes avenues, to sex, organized protest, armchair radicalism, and unusual residential arrangements. It was all very expressive and liberated until the social costs and the political implications became evident.

The number of broken bodies, minds, and lives resulting from the pursuits of the drug subculture has been appalling. Families have been permanently scarred. Moral standards have been tested to their very core. Although a monumental public expense, the cost of medical care for the drug-wounded has been insignificant when compared with the cost of losing a substantial and precious portion of a generation of American youth. Despite the fact that the drug subculture has receded from public view, it continues to maintain a major and politically influential industry. Today, cocaine is the fashion at the high end of the economic scale and deadly angel dust at the low end. The personal, economic, and social costs of the drug subculture's exercise of its personal freedom will undoubtedly be with the nation for decades to come.

The problems of the drug constituency will continue to spread into many corners of the body politic, debilitating it and diverting it from healthier pursuits. Nearly every issue involves economic and social costs. How much public money should be dedicated to research the problems of addiction and drug therapy? To what extent should the taxpayer bear the costs of mental institutions, hospitals, and rehabilitation centers that house and care for those broken bodies and minds? What will it cost to wean the poor and the young away from their addictions into more wholesome lives? How much policing will it take to stop the tide of narcotics from overseas suppliers? Whose economic and political ox will be gored if the police and the courts succeed in putting the drug industry out of business?

A more sensitive question bears upon the relationship between the drug subculture's buyers and sellers on the one hand and the Democratic party on the other. Senator Estes Kefauver's investigation of urban crime in the early 1950s uncovered embarrassing connections between Big Crime and small Democrats in several cities. The disclosures transformed Kefauver into something of a national hero and generated his presidential candidacy. The brush also tarred the party's image. While similar connections and traumas are not likely to disturb the Democratic party today or in the near future, an offshoot causes a problem. The problem was probably best stated by the televised shots of young Democrats and young Republicans at their respective 1972 presidential nominating conventions. The young Democrats appeared as long-haired, disheveled, multicolored, and radical hippies. In contrast, the young Republicans were well-barbered, clean-cut, Caucasian, and true-blue flag-waving patriots. Grassroots Democrats were not happy with the difference.

The difference is also electoral. Can a Democratic candidate in certain areas of the nation, for example, take a strong stand against the sale and use of street drugs without diluting his or her commitment to personal freedom and alienating a large part of the invisible drug constituency? How should a Democratic candidate advise a community to deal with the long-term consequences of drug use? The issue and the constituency may be out of view but they are nonetheless real. Democrats looking for guidelines will perhaps want to reexamine the nation's experience with Prohibition.

Less bizarre but almost as controversial is the sexual-preference constituency. The number who have "come out of the closet" over the past two decades suggests a surprisingly large closet. Not all are homosexuals; many are devoted to personal freedom, privacy, sexual experimentation, or are simply antipathetic to existing social norms. Together, gays, lesbians, and sexual-freedom sympathizers add up to significant political numbers. In addition, they tend to concentrate in particular sections of central cities where they have become well-organized politically and, as cohesive voting coalitions, have become the pivotal vote in an increasing number of local and state elections. A large part of this constituency tends to be Democratic, usually exercising influence in Democratic primary elections or in the general elections, by its decision on whether or not to vote.

The sexual-preference constituency has traveled the same political route as the feminist and other psychocultural minorities: at first, through consciousness-raising and protest against discriminatory social norms; as public attitudes become more sympathetic, by lobbying and electoral mobilization of its own and friendly constituencies; after acquiring political legitimacy and financial resources, by mounting campaigns to change statutes and bring legal challenges in the courts; and next, through electoral participation to help or hinder the election of particular candidates and parties.

With electoral clout has come a crescendo of constituency demands and difficult policy issues, not all of them political. Can gay or lesbian couples be married, with all the legal ceremonies, rights, and responsibilities that accrue to heterosexual marriages? Can medical insurance and other fringe benefits of employment cover the dependent member of a homosexual couple as they do family dependents? Where these questions have been raised, as in San Francisco, religious leaders of all types have rushed to the public forum to defend the traditional family. But the issues are not as simple as they seem and the sexual-preference constituency will continue to test the meanings of such comfortable terms as family, equal rights, freedom, and privacy. Rewriting definitions is likely to be a part of the work of Democratic party leaders for decades to come.

Sexual-preference lifestyles manifest themselves in other ways, augmenting in varying degrees the size of the constituency. There are the Swinging Seniors emerging in numerous retirement enclaves. Yes, there is sex among the elderly, more and merrier than suggested by ancient stereotypes. Encouraged by good health, affluence, free time, and sociability, and uninhibited by family or occupational duties or fears of pregnancy, some seniors—both married and single—have been setting aside traditional sex mores with almost unbecoming alacrity. They may also be among the invisible troops of the sexual-preference constituency.

Developing more overtly is the phenomenon of unmarried families. A growing number of heterosexual couples are cohabiting *as though* married, sharing household costs, duties, and privileges. Frequently, these relationships, if long-lasting, fall within the purview of common law marriage. Often children are born of these couples. Various welfare programs, most notably Aid to Families with Dependent Children and the food stamp program, are criticized for *causing* unmarried families and absent fathers. It is a hair-splitting question whether unmarried families are part of the sexual-preference or the restructured-family (see below) constituency. What counts politically is the reality of their situation. Whether by preference or compulsion, most tend to be among the poorer sectors of the electorate and, hence, a special concern of the Democratic party.

The residential neighborhood has always been a major component of a lifestyle. In earlier times neighborhoods were divided between the clustered estates of the wealthy and the seedy streets of the poor "on the other side of the tracks." With immigration came ethnic and nationality ghettos. Over the decades, the rural population—mostly white—moved to the cities. After World War II, internal migration brought blacks into the center of cities and moved whites out to the suburbs. Today, there are signs of new trends. Clean industries such as high-technology production or research centers are locating in formerly rural areas, encouraging a more pastoral type of suburban living. Retirees, environmentalists, upper-income professionals, and minifarmers are retreating from urban centers to the countryside. In contrast, young Yuppies with more casual racial attitudes and an eye to the future of urban real estate values are settling in the gentrifying neighborhoods of the cities. Wherever they reside, country or city, these individuals are adopting new lifestyles and altering the politics of their communities. Precinct captains, if there are any, have all they can do to keep up.

There are innumerable other subcultures with distinctive lifestyles: nutrition faddists, technology buffs, exercise enthusiasts, and so on. Taken together, they reflect the diversity of American life. But most do not have the breadth and durability that would make them significant party or electoral constituencies. And there is one further group, one that *may* become another invisible but potent constituency, made up of those who spend most of their income-producing energy working in or around the underground economy. These are the moonlighters who take compensation in cash or in unrecorded exchanges of goods or services, who engage extensively in barter in order to obtain their basic living needs: shelter, food, clothing, personal services. Their principal objective is to avoid the tax collector. For many it is also a lifestyle focused on the needs of the present, one that avoids the constraints of steady and routine employment and depends on community largess in times of crisis. These undergrounders are not necessarily lazy, irresponsible freeloaders. It is a constituency that simply objects to the work ethic, taxes, and the accumulation of wealth. What the party can do with and for the growing number of undergrounders will not be easy to discern or accomplish.

Recreational Constituencies

There are many familiar constituencies in this category, some with tremendous influence: fishermen, hunters, campers, horse-race fans, to name just a few of the more obvious. Recreation and sports are highly valued in American society, possibly the outgrowth of the religious sabbath as a day of rest and of free enterprise as a spur to the competitive spirit. It is therefore hardly news to note that recreational constituencies in the United States are numerous in membership, often highly organized, and capable of producing legislative and electoral results that favor their interests. Many have long-established and powerful lobbies, for example, the National Rifle Association. Is there a candidate for office that fails to publish a picture of himself or herself with a fishing rod, on a horse, playing softball, tossing a football or basketball, carrying a hunting gun, or otherwise displaying his or her attachment to a recreational or athletic interest?

In addition to the traditional leisure-oriented constituencies, new leisure groups with particular expectations and substantial resources are already in sight. The centuries-old Puritan work ethic is being challenged by a new leisure ethic; play has become an *essential* part of the pursuit of happiness and the full life. As a consequence, the production and sale of sports and recreational equipment is a multibillion dollar sector of the economy. Gymnasiums, health spas, and other recreational centers abound. Attendance at sporting events is sometimes better measured by players' salaries than by the number of tickets sold. National, state, and local parks and related recreational facilities are constantly being used more intensively. Interest in the performing, visual, plastic, and other arts and crafts mounts, together with demands for greater support from the public treasury. Postdegree and nondegree courses of instruction at secondary and postsecondary schools are prospering. There seems to be a travel agent at the corner of every city block as vacationers, retirees, and others indulge in recreational trips and tours to all corners of the nation and the world. This is a big constituency, including people of all ages, incomes, and social strata.

Several consequences flow from the rise of new recreational constituencies. Educators (particularly those on the public payroll), the media, and artists often seem to be earning their living as recreation managers rather than by pursuing their primary occupations. Public schools, colleges, and universities are called upon to provide leisure-oriented curricula, frequently at the expense of more traditional and demanding instruction. The media, particularly television, must respond to their audiences' insatiable appetite for predominantly escapist entertainment, all too often sacrificing the media's great potential for disseminating information, knowledge, and truer reflections of the world at large. Artists are increasingly involved in mental health, geriatric, and commercial endeavors, none particularly pertinent to their creative work. With their aspirations and functions thus diverted and commercialized, the members of these groups have become more self-aware and politically articulate. There are many Democrats in this constituency, and likely to be more in the future.

In the realm of sports, the political pot is likely to boil and bubble with growing intensity as divergent athletic, financial, and community interests clash. Entire towns and cities have become major recreational centers, with concomitant problems of adjusting local economies and public services to the visitor trade, for example, the towns around Lake Tahoe, the communities of and near Vail (Colorado), Atlantic City, and other places. Cities are battling to acquire or to keep baseball or football teams, incurring great costs in stadium construction, traffic control, and other requirements. Colleges and universities are debating where to draw the line between amateur and professional in the management of talent for their athletic teams. Politicians are already part of this scene.

As the economic and social consequences of these many recreational activities and industries expand, so too will the organization of their consumers and providers. The trend is not new, nor is the relevance of these constituencies for party and electoral politics. The forecast here is: the greater the economic and social consequences, the more significant the consumer and provider organizations of the leisure-oriented; the more organized the leisure-oriented, the more influential their cross-cut of other Democratic party constituencies. Given the rapid spread of the leisure ethic, this trend will soon begin to bring these issues to the desks of party leaders and will continue to do so for long into the future.

Families

According to most anthropologists, sociologists, and clergy, families are the basic platoons of society for purposes of social organization and human socialization. Yet forecasters see the families of the United States marching off in different directions in the foreseeable future. The consequences they predict often has more to do with the personal optimism or pessimism of the forecaster than with any available trend data. Of one thing we may be certain: the family will continue to be a primary focus of public debate and policy.

What will be some of the characteristics of American families over the next half century? Families will have smaller homes, more divorces, more remarriages, both spouses working for income, fewer children, more single female parents, and greater residential mobility. The smaller homes will be a consequence of higher construction costs and mortgage rates. The trend toward zero population growth will result in fewer children, except, as noted earlier, among the families of the new immigrants and the very poor. Serial marriages will create networks of stepfamilies, that is, a new kind of extended family. Divorce and unmarried cohabitation will increase the number of single parents, mostly female. Residential mobility will accompany occupational mobility and the divorce rate. If most forecasters are to be believed, the American family of the future is going to acquire some of the characteristics of a revolving door.

One consequence for public policy and party politics will be an intensificiation of issues already evident. Many of the issues center around the care and rearing of the children of working parents, married and single. As in so many other societies, the day care of children will come increasingly under governmental management. Preschools, kindergartens, and elementary schools will be restructured to provide full day supervision of the children of employed parents. Coincidentally, greater knowledge of the learning process in small children will provide ample educational justification for incorporating the very young into the school system and for extending the school day. At the workplace, arrangements for accommodating the parents of very young children will be more available through flexible hours, parent leaves, and infant care facilities.

Typically, the debates will get to the bottom line, money. Who is to pay for day care, restructured school days, and workplace arrangements? Taxpayers with grown or no children will surely balk. Parents may pay users fees but these will hardly cover the costs. Activity volunteers (see above), if available, may ease the problem of personnel and costs, but they will require recruitment, training, and close supervision, particularly if systematic instructional programs are pursued. Facilities and equipment will add to the costs. Inevitably there will be party differences regarding goals, programs, and financial support. There will also be an intensely concerned constituency of working parents assessing these goals, programs, and methods of financing. Furthermore, as the decades pass, better-educated parents, of which there will be growing numbers, will want better care and education for their children. This could be another formidable constituency for the Democratic party in its traditional role as defender of the educational enterprise.

Media Constituencies

The Information Society will—already does—surround the individual with communication media: television, radio, newspapers, magazines, books, films, telephones, computers, and combinations of these. Media users and audiences tend to match-up in special ways. Some people are readers and stay for the most part with books, newspapers, and magazines. Others, perhaps most, are picture viewers and watch television and film. Many prefer to listen, for which there are radio, records, and audiocassettes. The talkers prefer to use the telephone.

These matchup tendencies will undoubtedly diversify and intensify with new equipment such as videodiscs that replace books, dissemination technology such as cable televison, and the individualization of entertainment in the home and instruction in the schools. The latter development will be consistent with the increased confirmation that student learning efficiency often varies with the sensory capacities of the individual. Some learn best by reading, others by listening, and still others through pictorial images. Holography may create entire new audiences and a new communications economy as three-dimensional images of museum exhibits, athletic events, operas, ballets, and other events are brought into the home from places devoid of live audiences and for fees commensurate with the costs of the event.

The electoral implications of "media constituencies" are already well known among campaign managers. Lower socio-economic status persons tend to listen to the radio. Nationality minorities can be reached through "narrowcasting" (as distinguished from broadcasting) over foreign language radio and cable television stations. The more affluent read newspapers and other printed matter. Children spend as much, or more, time watching television as they do in the classroom. A newcomer to politics can acquire renown—name-familiarity—within weeks by intensive use of television, enough to upset a party's best candidate or strategy. The public relations and campaign textbooks are filled with data about and guidelines for appealing to media audiences of almost every conceivable kind.

How will so many communications media and so many audiences affect the future Democratic party? In two ways. In the first, the proliferation and specialization of mass communications will expand the communications constituency in general. Media providers and their audiences will continue to be a silent partnership of influence over political leaders concerned with image as well as reality. How will the audience perceive a political message on television? Will it reach the right audience on a particular radio station? Through which channel ought a message be sent to the party regulars? Increased party use of the media will make media audiences even more influential than today. The general media constituency will also be a powerful claimant for statutes and resources favorable to mass communication facilities and services. The party's leaders will need to attend to the electoral and policy implications of such claims.

The second way in which the proliferation of media constituencies is likely to affect the party will be as a filter between the leadership and the rank-and-file and between the nominees and the voters. The direct face-to-face campaigning of the stump or the rear platform of a train is already a political antique. The full text of a leader's speech and the give-and-take of spontaneous public debate will become a rarity. The very specific message for a very specific group of citizens will have to find its uncertain way through a maze of narrowcasting and specialized channels. As frustrated party leaders begin to grasp the fact that they are losing control over one of their primary functions, political communication, they will probably consider returning to the nineteenth-century practice of establishing and managing the party's own specialized media: a party daily newspaper, a radio network, a cable television channel, a Democratic party book-publishing company, and more. Other technologies—teleconferencing and computer-assisted conferencing—are likely to be added as major management instruments if the party works seriously on the challenges of grassroots organization discussed earlier.

One somewhat surprising source of media-related issues will emerge from the rapid development of worldwide communications. Worldwide telecommunication, a world press, and the development of images and symbols understood among all peoples will inevitably magnify the effects of world events upon the domestic politics of the United States, and, therefore, of the Democratic party. Even more than at present, the party will have a global constituency and the "precincts" of the world will become matters of practical concern for party leaders.

In general, the new constituencies—lifestyle, recreational, family, media, and undoubtedly others—will be distinguished by their social preferences rather than their economic or residential circumstances. Their basic living requirements taken care of, these constituencies will become concerned with *how* they live together, *how* they spend their leisure time, and *how* they remain in communication with the rest of the world. At present, most are more or less visible and relatively organized. The attitudinal and electoral implications of each of the new constituencies are likely to grow. As with other of their constituencies, Democratic leaders will need to follow these trends closely, understand them carefully, and determine how best to fit them into the party coalition.

THE GLOBAL CONSTITUENCIES

After World War II, the United States joined the world, reluctantly. The deed required new involvements and new costs that most Americans would have preferred to avoid: rearmament and establishment of this country's first full-sized, full-time military force; responsibility for breathing life into an infant United Nations; assumption of the role of policeman for the world; transmission of aid to allies in dire economic distress as a consequence of the war; leadership of the world's largest military alliance (NATO); and entrapment in unsought wars in Korea and Vietnam. In little more than a quarter of a century, the United States learned major lessons in world politics and became the major contributor to change in a rapidly changing world.

Global shrinkage—in time and space—has been another aspect of change that has virtually incorporated the rest of humanity among the constituencies of the political parties of the United States. A Berlin crisis in 1948, a Suez crisis in 1956, a Cuban missile crisis in 1962, an Iranian hostage crisis in

1980, a terrorist attack on Marines in Beirut, a landing of American troops in Grenada . . . and immediately significant repercussions are felt in United States public opinion and elections. A Sadat or a Begin will compete for support among American citizens and politicians by appearing before audiences in the United States and even before congressional committees. Television brings an undeclared war in Vietnam or a famine in Ethiopia into American living rooms, and viewers are quickly moved to political responses that would have taken months to materialize only a single generation ago. The global constituencies may not cast ballots in the United States, but they exercise almost every other form of influence on American politics.

Americans have been less than perfect in the global game, and there have been blind spots. For example, there have been many uncomfortable military alliances with dictatorial regimes in the interest of national security. Often these alliances neglected the longer term security that comes with promoting pluralist and democratic societies. Emerging supranational institutions, initially responsive to American approaches to world affairs, have recently become centers of anti-American or anti-Western coalitions, for example, the International Labor Organization and UNESCO. The politics of these supranational institutions, while frequently poorly understood by Americans, has had domestic political consequences in the United States for public opinion and party leaders.

One development has been particularly misunderstood, namely, the emergence of a nascent transnational political party system. Historically, political parties have been a special American contribution to human institutions. Political parties in the colonies and during the early days of the Republic added a popular electoral dimension to the parliamentary party concept that was born in seventeenth-century England. American elections have since been one of the wonders of the world, producing enough noise and apparent confusion to keep foreign observers doubtful about our national sanity. Yet contemporary Americans—both leaders and general public—have hardly noticed the growing importance of transnational parties since the end of World War II.

There are several reasons for this neglect or oversight: an antiparty tradition in the United States; recent shifts among voters from party loyalty to independence; a foreign policy doctrine of nonintervention in the internal party politics of other countries; the belief that the American party system is uniquely coalitional and incompatible with the presumably more monolithic ideological parties elsewhere; and the sense that there is something subversive about international party movements. It is also true that an emergent institution may be difficult to recognize while it is still abornin'.

Some transnational party movements are more than a century old; others have become significant since the end of World War II. The Communist internationals, the first of which was founded in 1848, have evolved in several phases: the Second International was established in 1889 and disbanded in 1914; the Third International (Comintern) started in 1919 and dissolved in 1943 during World War II; the Communist Information Bureau (Cominform) was created in 1947 and terminated in 1956.

One outgrowth of the Comintern era was the Foreign Affairs Department of the Communist party of the Soviet Union, established in 1943, with regional and country desks. This department was later divided into two which still function today. The first is the International Department, with connections among nonruling Communist and other parties throughout the world. The International Department also works closely with the World Peace Council, a "front" organization that coordinates the activities of nonparty Communist groups around the world. The second is the Department for Relations with the Communist Parties of the Socialist Countries, which follows the activities of regimes controlled by Communist parties.

In the 1980s thus far, some ninety-six Communist or Communist-affiliated parties exist among the approximately 160 nations of the world. If viewed globally, it would appear that there are as many factions in the world Communist move-ment as there usually are within the Democratic or Republican parties, if not more. Some Communist parties fall closely within the sphere of the Soviet party, others follow the Chinese party, and still others assume the independent line of the Yugoslav party. Different times and circumstances influence the degrees of cooperation between Communists in different nations, for example, between the Soviet and Hungarian par-ties or the Chinese and Albanian parties. All, however, seek to place their leaders in control of their national governments through revolution or election. All conduct campaigns to win popular support for their leaders and policies. Most believe in "dictatorships of the proletariat," that is, one-party author-itarian or totalitarian political systems.

Ideologically and historically, Communists perceive the world as a single political system made up of many national subsystems, much as the Democratic or Republican national committees might view their respective organizations or fac-tions in the fifty states. The geographical difference is signif-icant. Soviet assistance to Nicaraguan Communists, for example, is *not* considered intervention in the political affairs of another nation, but rather as political aid to fellow-partisans in a world-state; in this view, national boundaries are merely human devices. In contrast, the Democratic or Republican national committees, while sending assistance to their state parties with similar motives, do so with cautious respect for local sovereignty, even within a single nation. The notion that Democratic and Republican national committees should send political aid to fellow-pluralists *in other nations* has only very recently begun to appear as a legitimate American party activ-ity, but one that runs up against American nonintervention attitudes. As we shall see below, United States political party aid to democratic parties overseas is still a highly controversial program whose future is likely to have important conse-quences for the Democratic party.

Non-Communist transnational party movements con-tinue to acknowledge national boundaries and national sovereignty but nevertheless pursue programs of cooperation with fellow-partisans across national boundaries. The eventual effect, of course, will be to pay less and less attention to national boundaries and national sovereignty, not a surprising trend in an increasingly interdependent world. Among these transnationals are the Socialist International, the Christian Democratic International, and the Liberal International.

Socialists accept a pluralist politics and usually seek change through nonviolent parliamentary methods. Socialists are *not* Communists although there often is good reason to be confused about the two. Both are progeny of the same seminal theoretician, Karl Marx. Both have a common organizational history growing out of the First Socialist International (1864–1877) and the Second Socialist International (1889–1919). Communists often refer to themselves as Socialists, although the reverse is never the case. From time to time since World War I, the two movements have adopted "united front" tactics during which they become a coalition to achieve limited objectives, for example, the removal of a regime, a victory in an election, a victory in a labor strike, or the control of a legislature.

Confusion notwithstanding, the Socialist International has been active and frequently highly successful since World War II. Today, there are nearly fifty member parties and fifteen consultative parties throughout the world. These parties usually take the names Social Democrats, Labor, or Socialist. Social Democrats in Europe have worked together to win a plurality of the seats in the direct elections of representatives to the European Parliament.

The Socialist International has factions: a right wing that is determinedly anti-Communist and anti-Soviet; a left wing that favors united-front coalitions with Communists, as in the first Mitterand cabinet or the civil war in El Salvador. The International at times pursues a mixed strategy: arms-length relations with Eurocommunists but military collaborations with Communists in Third World civil wars against authoritarian regimes. Under Willy Brandt's leadership, the International is aggressively endeavoring to build affiliated party organizations in Latin America, Africa, and Asia.

Equally aggressive is the Christian Democratic International, also with approximately fifty affiliated parties in almost as many countries. The Christian Democrats are second only to the Social Democrats in transnational influence in Europe, most specifically in the European Parliament. In the direct election campaigns, cooperating Christian Democratic parties named themselves the European People's Party. In Latin America, Christian Democrats are perhaps the strongest partisan counterforce to various versions (Castroist, Maoist, etc.) of Communism. An outgrowth of nineteenth-century Catholic political movements, contemporary Christian Democrats tend to be secular and nonconfessional in doctrine and conservative in public policy orientation.

The third of the pluralist transnationals is the Liberal International. Some 40–50 national parties are affiliated, the principal of which are the Liberal parties of Canada and Great Britain. Liberal parties are also prominent in Japan, Australia, and Latin America. With typical liberal individuality, the national affiliates of the Liberal International display a wide range of policy orientations except in their united opposition to totalitarianism, defense of freedom and human rights, and dedication to the dignity of the human individual.

There are other lesser transnational parties: the Conservative (International Democratic Union) and the pan-Arab Ba'th parties. In the past there have been the Fascists, the International Peasant Union (the Green International), and the Aprista (Alianza Popular Revolucionaria Americana) parties in Latin America.

What does all this have to do with the Democratic party? By 2032 the Democratic party will be a leading affiliate of one of the transnationals. The Republican party already is, having joined the conservative's International Democratic Union. Which will the Democrats join? The choice is likely to be between the Socialist (Social Democratic) International and the Liberal International.

When the time to join arrives, the issue is likely to shape up as a battle between the more ideologically leftist Democratic delegates to the national conventions and the more moderate leadership in the party's state and congressional organizations. In many respects, the disagreement will be semantic and perhaps a consequence of historical circumstances. Jeffersonian democracy emphasized a strictly limited role for government in the lives of the citizenry. Jacksonians gave government responsibility for defending the less affluent or less fortunate by laying constraints upon the conduct of the wealthy. After the turn of the century, Bryan and Wilson advocated vigorous governmental intervention in the economic and social policies of the nation. Franklin Roosevelt's New Deal implemented Wilsonian interventionism to a previously unimagined degree. The New Deal legacy has been a blend of governmental activism that proximates collectivist economic policies and civil libertarianism that protects the political individual and minority groups.

Semantic issues will probably enter the argument in two ways. The average American's impression that Socialists and Communists are alike will make it extremely difficult for the more left-leaning Democratic leaders to carry forward an affiliation with the Socialist International. Such an affiliation simply would not sell in Peoria.

In contrast, the Democratic party is already reputedly the liberal of the two major parties, and nomenclature alone would make it easy to affiliate with the Liberal International. The objection to such a move would be the outdated perception that the "European-type" liberals are predominantly laissez-faire capitalists. The perception could be corrected by a reading of the Liberal Manifesto of 1947, the Liberal Declaration of Oxford of 1967, and the Liberal Appeal of 1981. It will come as a surprise to many that the latter appeal is in many respects interchangeable with the Democratic party platforms of the 1970s and 1980s.

The Democratic debate over affiliation with a transnational party could serve another positive function, namely, a reconsideration of the modern meaning of liberalism within the party. The orientations of the Liberal International could well make a major contribution to such a deliberation, particularly in the reconciliation of labor, civil rights, and Yuppie economic policy postures. Above all, the debate could become the occasion for setting aside some of the archaic concepts and enmities of left, center, and right liberals in the party.

If the debate is prolonged, it may lead to a kind of enduring Democratic factionalism that correlates with the transnational affiliation options, that is, a pro-Socialist left, a pro-Liberal center, and a pro-Christian Democratic right. Under such circumstances, each faction could organize itself along lines familiar to the party, that is, with organized groups similar to Americans for Democratic Action or Coalition for a Democratic Majority. A sustained factionalism of this kind would probably occur if the party continues to fail in its bids for the presidency or if any one faction fails to achieve clear ascendancy when holding that office.

Apart from the question of affiliation, the growing awareness of the emergence of a transnational party system is likely to affect party conduct in a number of other ways. Foreign policy issues will be formulated as *world* issues. The policies of nonintervention in the politics of other nations will be questioned, revised, and brought into conformity with the conditions of an interdependent world. Ideology will take on a more comprehensive and consistent meaning in factional and interparty debates. An accent on ideology is likely to make party politics more attractive to young Democrats, particularly those who are more idealistic and oriented toward world issues.

Democratic leaders will be in closer contact with their counterparts in other countries, and this is likely to have an impact on both the structure of the party and its approach to many issues. For example, the Democratic National Committee will need staff to work with overseas contacts and to keep the leadership current on world issues of importance to the party. Steps in this direction are already being taken with the formation of the National Democratic Institute for International Affairs, an auxiliary of the Democratic National

Committee. The Institute was established in 1983 in conjunction with the establishment of the National Endowment for Democracy, part of the Reagan administration's Democracy Program. There is also a National Republican Institute.

As for issues, some that were traditionally domestic are no longer so; for example, unemployment in the United States has become an integral part of the problem of global unemployment. Party platform-writing will have to respond to these changes, probably with the help of the National Democratic Institute. Reread the first chapter of this book and recall the issues that will be global in nature by 2032.

How will the Democratic party adjust organizationally to changing world institutions between now and 2032? There will be dilemmas aplenty, particularly since the party has a traditional tendency to focus on local and state politics at the expense of foreign policy and has recently softened its supportive posture on behalf of building world institutions. As national involvement in world institutions increases and national sovereignty diminishes in the swirl of world politics, the meshing of party goals, platforms, and organizational activities at two levels—national and global—will bring much grinding of gears, debate, and frustration.

The dialogue about transnationalism and party-relevant international affairs will probably sound like a replay of Hamilton versus Jefferson, that is, centralization versus states'-rights decentralization, or, in today's circumstances, globalization versus national sovereignty. It may be difficult for a states'-rights party like the Democrats' to support a Hamiltonian program of global institutionalization. An added dimension to this difficulty will be the likelihood that multinational corporations will adopt a twenty-first century version of nineteenth-century liberalism, becoming proponents of world governmental centralization to enhance international economic stability, to discourage international wars, and to facilitate the growth of consumer markets and free trade.

As Democratic leaders and factions ponder the pros and cons of transnationalism and globalization, the American voter will be acquiring related interests and attitudes. A growing proportion of the electorate has in recent decades become better informed and more intensely interested in world affairs. This is undoubtedly a consequence of more education, televised world news, increased travel abroad, and a growth in world affairs citizen groups. Connections between foreign and domestic policies will be more explicitly identified, explained, and defended. Voter interest in the peace-with-security issue is likely to spread as the generations born after Hiroshima mature and assume leadership positions. Democratic party campaigners, who in the past gave highest priority to domestic issues, will be at pains to demonstrate the party's capacity to slow the arms race, maintain the safety of the nation and our allies, prevent war, promote international peacekeeping, and build sturdy global institutions in which American interests are well served. Evidence of such prowess will be difficult to provide so long as the party refrains from or remains divided about its own active participation in world-politics and world institution-building.

ELEVEN

Dilemma and Destiny

The above has been a relatively loose sampling of the future of the Democratic party and a free-wheeling overview of the issues of the future. If a terribly mixed metaphor may be permitted, has the destiny of the Democratic party already been drawn in the sands of time by the finger of Fate? Or are the innumerable policy and organizational issues raised here human dilemmas subject to human deliberation, choice, and happy endings? How much of this discussion should consist of inexorable trend lines, either-or choices, and blank pages? How much is destiny and how much dilemma? Or should this book simply be offered as a provocation—a target for brick-bats and ridicule, to be dismissed as another agenda of worries for an overwrought party leadership?

The fact is that some things have always been, are, and

will continue to be, while other things are very likely to be. The human enterprise is probably most unique in its capacity to remember the past, recognize and operate in the present, and anticipate and plan for the future. Civilizations have produced persons and institutions that specialize in recording the past, making present choices, and designing goals for the future. The Democratic party, as it approaches its 200th year, is an institution that has done and must continue to do no less.

THE DEMOCRATIC PARTY'S DESTINY

"Destiny" is a bit dramatic, but it makes the point succinctly. There are some things that the Democratic party has always been and will undoubtedly continue to be. These basic party characteristics and trends provide the framework within which its future is likely to evolve.

The Democratic party will continue to represent the less fortunate even at times when there are few citizens who perceive themselves as in this category. The party's problem is not to mark a dividing line between fortunate and unfortunate but rather to help those at the bottom of the socioeconomic scale better to understand the relative inequities they are experiencing and better to advise these citizens what they can do about rectifying the situation. The issue is not the poverty line or the color line or any other line. Rather, it is a matter of redefining the criteria for perceived injustice, which could range from personal loss of employment to community loss of a baseball team.

The Democratic party will continue to measure policy success or failure in terms of people rather than money. Are people working, healthy, happy . . .? Money, after all, is a human artifact whose negotiable value is determined in human marketplaces. Perhaps the most important thing to do with money is to keep it circulating. For Democrats, affluence is, in the first instance, how many citizens are receiving and spending money and, only secondarily, how many dollars are in the treasury. When Democrats lose interest in policies that circulate money, they deny themselves a fundamental party thesis and a great many votes.

The Democratic party will continue to serve as the nation's principal civic recruitment and induction institution, Americanizing newcomers and introducing them to the political process—immigrants, nonvoters, and other new constituencies. With its urban and rural machines gone, the party has not recently gone about this task as successfully as in earlier times. The task has been complicated by the conflict between representing the traditional constituencies or the new ones—blacks, women, youth, and Hispanics. The cost to the party for providing this service, ironically enough, is often lost elections until the newcomers organize themselves into strong coalition partners.

Democrats will continue to fight like hell among themselves, the Gemini curse. Factional battles will be marked, as usual, by inadequate information and ideological rigidity. The greater risk here is not the scars of the internecine fighting but rather the prospect that the factional winner will be unrepresentative of the Democratic electorate.

The party will always want for operating funds. It can enjoy a surfeit of rank-and-file workers if it attends properly to their recruitment and management. The need for and ardent pursuit of money, important as this is, has in recent years been a distraction from organizing people. Money is of course necessary, but only people vote.

Representation of the less fortunate, redistribution of the nation's wealth, recruitment of new citizens, rambunctiousness within its factions, and rank-and-file organization are the five Rs that have consistently concerned Democrats. The party is certainly destined to be concerned about them far into the future. The five Rs reflect the party's basic personality, with which its leaders will have to deal, for better or for worse.

THE PARTY'S DILEMMAS

It is one thing to be locked into a basic personality and another to cope with difficult matters of choice, although the two are related. The former smacks of destiny about which there is little choice; the latter involves hard choices, but choices nonetheless. If nothing else, the Democratic party will have many dilemmas of choice over the next decades.

How should the party go about designing comprehensive and well-integrated programs of public policy that are effective in achieving broad goals rather than merely in distributing political crumbs to every supporting constituency? As a coalition playing nonzero-sum games, Democrats are not likely to find easy solutions to this question. Every vote counts. Every member of the coalition counts. And, for Democrats, everybody deserves equal treatment. This set of requirements rarely adds up to comprehensive and well-integrated programs, for which setting priorities and acknowledging inequalities are mandatory. How many New Deals can there be, requiring, as Roosevelt's did, a relatively well-orchestrated programmatic response and a coalition consensus premised upon open-ended growth for all constituencies?

If the party is to serve as representative of particular constituency interests, how should it proceed to help build and lead those constituencies? The discussion above makes clear that this is another of those easier-said-than-done projects. How exactly should the party go about giving institutional, technical, and statutory aid to the labor movement, the farm economy, the array of needful minorities, and the newly emerging constituencies? Regardless of the necessity for helping rebuild or restructure its constituencies, will such efforts not bring cries of interventionism and charges of "selling out" to the interests? How much will direct action be self-defeating?

In what ways and to what extent should the party take futuristics (modestly displayed in parts of this book) seriously, and with what organizational mechanisms? The world and the nation are changing in ways that are quite discernible now but there are equally certain surprises hidden in the future. Foresight and the design of collective goals are fundamental responsibilities of political leaders. How can the Democratic party best serve in this anticipatory role and as an unofficial but influential planning agency for a dynamic and rapidly changing society? Can the party, following its states'-rights tradition, devise, for example, new mechanisms of decentralized local planning that avoid bureaucratic intrusions from the federal center, that is, a kind of localized or federalized national planning process?

How should the party go about rectifying and clarifying its reputation as the liberal party of the United States? This dilemma leads to philosophical issues of substantial depth and difficulty. Jeffersonian liberalism (which frequently seems to have been coopted by the Republicans) and European liberalism have emphasized the principle of limited government and maximum citizen and local prerogative. New Deal liberalism, however, preferred collective action and governmental intervention. The party has strong impulses toward political decentralization on the one hand and collectivist forms of social democracy on the other. It will not be easy for Democrats to come together on issues of liberal principle and practice. A closer look at the experiences of European liberalism may provide helpful guidance.

Historically, the party has been, time and again, deeply divided on issues of war and peace and the management of international affairs. One aspect of this dilemma is that many of the party's constituencies tend to give higher priority to domestic issues such as unemployment, inflation, and civil rights than to foreign affairs. The party also has a substantial pacifist and antimilitary element, whether the occasion is the Civil War or the Vietnam War. Of the Democratic presidents who have pursued assertive internationalist programs— Wilson, Roosevelt, Truman, Kennedy, and Johnson—only Roosevelt and Truman can be said to have achieved their stated goals without major political mishap. Today and in the future, however, the domestic priorities will necessarily have to be reformulated to take into account global interdependence and the growing relevance of supranational institutions for American well-being at home. Erasing the artificial line between domestic and global formulations of issues will require the best intellectual and linguistic dexterity that the party has.

How should the party proceed to protect its organizational integrity from exploitation by candidates who use its name and resources and by institutions (press, PACs, etc.) that are undermining its influence? Should the party, for example, require its nominees to sign a written contract agreeing to funnel all the campaign contributions they receive through the accounting system of an appropriate official party committee, with the party retaining a small management fee for overhead? Should each party nominee be required to register complete biographical material about himself or herself with a party committee, including past voting or administrative decisions if previously in public office? Should the party invent a platform-writing process that is continuous rather than periodic, with significant rather than perfunctory input from local sources, perhaps as part of a nationwide local planning process?

How will the party devise ways to create a new nationwide grassroots organization in which live party workers are in regular touch with live voters, that is, where human contact is real, sustained, and meaningful? Democratic voters need personal contact, not mail fundraising solicitations. If grassroots organization continues to be neglected, the Democrats may become a party without a constituency, even though there are constituencies out there in search of representation.

Between now and 2032, the nation and the world will experience profound physical, economic, social, and political changes. The management and facilitation of these changes will continue to be a special challenge for the leaders of one of the nation's and the world's most tested instruments of change, the Democratic party. Basically, a political party is an organization seeking to install its leaders into the offices of government and thereby to obtain for its leaders the necessary initiative and influence to make public policy. A party is naught without leaders and not much if its leaders cannot win public office. For lack of leaders, the Democratic party may be lost. Without the Democratic party, constructive change in the United States may be lost. It is incumbent upon Democrats to recruit, train, and nominate the kinds of skilled political leaders, managers, and brokers that have in the past taken the party to its proudest moments in the service of the nation. This process of recruitment, training, and nomination cannot and must not be left to chance.

There are indeed dilemmas ahead for Democrats, not to mention pitfalls and political pathologies. In the latter category loom the ancient foes of survival and progress: inattention; inertia; timidity; ignorance; cupidity; pessimism, and the unwillingness to discuss and debate. Tomorrow's Democrats will need to develop innovative ways in which to worry together about the condition they, the nation, and the world will be in during that bicentennial celebration in 2032.